Fair Wind and Plenty of It

Fair Wind
and Plenty of It

A MODERN-DAY TALL SHIP ADVENTURE

RIGEL CROCKETT

VINTAGE CANADA

VINTAGE CANADA EDITION, 2005

Copyright © 2004 Rigel Crockett

Published in Canada by Vintage Canada,
a division of Random House of Canada Limited, Toronto.
Originally published in hardcover in Canada by Alfred A. Knopf Canada,
a division of Random House of Canada Limited, Toronto, in 2004.
Distributed by Random House of Canada Limited, Toronto.

www.randomhouse.ca

Page 393 constitutes a continuation of the copyright page.

Library and Archives Canada Cataloguing in Publication

Crockett, Rigel
Fair wind and plenty of it : a modern-day tall ship adventure
/ Rigel Crockett.

ISBN 0-676-97635-2

1. Crockett, Rigel—Travel. 2. Voyages around the world.
3. Picton Castle (Ship) I. Title.

G440.C846A3 2005   910.4'1   C2004-905232-2

Text design: CS Richardson

Printed and bound in the United States of America

2 4 6 8 9 7 5 3 1

To Ariel

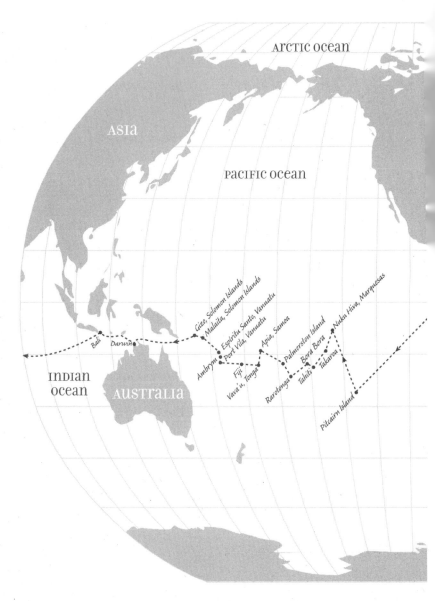

The First Circumnavigation of the Barque *Picton Castle*

Barque *Picton Castle* Sail Plan

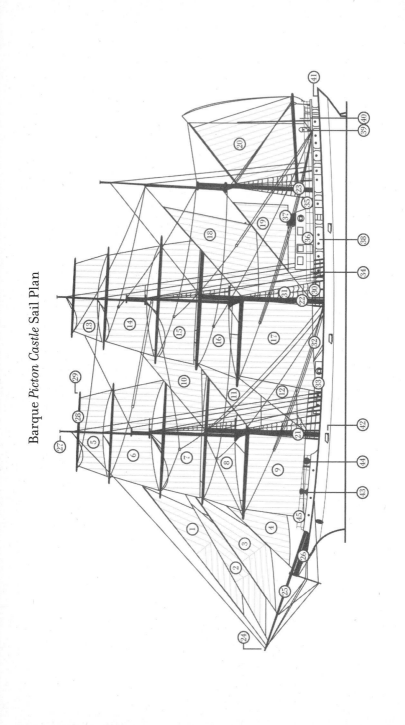

Barque *Picton Castle* Inboard Profile

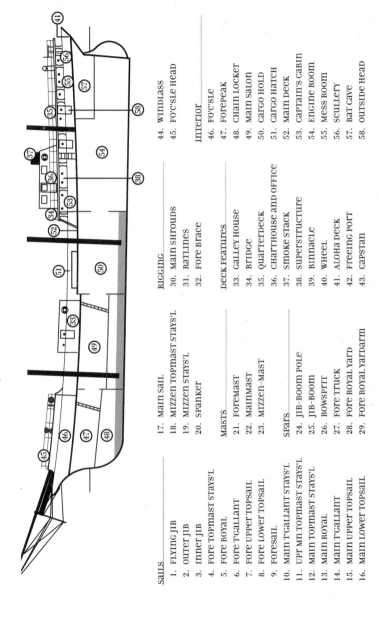

sails

1. FLYING JIB
2. OUTER JIB
3. INNER JIB
4. FORE TOPMAST STAYS'L
5. FORE ROYAL
6. FORE T'GALLANT
7. FORE UPPER TOPSAIL
8. FORE LOWER TOPSAIL
9. FORESAIL
10. MAIN T'GALLANT STAYS'L
11. UPPER MN TOPMAST STAYS'L
12. MAIN TOPMAST STAYS'L
13. MAIN ROYAL
14. MAIN T'GALLANT
15. MAIN UPPER TOPSAIL
16. MAIN LOWER TOPSAIL
17. MAIN SAIL
18. MIZZEN TOPMAST STAYS'L
19. MIZZEN STAYS'L
20. SPANKER

MASTS

21. FOREMAST
22. MAINMAST
23. MIZZEN-MAST

SPARS

24. JIB-BOOM POLE
25. JIB-BOOM
26. BOWSPRIT
27. FORE TRUCK
28. FORE ROYAL YARD
29. FORE ROYAL YARDARM

RIGGING

30. MAIN SHROUDS
31. RATLINES
32. FORE BRACE

DECK FEATURES

33. GALLEY HOUSE
34. BRIDGE
35. QUARTERDECK
36. CHARTHOUSE AND OFFICE
37. SMOKE STACK
38. SUPERSTRUCTURE
39. BINNACLE
40. WHEEL
41. ALOHA DECK
42. FREEING PORT
43. CAPSTAN

44. WINDLASS
45. FOC'SLE HEAD

INTERIOR

46. FOC'SLE
47. FOREPEAK
48. CHAIN LOCKER
49. MAIN SALON
50. CARGO HOLD
51. CARGO HATCH
52. MAIN DECK
53. CAPTAIN'S CABIN
54. ENGINE ROOM
55. MESS ROOM
56. SCULLERY
57. BAT CAVE
58. OUTSIDE HEAD

TABLE OF CONTENTS

Map / vi
Diagram / viii

This is the pleasure of life at sea,—fine weather,
day after day, without interruption,—fair wind,
and plenty of it,—and homeward bound.

Richard Henry Dana
from *Two Years Before the Mast*, 1840

CHAPTER 1

Gale Warning

25 November 1997
Beginning of World Circumnavigation
Bound for Panama from Lunenburg Harbour, Nova Scotia,
Canada

As EVENING DEEPENED, SWELLS GREW HIGH. DRIVEN across the North Atlantic, they rolled under us and smashed into white against the snowy bluffs that cradled Lunenburg Bay. The *Picton Castle* had felt so large and steady there. Now, as we ploughed into the wide ocean—pitching, rolling, testing the concrete ballast that we'd poured—she felt small.

I tightened my grip on her wheel for balance and thought of our thirty green fare-paying crew. Most, unaccustomed to rough nights underway, grew seasick and cold on deck and below. We pressed farther from land and the strengthening wind piled the swells steeper. It kicked up whitecaps, tore them into spray.

The air was below freezing. I pulled my hat down over my ears, lifted my wool collar against the cold wind that blew over the stern. The ship, 179 feet overall, rocked so that her iron freeing ports, meant to shed water from the deck, opened and slammed shut with a string of clanging reports. In a still harbour the deck sat just three and a half feet above surface. In a rolling sea, water sprayed aboard on the low side and surged across the deck in torrents. She was wetter than I'd thought she'd be.

Above the engine's deep chug, a near gale-force wind whistled in our new rigging. It had been a while since a square-rigger had sailed out of Lunenburg harbour. From the 1860s to the 1880s, Lunenburg was home to an impressive fleet of twenty-five to thirty square-riggers that carried cargoes all over the globe. By 1912, the last of them had her yards removed so she could be handled with fewer crew and scrape by for a few more years in an industry doomed to fade away. In late November 1997, I looked up to our topsails, lashed to their yards just days prior. Two on the fore, two on the main. I was impressed that the Captain had set the uppers in this wind. Twenty-five days behind schedule, he hungered to make distance south before the storms of winter could lock us in, before they could rob his last chance to hold the confidence of the fare-paying crew who'd helped finance his voyage.

Chief mate Brian held the rail for balance as he walked aft from the charthouse to the end of the quarterdeck where I steered. Under the shade of his sou'wester I could see his brown, close-set eyes. He fixed them on mine, like he always did when delivering an order. "Come right to south."

"Come right to south," I repeated, and then leaned into the wheel, feeling relieved to steer away from this cold, away from the disappointments of my Lunenburg summer. Crew tugged on the braces to pivot the yards as we changed course. If everything went well, we'd fetch the tropics in a week. Then the order would be *steer west*, and it would stay west until we'd circled the globe.

Dressed in a long black raincoat and knee-high rubber boots, Captain Dan Moreland stepped from charthouse to quarterdeck and mustered his watch. I felt my toes clench in my boots and made an effort to relax. The man looked tired from our four-month sprint to ready the ship. The grey patch on the chin of his beard had grown, and his face seemed long. He spoke a couple of clipped sentences and disappeared back into his charthouse, leaving the management of his watch to Jesse, his lead able-bodied seaman.

Jesse, with a few days' scruff on his cleft chin and a ponytail pressed down by his wool hat, sent one of his professional watchmates to relieve me at the helm.

I walked towards the charthouse to report that I'd been relieved and noticed that many of Jesse's crew were women. Some of them looked uncomfortable, likely wondering why they'd each spent $32,500 (U.S.) to be here.

"If you fall overboard," Jesse said to his watch, "jam your marlinspike in your eye, because there's no way you'll be rescued." His watch laughed nervously at the severity. I chuckled too. I was not quite so serious as Jesse. Probably it was reflected in my rank—a second-string able-bodied seaman, below the bo'sun on our watch. Still, Jesse was right. A man overboard stood next to no chance in this water.

I worked my way forward to the fo'c'sle for a few hours' rest before my next watch. I climbed into my upper bunk, drew the curtain, flipped on my fifteen-watt reading light and settled my shoulders against the bulkhead. At about thirty inches, this fo'c'sle bunk was wider than most in commercial ships, and I was one of the lucky few with a porthole. No doubt it would be a luxury in the tropics, though now condensation and ocean spray obscured its glass, sparkling emerald in the starboard sidelight.

I grabbed my journal from the shelf beside me. Pulling up my knees to prop the book, I slammed them noisily into the guitar I'd strapped to my overhead. I muffled the strings, and with hands stiff from cold I wrote:

It has been many months since I've written an entry. I've been working like a dog on the ship and finishing my sea chest. What few thoughts I've put on paper I have sent to Ariel.

These months have been poignant. I've gotten to know Dad much better. He's a sage man and carries a lot of sadness. His eyes were filled with tears when we sailed off the dock. Laurel cried on my shoulder last night. I didn't expect it—my sister and I have been so aloof lately. I love Laurel. She seems both grown up and a little girl. Mom cried today.

The last few months have held a lot of disappointment. I avoid the Captain. My father is worried about the voyage.

I feel I've grown a lot here. Everyone has.

Here I go. Homeward bound.

When watch duty came around at 20:00 hours, chief mate Brian ordered me back to the wheel. The sky was near black except for a spattering of stars visible through a rip in the clouds. The seas had grown more turbulent and cold wind grabbed at my throat. A brass hood with a glass window like an old-fashioned diving helmet had been placed over the binnacle. Inside it, a red light illuminated the compass card that swivelled and kicked. I held the wheel and tried to get a sense of the conditions. The sea was on the quarter, not quite from the stern. It pushed us around, corkscrewing the ship through the water. Yaw, roll and pitch. After a while bo'sun Josh, our stocky, bearded watch leader, told me to help a new crewwoman learn to steer.

Patricia Lynch, a Boston lobbyist, was one of the few crew not seasick. She stood beside the wheel and leaned towards the compass, squinting over pharmacy reading glasses that were obscured by salt spray. Her hands clutched the spokes of the helm tightly, partly to steer, partly for balance. In the light of the compass I noticed she wore mascara and lipstick. I smelled expensive perfume on the cold northwest wind.

"A touch left," I said. "Just a few spokes. Now bring the wheel back amidships. That's good."

"I can't see a fucking thing," she said in her smoky voice, and laughed a full, raspy laugh.

I liked her spirit. "Try steering for those three stars over there . . . those ones, in a row, Orion's belt."

Patricia steered for Orion while the wind built to the predicted gale force. The temperature continued to drop. Icy wind tore the tips of waves into long streaks of foam that glowed pale white in our stern light.

The ship stood up well to the growing wind and her high square sails helped dampen her motion, though when the seas caught her right, she rolled through eighty degrees, swinging her tall masts like chopsticks. Standing near bow or stern, you could sometimes feel her drop from beneath us. She put her nose down. A burst of speed; she headed for the trough. She nearly stopped, blasting salt water over the bow. When we were deep in these troughs, the tops of the swells covered the horizon, even looking from the quarterdeck, with eyes sixteen feet above water.

"Are you OK, Patricia?"

"Oh, I'm fine." She tilted her head back and laughed, her lipstick deep red in the dim light of the compass. "I just feel like I'm in a movie."

Patricia's spirit reinforced my idea that laughter and activity ward off seasickness. I'd learned to act as if the ailment didn't exist. Acknowledge that knot in your gut or the sting of a headache and seasickness will overpower you.

At 2200 hours, bo'sun Josh had the helm relieved. In one of his typically descriptive orders he told me to take a watchmate on a ship check. "Buddy up," he said. "Look in all the compartments, look for water, make sure no one's hurt, tend the coal fire in the galley stove, make sure there's no fire anywhere else, look in the hold to see if the cargo is secure, but don't go in if you don't have to."

We threw a little coal in the stove's firebox. Kettles fenced in on the stovetop rattled. They held coffee that our eccentric cook had sewn into mesh bags and left to boil for God knows how long. That coffee-making technique and her delegation of all cooking duties in Lunenburg were some of her less welcome efficiencies. We walked forward to the fo'c'sle, into the quarters of my fellow ABs, or able-bodied seamen. We heard the scrape of sea chests moving in their lashings and the slap of wet foul-weather gear against bunks and bulkheads. The compartment pitched, yawed, rolled, dropped, stopped.

The main salon, though it moved less, was a disaster. The sickly sweet smell of supper was still there, but it'd been altered by the acrid smell of stomach juice, accompanied by the retch and splatter of barf hitting buckets. A peek in the cargo hold revealed that the goods on the starboard side had settled. On the port side, a haphazard stack of used bicycles reached nearly to the overhead and teetered precariously. We climbed the broad main-salon ladder to the deck and waited for a swell that'd just piled over the rail to roll to the low side of the ship. Leaning into the wind, holding on to the rail on the ship's high side, we headed quickly to the stern of the main deck, a place we called the aloha deck. This was where the seasick people were. They'd come for the abundance of fresh air.

In the light shining from the mess, I saw their pallid faces twisted in pain. A seasick sailor leaned over the rail next to the spare lube oil barrels. I knew that horrible feeling—a head full of worms, a diseased animal in the stomach clawing its way up.

We climbed the ladder to the quarterdeck and waited until midnight, when the next watch relieved us. It felt about time. The small patch of clear sky had long since been choked in by thick cloud, which drove a cold rain. We gathered by the charthouse, where chief mate Brian accounted for us, looked everyone in the eyes and said good night. As I turned to descend the ladder, making sure the greenest hands made it safely to the main salon, bo'sun Josh clamped his hand on my shoulder. I turned to look at his face, inscrutable beneath beard and sou'wester. The red charthouse light emphasized the bend in his nose, busted three times, once by marlinspike. "Rigel," he said, "sleep with your boots on."

I rolled my foul-weather pants down over my boots and wedged them between a couple of sea chests below my bunk. I figured the bo'sun's comment was exaggeration, but if his instinct proved right, I'd be able to jump into them like a fireman. I climbed into my bunk with my clothes on and wedged myself in with dirty laundry, pillow and blankets to keep from being thrown around. They were all wet from condensation and the fo'c'sle smelled dank. I felt like a pig in a cement mixer. A confused sleep took me, interrupted by the hourly passing of crew on a ship check, the jarring smack of tall waves against porthole, the racking shudder of the bow sliding sideways down the face of a swell. Heavy rolls made the foul-weather gear stand out from its hooks. Heavy rolls left me clutching to stay in my bunk, thinking for a moment of the events that brought me here.

CHAPTER 2

Beginnings

I WAS CONCEIVED THE DAY MY FATHER LAID THE KEEL for his first boat. This boat, which he built in the barn next to our house, was the product of his soon-to-be wooden boat-building company, the Rose Bay Boat Shop. At the time, Bob Crockett was an apprentice at Stevens and Sons Boat Yard, near Lunenburg. My mother, Sue, was a sail-maker for the same family. When I was born, they were helping to build a small square-topsail ketch, the *Sheila Yeates*. The ship had been commissioned by a bright-eyed man in his early sixties named Geoff Pope.

Geoff became a close family friend. So it was no surprise that nine years later when his ship sailed to Halifax, he and his small crew visited our house. Geoff sat on the floor of our living room and leaned his back against the bricks that framed our fireplace, leaving the couch and chairs for his crew. It was there that he asked my dad if I would like to sail from Halifax to Quebec in his *Sheila Yeates*. My dad then asked me, adding that it would be a once-in-a-lifetime experience. I said yes.

Over the next three summers, sailing with Geoff, I saw icebergs and whales, the green banks of Gaspé and the misty cliffs of northern Newfoundland. I was captivated by the mysteries of rope, and I admired old Geoff as he climbed in the rig, hauled lines and moved about his deck.

I remember Geoff spoke sometimes of the Brigantine *Romance*, a ship he'd sailed in as fare-paying crew at age fifty-five. This experience had affected him so profoundly that it led him to build his own ship and sail her to places like Greenland, Iceland and Scotland. Geoff pronounced the name "Ro*mance*," emphasizing the second syllable. I figured it was just one of the many small things that made my hero different from everyone else.

As I grew older and met more sailors who'd sailed in the *Romance*, I realized that the pronunciation was important—a badge that marked their membership in a family they called the Marineros. This was the name given to them by their hard-nosed captain, Arthur "Skipper" Kimberly, who'd sailed in American three-masted cargo schooners and a Swedish four-masted barque in the final days of commercial sail. By then, owners were forced to run their ships with no margins for capital improvements, replacement ships or anything but the barest of living conditions for seamen. Wages were often in the negative after they'd signed off a long voyage and paid back the company store for oilskins bought on credit. Seamanship was the best in the world, though, and that is the legacy Skipper passed on to his Marineros.

When I was twelve and had made three passages in the *Sheila Yeates*, Geoff called me from Traverse City, Michigan. "Hey, Rige," he said, "how are you? Look, if you can get to Traverse City tomorrow, there's a berth for you in a 120-foot Gloucester fishing schooner, the *Ernestina*. You'll sail as cabin boy."

I was excited, but also a little hurt that Geoff hadn't invited me back aboard his ship. Still, the feeling passed the next day when we stood together by the helm of the *Ernestina*, docked in Traverse City, and I realized that he had bigger plans for me. I could hear the awe in his voice as he looked down the *Ernestina*'s sweeping deck. "Lookit, Rige. She's as big as a city block."

The *Ernestina* did seem that big to my twelve-year-old eyes, and beautiful too.

Soon, Geoff introduced me to her captain, who had restored the *Ernestina* from an abandoned, half-sunken hulk to her former state as a beautiful and seaworthy schooner that had once reached farther into the Arctic than any other sailing ship, and had run passengers from the Cape Verde Islands to Massachusetts from 1948 right up to 1965. He had even won an act of Congress to reinstate the American flag to that ship. His name was Captain Dan Moreland, and he was a Marinero of the first degree. He'd been chief mate of the *Romance* at age twenty-two, on her first voyage around the world.

By chance, the same day I met Dan Moreland, I also met Dennis Conner. He was at the height of his fame that year, having just won back the America's Cup, redeeming his name after being the first American skipper in 132 years to lose it. I'd watched Conner's saga closely because my dad's boat-building company, which had long since outgrown the barn next to our house, had won a contract to build two of the contenders for Canada's entry in the Cup race.

Despite Conner's fame, I admired Captain Moreland more. Conner seemed uncomfortable in his skin, awkward, with his chubby, sunburned cheeks. By comparison Moreland was slender, and cool in his Panama hat. Whether he was feeling charitable, inviting the crew back to his cabin to share some rum and old writings about the *Ernestina*, or grumpy, making the first mate squirm, he had the respect of all aboard. I could see it in the way they acted around him, a little like schoolchildren encountering a favourite teacher on summer break. I noticed that a lot of them imitated the way he dressed, sometimes taking on his facial expressions. I'd even caught myself a few times searching the corners of my mouth with my tongue like he did when concentrating—docking the ship, or that time the next year off Newfoundland when the wind was so strong that the mainmast took on a standing vibration and the port rail touched the water.

After that first summer with Moreland, my course was set: I wanted to be a tall ship captain too, and develop all the skills I could. When I returned to Rose Bay, I read *Dove*, about a sixteen-year-old's solo voyage around the world, and I hounded my dad to let me build a wooden boat.

I searched through his books and the books at the library. Following his advice that a boat should be as long in feet as her owner is old, I found plans for a beautiful twelve-footer. Its gaff-rigged sail and lapstrake sides appealed to my identity as a traditional sailor. But to my dad, who'd recently extricated himself from his boat-building company, my boat had the unsavoury feel of a project he might have to finish himself.

That fall, my parents took a week-long vacation. They left my younger sister, Laurel, and me with a babysitter, and a thick book on boat building to help me understand the weight of my ambition. I read the first chapter. Then, considering myself qualified to begin, I pulled out three sheets of Dad's most expensive ¾-inch mahogany marine-grade plywood, nailed them to the floor of his shop and began to loft my boat, starting to draw it up full-size.

At the end of his vacation, when Dad entered his shop, he hid his regret for the damaged plywood, telling me what a good job I'd done. Over the next three years he was with me whenever I hit a hard spot, until my boat was finished.

The year I completed my boat, Dad and I sailed with Geoff in the *Sheila Yeates*. Together we had a brilliant downwind passage, dodging small icebergs through the

Strait of Belle Isle, finally disembarking in St. Anthony on the northern tip of Newfoundland. Geoff and his remaining crew of seven planned to continue to Greenland, Iceland and the Shetland Isles. Dad and I ached to continue, but we had obligations back home. Still, we were so torn by the decision that we left it to a coin toss.

Go home, the coin said.

"Best two out of three," we said.

Go home.

We were in the kitchen days later when Dad found a short article in *The Halifax Chronicle-Herald* about a small wooden ship that had sunk in pack ice, south of Greenland. A quick call to the *Herald* confirmed it: the *Sheila Yeates* had gone down. All hands were saved.

My first regret in life was not being there. Though I had no death wish, I felt I had somehow let the ship and my friends down. I believe the memory of that feeling made me sail in the untried *Picton Castle* into this late November gale, when a whole lot of us were feeling awfully dark.

One year after the sinking, Captain Moreland sent a letter encouraging me to apply as a deckhand on an engineless, square topsail schooner called the *Shenandoah*. "Captain Bob Douglas," he wrote, "is about the best schooner sailor there is and his *Shenandoah* is magnificent."

When we came to anchor on my first day aboard, I tried to show my considerable sailing prowess by lowering the peak of the heavy gaff that supported the *Shenandoah*'s foresail. Taking the taut halyard from its belaying pin to ease it down under control, I accidentally let the line slip and the gaff plummeted. Embarrassed, I tried to stop its fall by clamping my hands around the free-running line. It lifted me off the deck. Hard manila fibres tore soft flesh from my hands.

I wasn't even required to be on deck that day, or indeed that week. I was on galley duty, and my only obligation was to wash dishes four times a day and help the cook prepare food for forty. All week the hot dishwater hurt my hands, and every day the work dragged on well past midnight and began again at six.

Still, Captain Moreland was right; it was good training. We sailed the ship hard every day, and because of my enthusiasm I spent a lot of time in the rig. I quickly learned how to keep a rhythm while running up ratlines. Soon I became comfortable enough to complete an old *Shenandoah* rite of passage called trucking. It was a feat named for the small disks, or trucks, that protect the end grain at the very tops of the topmasts. One day, sailing towards Nantucket, after I'd sewn a patch in the highest square sail, I decided to just keep going up. I shinnied the greasy topmast until I stood upon the hounds, where the highest rigging converged. I placed my hands on the truck at chin level and hoisted myself atop the mast. *Shenandoah*'s seven sails billowed like clouds beneath me. Her flag snapped at my ankles.

That first summer, the *Ernestina* sailed into *Shenandoah*'s harbour on Martha's Vineyard. I'd heard that Captain Moreland had been fired from his command of that ship, but I took a boat over to see. Even before I reached her, I could sense his absence. The mainsail was furled differently from the foresail. Captain Moreland would never have allowed such a lapse in attention to detail.

That night, I met up with a couple of fellow sixteen-year-olds from the *Ernestina*. Like me, they had sailed under Moreland and looked up to him. We walked along the cool cobblestone and confided in each other. Things were worse than I'd thought. Not only had our captain been fired, he'd also got a divorce and a large tattoo of a Chinese dragon on the soft part of his forearm.

They told me he was fired because of some bad accounting work and that his divorce involved some intrigue. I imagined the details: his wife must have cooked the books. Then he took the fall, divorced her in disgust and got a tattoo in an act of anguished self-abuse. I never did ask for the truth. It didn't matter to me.

Captain Moreland had made one more change that year. He'd created a plan that became legendary in the gossipy world of tall ships, one that would free him from the threat of being separated from his vessel by bureaucracy: find an old, steel steamship with lines like a sailing ship and convert her into a square-rigger with funds raised from investors. Then, in the tradition of Arthur "Skipper" Kimberly and Irving Johnson, he would voyage around the world with a fare-paying crew. Not only would he be captain of the ship, he'd be president of the company that owned her. It sounded to me like the perfect plan.

Just before my third summer in the *Shenandoah*, Captain Moreland sent me a volunteer application for the US Brig *Niagara*, where he'd been chief mate for some time. I had already committed to the *Shenandoah*, so my father filled out the application and got in touch with Moreland.

Even before my dad joined the *Niagara*, Moreland let him in on his project. He knew that my father's shipbuilding skills, business knowledge and connections in Lunenburg would be a help to him. What my father desired was the voyage. He'd dreamed of sailing around the world ever since he was a kid, and even bought an old sailboat for the purpose, which he kept in the shop and worked on in his spare time. United by mutual goals, friendship and professional respect, Dad joined Moreland and his team almost immediately.

I read their correspondence and business plans. I pored over the drawings and followed the progress. In 1991, Moreland had found a ship in Norway that met his criteria:

she had a working diesel engine but was originally powered by a modest 91-horsepower steam engine. To compensate for the low power of that engine, her designers borrowed the hard-won lessons applied to latter-day sailing ship design. They gave her a lean entry, a clean run, substantial dead rise and a long keel like a square-rigger's.

Her riveted steel hull was sound, too, the surveyor's results showed. Commissioned by the Royal Navy in World War II, the HMS *Picton Castle* had even withstood a mine blast under her bow. That explosion had lifted her out of the water, yet she was for the most part undamaged. From fishing the North Sea to running cargo along the coast of Europe between Portugal and Murmansk, the *Picton Castle* had proven herself seaworthy in the worst weather short of Cape Horn. And to Moreland, who like many mariners is a touch superstitious, "she just felt like a happy ship," he wrote us in a postcard.

In May 1993, Moreland and his small crew boarded their happy ship in Norway. They had a brief orientation with the ship's systems, finding layers of shoddy repairs that the Captain evaluated with characteristic sarcasm as "highly economical." Soon they moved her to a Danish shipyard on the island of Aero, and for four arduous months laboured to make her seaworthy for passage across the Atlantic. Lack of funds, however, stalled the ship in Ipswich, England, where they would spend a lean and uncertain year while Moreland collected enough money to bring her across the Atlantic to New York, finally running up his credit cards to keep the crew fed.

In the winter of 1994, Dan Moreland left his ship at her derelict wharf in Manhattan's South Street Seaport Museum to visit our house in Rose Bay. I had hitchhiked home from college to spend some time with my old friend. Together we walked around the neighbouring town of

Lunenburg, looking at the shipyards, chandleries, black-smith's shops and block shops that had run continuously since the age of sail and would make the conversion possible. We talked about books, space travel, music, human-powered flight and ships. He took me seriously, and I loved it. I told him that I wanted to be part of his crew.

That evening he made a phone call and set me up with a job in the US Brig *Niagara*, a ship that, despite his leaving, still had a high quotient of Marineros. He wanted to be sure I'd be properly trained when the time came.

That night was the first of many that I lay awake picturing the voyage, shaking in anticipation of the adventure.

CHAPTER 3

Picton Castle

*Lunenburg, Nova Scotia
August 1996 to May 1997*

Naysayers called her the *Fiction Castle*. Many in the industry seriously doubted that her black hull, dented and blotched burgundy by rust, would ever part the water of Lunenburg harbour. Much more, they doubted that this sixty-nine-year-old North Sea trawler could be converted in just eighteen months into a seaworthy three-masted barque, ready to circumnavigate with thirty fare-paying crew.

Adding fuel to their doubts were the two years the *Picton Castle* lay dormant in New York, docked first in Manhattan and later at the Hudson River Maritime Museum in Kingston. But we believers knew that this was neither failure nor laziness. Moreland was simply biding his time, waiting until he had sufficient funds to do the conversion in one go rather than sabotage his project, as so many others had sabotaged theirs, by working in fits as money trickled in, thus wasting time, frustrating participants and destroying the confidence of backers by moving too slowly.

Then, in early July 1996, one of the ship's first investors decided he wanted to see the ship converted and tied to a pier at an event he was hosting seven weeks later in Bristol,

Rhode Island. To that end, he would channel $750,000 into the project. This money would get the *Picton Castle*'s conversion well underway.

Perhaps Moreland's doubters didn't know the great effort and commitment he could get out of people. Those of us who came to Lunenburg knew. We'd seen it ourselves. We'd listened to what people said of his leadership. Some compared him to Tom Sawyer with his whitewashed fence; others preferred the example of Darth Vader. Nonetheless, one thing was clear: if anyone could do it, Moreland could. And when his *Picton Castle* motored into Lunenburg, we followed him like baby sea turtles follow the moon.

Brian Donnelly watched the ship arrive. At thirty years old, he had already retired from sailing-ship life when the Captain told him he'd make it worth his while to lead the rigging of the ship's three lower masts. Brian was also the Captain's first choice for chief mate on the circumnavigation. I believe Moreland had found compatibility between their military leadership styles and fine seamanship skills when they'd worked together aboard the US Brig *Niagara*.

Fresh out of military high school, Brian had cut his teeth aboard the Brigantine *Romance*. Like Moreland, Brian worked his way up to be chief mate under Captain Arthur "Skipper" Kimberly. Under Skipper, Brian learned his seamanship ethic, but sadly, by the time Brian signed aboard the *Romance*, Skipper was nearing retirement, his ship was plagued with rot and her glory days were far behind. The ship's two circumnavigations, nicknamed WWI and WWII, were defining experiences for the *Romance* sailor and had become the stuff of legend.

So, ever since Captain Moreland announced his plan, Brian had hoped he would be chief mate of the *Picton Castle*. He also hoped his girlfriend of four years, Beth, would leave her medical residency to be the ship's doctor. Still, Brian's dream was tempered by reality. He had monthly child support payments to make, and Beth had med-school-sized student loans to pay. Generally, American traditional ships run on a shoestring budget, and the *Picton Castle* would be no different. Captain Moreland could probably find any number of competent mates willing to work for little more than the privilege of sailing under his respected command. There were other doctors in the world, too—many with more experience, no student loans and a willingness to crew the ship for free. Brian had been prepared to put aside his dreams in favour of his responsibilities when Captain Moreland made it clear: Brian and Beth were his first choices in key personnel. He'd commit enough money for them to meet their responsibilities, and then some.

From the moment the *Picton Castle*'s lines hit the dock in Lunenburg, the ship was a frenzy of activity. The Captain, in his usual style, had a staggering list of projects to complete. There were three lower masts for Brian to rig that would form the foundation of the ship's rigging. But before those masts could be installed, or stepped, the deck needed three reinforced holes, or mast partners, to accept them. Unfortunately, in the case of the foremast there wasn't even a deck to cut a hole in, only a gaping cargo hatch, large enough to load a Sherman tank. The masts themselves had to be fabricated out of twenty-inch steel pipe. For support, each mast needed shrouds and stays, heavy wire ropes that secure the top of the mast to the deck. These massive wires attach to the ship by eyes formed at their ends. To make an eye, one must bend the wire back on itself and secure it with rigging seizings, handmade, noose-tight wire windings. But first, every one of Brian's shrouds and stays would have to be coated in tar, bound in tarred linen and finally wrapped tightly in marline, a process called parcelling and serving.

Leading by example, Brian pushed his crew to do the best they could every day. I joined his rigging crew for a weekend before starting my last year of university. I was helping Brian form an eye in one of the massive shrouds. He had bent the great cable back on itself and was binding both parts permanently with a rigging seizing, levering the turns of wire tight with a heaver, a wooden tool the size of a baseball bat. I watched him closely. Lean muscle tensed along his arms. Probably once a skinny kid, Brian's fifteen years of physical work in ships had given him a labourer's build: solid arms, strong back, straight shoulders. Leaning his sinewy body into the heaver, he seemed an extension of his work, a powerful coil of energy. Bits of thinning reddish hair curled from beneath his engineer's hat. Brian was raised Boston Irish and looked the part. Long red stubble bristled on his angular face. I could see freckles on the backs of his tarry hands, and hairs that glinted like golden threads as he gripped the heaver, winding, binding an eye in the shroud. His close-set eyes were locked on his work.

Captain Moreland approached and stood close behind Brian. The silent scrutiny of his superior was putting Brian on edge. His jaw muscles rippled with tension. A single vein that ran up his forehead began to pulse and swell. He leaned hard into the heaver. The wire stretched and flattened, heating up as he wound it around the shroud. Tar oozed down.

The Captain left. Brian relaxed a little.

"Do you hate him yet?" I asked jokingly, thinking of our captain's reputation for driving his mates.

He was silent, still focused on his seizing—thinking. Then he spoke.

"I love him for doing this."

There was a world of work to do before the Captain could turn back the clock on his ship to the end of the nineteenth century. A curving clipper bow had to be fabricated and installed to cover the ship's vertical "plumb bow" that had stood straight as a soldier for sixty-eight years. That new bow would change her place in ship lineage, closer to the fast wooden clippers that ruled the oceans in the mid-1800s. Steel hawse pipes had to be tunnelled from the deck through the new bow for the anchor chain. The Captain wanted an old-fashioned, manually operated anchor windlass to be forged at the Lunenburg Foundry. Its pattern would come from a collection in the stock room that dated from 1891, and it would be installed on the fo'c'sle head, or forward deck. Unfortunately, that deck was rotten and had to be replaced and caulked. A steel bowsprit needed to be fabricated and installed, protruding forward over the new clipper bow. Back aft, the wooden quarterdeck planks also needed replacing. Skylights had to be installed; so did a new deckhouse for the galley. A new teak railing was to girdle the quarterdeck. Far below, in the vaulting cavern of the engine room, the ship's engineers were overhauling the main engine, replacing the piston rings, cleaning out the gearbox, refurbishing the heat exchanger.

These jobs, and seemingly hundreds of other carpentry, blacksmithing, engineering, cleaning, chipping and painting tasks needed doing in the upcoming seven weeks. It was too much for a newcomer to Lunenburg to orchestrate himself, even a newcomer as resourceful as Captain Moreland. So my dad joined the conversion effort four days after the ship arrived in Lunenburg. Youthful and with a cackling laugh, he helped manage with delighted enthusiasm. At the peak of the conversion effort, Bob had ramped up most of the 125 workers who were advancing the ship towards her new identity.

The seven-week conversion of the *Picton Castle* was a tornado of effort. To the surprise of many, the Captain's ambitious goals were accomplished and he made it to his engagement in Bristol by the promised date, letting go the anchor just as the guests arrived.

After Bristol, fundraising tapered off. The ship's conversion was perhaps a third complete, but for the year and a half remaining until the beginning of the voyage, the operation needed its belt tightened. Welders worked on the ship sporadically. The Captain, with my father's assistance, continued to raise funds and court the fare-paying crew who would share the cost of the voyage and, hopefully, provide the company with its profit margin. The Captain's core professional crew stayed aboard and continued to rig the ship. They worked forty hours a week, did the dishes and put in about three extra hours of domestic cleaning on Saturdays. In exchange, they got a bunk, three daily meals, $100 a week and a shot at being crew on the voyage. During the winter, my father understood he'd secured himself a berth on the voyage. He was to be the morale officer and the Captain's alter ego. He was also charged with managing the ship's finances.

As a kid, I hadn't counted on voyaging with my dad. I knew from his solitary hours restoring an aluminum boat in his old boat shop that he hadn't counted on me voyaging with him, either. But after the refit I felt he had a strong claim to voyage.

While he worked on the ship, I struggled to finish the final year of my physics program, which I'd taken up instead of literature because of a childhood interest in human-powered flight. I wasn't a talented physicist. As a result, I was always busy looking for projects on billiards and ship stability, every day proudly wearing an oval pin with the *Picton Castle*'s dragon logo enamelled on its face.

My younger sister was next to join the ship. My parents were the first to tell me that she and the Captain were seeing each other. Laurel had always seemed older than her years. In truth, she had always felt a little like my older sibling, and since seeing Danny she'd become interested in great literature and film. "Wow. Well, hey, I'm sure we can all keep things separate," I said to her on the phone.

Dad made a joke about a shotgun. He had no shotgun, would not use one if he had it, hippie that he was. As a family, we were more inclined to let each be his or her own person, not to judge, and to stick together.

Then I found out that Mom was coming. I loved my mom, but things were getting out of hand. *I'll sail in a different ship. You guys have fun.* I had a flashback to the back seat of my parents' car, a bag of smelly food at my feet, me and my sister fighting over the armrest.

The Captain was considering the wisdom of our whole family voyaging. Understandably, he was concerned by social entities with a structure independent of the all-important chain of command. But he seemed willing to give it a try. Besides, a ship in which the Captain has a girlfriend, or "queen bee," is a happier ship.

Then reality hit home. The crew started calling us Swiss Family Crockett. *OK, I'm outta here.*

No. I'll stick it out. I'll wear my pin and enjoy my last year of university. I will not step into the great blackness of withering job interviews, table-waiting or grad school rejections. I will join a project so improbable that it's fuelled on nothing but pure belief. I am a traditional sailor on the threshold of a life dream. My hands will harden on salt-encrusted lines. My back will darken under tropical sun. I will spear fish from our surging headrig, always pointed west. I will wander distant villages, penniless. I will eat papaya, mango and guava from the tree. I will rub coconut oil on a pair of brown Tahitian shoulders on a black sand beach. The hibiscus blossom behind her ear will smell like the too sweet perfume of my first crush. Is that what hibiscus smells like? I will leave Lunenburg

in one direction and return from another, a master of the art of
square-rig sail.

And until the day I stepped aboard, I worked like hell. I fell in love with Ariel, who had the same name as a famous clipper ship. I knew that the *Picton Castle* would mean our separation, and this gave me a feeling of nostalgia, or rather the anticipation of nostalgia, and the feeling grew as the date of our graduation approached. Each night, after working in the lab, I would scrunch through ankle-deep snow to her apartment at two a.m. And each night we'd make love on her futon, and while we slept we'd tangle our arms and legs more and more, so that when we awoke in the morning we would not know exactly whose limbs were whose and did not really ever want to sort it out.

On the first day of May 1997, I threw my bags over the rail and stepped aboard the *Picton Castle* as professional crew. With only six months until the voyage was to begin, her rig and accommodations were only half complete at best. Still, everything felt loaded with potential. From my first moment aboard, I enthusiastically tried to find my place in the ship's social structure.

My orientation began the first time I had lunch with the Captain and crew. I took a place next to Captain Moreland on the open-air bench at the stern, brimming over with the fond admiration I'd had for him since my youth. He turned his head towards me slightly. I noticed the shock of grey on his bearded chin and his slick ponytail that pulled thinning brown hair from his proud forehead. I caught the gleam of the slender gold hoop that hugged his right earlobe. His eyes were trained on me sidelong, pale blue with a glint of sarcasm. "Rigel, you realize that I'm your captain now and we can't be friends any more."

"Yeah." I moved away from the master towards the sound of the chuckling crew.

Lunenburg Summer

Lunenburg, Nova Scotia
May to September 1997

DAYS AFTER MY ARRIVAL ABOARD SHIP, I WAS ON THE dock helping Jesse, the lead rigger. I tipped my head back to see him standing comfortably on the crosstrees at the top of the fore topmast. With his scruffy hair loosely tied back and his wry smile, Jesse's rugged good looks balanced the refinement of his upbringing, evident in his perfect speech, his politeness and the fine books he'd read. Upon graduating from Dartmouth a few years before, he had chosen a career in traditional ships. He'd finally found an arena that challenged and excited him, and he worked and talked like he was making up for lost time, like the *Picton Castle* was his proving ground.

Jesse shouted down from his perch, instructing me to hoist the end of a large wire stay that lay coiled on the dock. He wanted to take the end of that wire, which formed a large eye, and pass it over the masthead, securing it in place

The wire rope was eighty feet long and slick with grease. I feared that as I hoisted this long stay up to Jesse, the weight of its tail would make it slither through my knot and fetch up on the eye, depriving Jesse of the slack needed to pass the wire easily over the mast.

"I think the wire might slip. Do you think I should put a quick seizing on it?" I shouted up to him on the crosstrees, knowing the wire wouldn't slip through a seizing.

"Well, it *is* heavy wire," the rigger shouted from aloft.

I was kneeling on the dock, finishing the seizing, when I heard the Captain's loud footsteps stop behind me. I turned to see his wooden-soled Danish clogs that not only made him a couple of inches taller but represented a pivotal phase in his life: four years as bo'sun of the Royal Danish Schoolship *Danmark*. In those four years he'd managed the maintenance of that magnificent ship and took part in the training of every young prospective officer in her home nation. I looked from his clogs to his canvas Carhart work pants to his flannel shirt, puckered at the sleeves by a black wool vest buttoned tightly about his slight paunch. I rested my eyes on his gold wire-rimmed glasses, his stern expression.

"You don't need that seizing," he said.

"Are you sure?" I asked, not sensing the insult I implied.

"Of course I'm sure!"

He walked away as I removed the seizing and hoisted the stay to Jesse. The great wire ascended, wilting on either side of my knot, not slipping an inch. Impressed that the Captain's knowledge allowed him to rig without wasted effort, I burned to learn more.

The wire reached Jesse. He grabbed its dangling eye, slam-dunked it over the top of the mast and seated it in place. He was ready to descend, but there were no ratlines on the shrouds for him to climb down. Jesse tied himself to the line I'd used to hoist the stay and I lowered him to the deck. We carried another stay from the rigging loft and laid it on the dock in a great coil of greasy steel wire.

"Now it's your turn," said Jesse, stepping out of his worn climbing harness and handing it to me.

As I tightened the harness straps about my waist, I heard the Captain's clogs stop behind me. I didn't look up from the straps. He spoke to Jesse in a clipped monotone, more accusation than question. "Why is Rigel putting on that harness?"

"I told him he could place the outer jib stay," Jesse replied, looking at the coil of wire on the dock.

"This is not one of those fair ships where everyone gets a try. You start a fuckin' job and you finish it."

"I understand," said the rigger.

The Captain turned to me. "Rigel, do you know what you're doing?"

"Yeah," I said, without much conviction. Though I understood Jesse's instructions, I'd never rigged a stay before. The Captain turned and walked towards the gangplank to board his ship. *Clack, clack, clack,* went his clogs. I felt his dissatisfaction. *What did you want me to say? Something more decisive? You like decisive answers. You like one syllable.*

The clogs stopped. Said the Captain, "Rigel, do you know what you're doing?"

"No." *Why did I say that?*

The Captain grunted something incoherent and walked aboard the ship, his clogs making a deeper clatter on the wooden gangplank.

I placed the outer jib stay without incident, but it was the last piece of rigging I touched for quite a while.

My first task as the ship's painter was to renew all of the brownish-yellow paint, called buff, that accented the black hull of our ship. I knew this colour well because every time I looked across the wharf, I saw the traditional two-man fishing boats, or dories, that the colour was named for.

They spilled from the door of Kim Smith's dory shop, supported over the harbour on stilts.

For the next month and a half the Captain shuffled me from one painting job to the next. I wanted to show that the ship needed my skills and efforts, but I was never able to do anything right in the eyes of the Captain.

After days of various painting assignments, the Captain told me to paint the end of the headrig, jutting forty-two feet off the bow of the ship. "Paint the end of the jib-boom buff, like a yardarm," he said, indicating a length with his two palms facing each other.

The end of the jib-boom was collared by an iron band and terminated with a stretch of wood the size of a large wine bottle; half of it was varnished, half painted buff from an old batch of paint. I shinnied out the long varnished spar to cover the old buff with the new, slightly yellower batch of paint. I was careful to cut a sharp edge as I painted, dangling precariously. This was an excellent chance to prove my painting abilities.

I finished quickly and was back on the dock when the Captain planted his clogs in front of me. He looked at me with angry eyes shaded by a flat-brimmed straw sailor's hat.

"Rigel, you're really making me wonder about you."

What did I do?

"Are you stupid?"

I felt like a scared animal.

"What is that?" His voice went up as he pointed at the headrig and leaned towards me.

"I painted it buff."

"I know you painted it buff! Rigel, look around you." He gestured outwards with his arms. "Look at all the work that has to be done."

I looked at the ship. The topmasts needed more stays. Those topmasts required yet another level of masts stacked above them. Those highest masts too would need stays. Then, ten horizontal yards the size of telephone poles needed to cross the masts at different heights. Between the yards, our square sails would be spread. Those yards hadn't been made yet. Neither had the sails. I looked at the wine-coloured streaks and blotches of rust that covered the black hull. She needed cleaning and painting, badly.

"We need a ship by July. Do you think that with all this work I need you to repaint that little nipple on the end of the jib-boom?" His pale blue eyes poked at me like accusing fingers.

"No."

"Paint the jib-boom pole, Rigel!" He pointed to the headrig. The oriental dragon tattooed on the belly of his forearm flashed in the sunlight. He held my gaze for a couple of seconds and walked away.

Still rattled, I carried my paint bucket carefully, like it held the remains of my self-worth, as I shinnied again to the end of the headrig. I painted from the nipple on back. I laid sheets of buff over the entire varnished spar. *I am on the road to redemption.*

I heard the clogs.

"What are you doing?" He seemed to be begging. He'd left a conversation with my father to confront me. His face was drawn into a pleading expression as he pulled off his straw sailor's hat like an upset baseball coach. "You should try to get back the money you spent on that college you just graduated from."

I looked at him blankly.

"Paint from the end of the jib-boom to the iron band."

My heart raced with embarrassment. I started to itch all over. *He wanted me to paint the wine bottle section and only the wine bottle section. That's what a jib-boom pole is.*

"Get some thinner and wipe that off!"

I could hardly clean up my mistake fast enough. Then I was walking on the dock, next to the headrig, when the

Captain planted his clogs in front of me. "Rigel, what were you thinking?"

"I thought you told me to paint the jib-boom."

"Oh, so it's my fault? Is that what you're saying?" He stepped back in his clogs.

This is not going well. "No. It's my fault."

"Look, Rigel. You've sailed in some of the best ships afloat: the *Ernestina*, the *Shenandoah*, the *Niagara*. They're all painted like this. Why don't you know this? I can't go around explaining every single job to everybody—that's why I hired professionals. You have got to get your head out of your ass. You know this stuff. Use your head."

Some days later, I was putting a coat of varnish on the oak rail that surrounded the foremast when I heard the clogs stop behind me. Kindly, the Captain said, "Rigel, put on some clean clothes for lunch. We're going out."

At lunchtime, glad to have a chance to talk, I met the Captain on the dock. I took a satisfied look at the fife rail.

"Pretty fife rail, isn't it, Rigel?" His voice was disarming.

"Yes, it is."

We walked to Magnolia's Grill. Old forty-five records and foreign money decorated the walls. I sat across from the Captain. Over his shoulder I saw a large print of the fast, engineless schooner *Shenandoah*. Under full sail, she screamed past the entrance of Nantucket harbour, not forty feet from the beach. I thought of how much I'd loved it when her captain pushed the envelope like that. We were the lost boys then. Then my heart sank. I saw the white-painted end of the jib-boom that I'd painted wrong on our own ship days before, and the white ends of the yards—the yardarms—shining as clear as the stars that frame the Big Dipper.

"There's the *Shenandoah*," I said, hoping to strike a familiar chord with the Captain.

"There she is," he replied, smiling.

After some small talk, we ordered fish cakes and got down to business. "You may have noticed that I'm being hard on you." A probing glance.

"Well, yeah. A little."

"I'm trying to pull you out of your apprenticeship. You know that first there's an apprenticeship, then the apprentice becomes a journeyman, then he becomes . . ."

"A master."

"Well . . . he becomes what's next. There are no master riggers anymore."

Not even you?

"Rigel, you've had the longest apprenticeship of anyone I've met. I also know that you were in school every winter, and that makes it harder to advance . . . When I was twenty-two, I was the first mate of a brigantine on a voyage around the world. Now, mind you, I was lucky in the extreme, and I wouldn't measure anyone by my accomplishments. But I had opened my eyes beyond the apprentice phase and was seeing things as a journeyman, and that is what I want you to do. So, when I am hard on you, I want you to know that it's not to be taken personally. It's in jest and . . . insult."

We talked about my family voyaging, about problems with alliances and problems with my lack of freedom. I said I could live with my whole family voyaging. We finished our lunch. He picked up the tab and we walked back to the ship.

About a month later, we got some rain. I'd been praying for rain since I started painting. I'd finished everything needing paint below deck. And since the deck was wet, there was nothing for me to paint there either. I was assigned to the rigging loft and worked enthusiastically. The Captain instructed me to cut a length of wire rope and splice an eye in each end. This would become a footrope, secured to the bottom of a yard for crew to walk on when they loosed or furled square sails.

I spliced the eye quickly, hammered it smooth with glancing blows and trimmed off the ends of the strands. I secured it at waist height and began serving over the splice with a serving board. I started beyond where the tucked wires terminated and began serving towards the eye. When the serving was an inch from the eye, the Captain approached. He stopped my work and said, "I am going to show you something you don't know."

I thought I knew the technique but felt too cowed to con-tradict him.

He tightened down the final turns of his special serving by wrapping the twine around his fingers and pulling hard. It was quickly looking like the serving I knew. Tarred mar-line dug into the thick hairy patches between his knuckles. He paused to look at me. "Use a fid for this. Don't ever let me catch you using your fingers."

He pulled the turns hard and I wished I'd risked saying I knew how to do the serving. Brian had shown me the summer before. I could now only listen.

He drew noisy breaths through flaring nostrils. "I shouldn't have to be showing you this stuff, Rigel. You should know that there's a world of qualified square-rig sailors who would be more than willing to take your job. You're mainly here as payment to your father for the work he's done for the vessel."

"Oh, I didn't know that." Pain of shame hit my gut. The feeling that I didn't deserve to be here crashed over me like a wave. *I am a lie.* My skin crawled with stinging sweat. I felt my face flush red. It deepened the humiliation. *It makes sense: Dad worked on the ship all winter. He knew how much this voyage meant to me. He arranged something to make sure I'd be allowed to go. Fuck! Why can't he leave me the fuck alone?*

"And you finish off the service like this." A toxic pause. "Shit!" He cast a hostile glance about the room. In his frustration he'd finished the service backwards. He took short, deliberate breaths as he spoke. "Normally, I would fudge it, but since you're watching, I will show you how to do it right." He redid the service properly. I watched silently.

My father drove me home in his truck that day for supper with the family. He sensed my hostility. "Hey what's wrong?"

"Nothing."

"Are you finding Captain Dan a little taxing?"

"Yeah, I guess. Listen, Dan told me I'm on the ship as payment to you for your work."

He looked confused. "Oh, so he's trying to turn you into currency now. We never talked about anything like that." He took a pause to think. "No, we never talked about anything like that."

"*Oh.*"

"Rigel, think about it. Do you feel any less qualified than the other crew?"

I make a lot of mistakes. But I have my strengths. I'm in a slump. I'm as competent as most in my capacity. I have skills to offer.

"Look, Rige, I'm sorry he said that. I don't think it's true."

Over the rest of the summer, the Captain had more lessons in store for me. One, I remember, went a long way towards curbing my brainfarts, my mistakes made from haste or perhaps from trying too hard. Once, after I'd made an annoying string of errors, he said very kindly, "Stop for a second and a half before you do anything. Stop and think." Later, he challenged me to a contest, hoping to raise my awareness by seeing if I could spot problems with the rigging project before him.

As the summer continued, the crew's hierarchy evolved. Second mate Karen Balog and bo'sun Josh Weissman, a couple, arrived together from Alaska in mid-May. Traditionally, the role of bo'sun was to manage all areas of rigging and ship maintenance except for the engine room and galley. But the Captain and Jesse were already handling the rigging with great speed, so Josh was put in charge of managing the ship's painting, thankfully providing a buffer between the master and me.

Almost two months after the bo'sun arrived, I got a temporary reprieve from painting. It was now less than two weeks before the ship was committed to a fundraising tour of Cape Breton for the last half of July. We still needed to step the highest masts on the fore, main and mizzen. We had to install, or cross, ten yards. The ship needed painting, cleaning, stowing. And of course she still had no sails or running rigging.

It was at this time that the Captain gave me the privilege of helping Jesse in the rig. He and I were to climb the shrouds without ratlines and step the highest tier of masts, the t'gallant masts, while the Captain orchestrated from below. He stepped the masts in the traditional way, without any assistance from cranes. The crew walked around the capstan, winching the spars aloft. It was arduous work, but beautiful. Jesse and I climbed the bare shrouds many times a day. We used our arms to pull ourselves up, and supported our weight by hooking shins and feet around the shrouds.

On one of these days, we hoisted a mast aloft only to find that the stays were too tight around the spars. Jesse sat on the top of the topmast like it was a seventy-foot-tall bar stool and hammered brutally to force the stays into place. I sat below him on the crosstrees, struggling to support the weight of the greasy wires to keep them from binding on the mast as he pounded. The heavy cables shivered as Jesse hammered. Though I was growing stronger by the day, I strained to hold them up. Sometimes Jesse could force the stays into place; sometimes they were too tight.

We worked while the sun set. We worked until the Captain told us the day was through. Then we slid down the rigging to the deck, muscles on fire. At the end of each hot day, with the evidence of our effort aloft, all of us felt we'd put in a mighty day's work and spent our remaining waking hours at the Grand Banker, the ship's adopted bar, drinking away our day's pay. First, draft. Then tequila to stay awake. Then more draft to wash it down.

The day we finished crossing the lower yards, Brian Donnelly and Beth MacDonald, the chief mate and ship's doctor, joined the ship, Brian having recently upgraded his master's licence. With four days remaining before our Cape Breton fundraising engagement, the command structure was finally complete.

Brian slid into the role of second-in-command immediately. With the Captain whispering directions over his shoulder, Brian crossed six more yards in two days, leaving all but the highest yards, or royal yards, on the deck. The ship looked bald-headed and incomplete, but at least she was a square-rigger now. Brian found time one night, soon after we'd stopped work, to tell me I'd improved as a seaman—that I was starting to think. The praise felt like cool rain after drought, but I had to admit to myself that I had the Captain to thank for my awakening.

We lost two cooks by the time we'd circumnavigated Cape Breton and were now fed by a twenty-year-old called Zed, who was originally hired to help us paint. Nearly as good at cooking as he was at painting, Zed made spaghetti almost every night.

The workload didn't let up, either. Though the officers now insulated crew from Captain, it seemed he only grew more domineering and arrogant each day. We, the crew, responded by competing with each other, scrambling to stay off the shit list. It seemed that part of the reason we worked so many hours was that no one dared be the first to stop. Cleanups went on with neurotic fastidiousness until every last line and every piece of twine and welding slag and grinding dust was swept or picked off the deck.

I tried to slide into invisibility. Every movement was calculated to help me disappear. *I take my meals outside because the mess is the haven of officers, and of crew who hope to be officers. I don't speak out of turn. I work as hard as I can in places shielded from the Captain's glare: forward of the foremast, the forepeak, forward of the galley house.* Soon, I encountered other crew on my reclusive path.

Twelve of us were in the professional crew. I often looked in the faces of my shipmates and saw my own feelings mirrored in their expressions: maybe things will get better when the amateur crew arrive. Things will have to get better. Either that or the voyage might just die of misery.

That was when my father quit.

The Captain had bullied him as well, acting surly and uncivil, coming down on him in public—using words like *stupid* and *don't you ever*—once because my dad was so insubordinate as to shout information to him across a dock, once because my dad interrupted a conversation between his daughter and the Captain. The Captain also berated him for things outside the realm of his job, in his personal life. My father, for his part, refused to be humble. He became less obedient, disrespectful.

For the Captain, this was impossible, an insult to the chain of command that just made things worse. The cycle of disrespect continued until one day my father couldn't swallow any more recrimination.

It was a Monday. I was home eating lunch, my day off falling on a workday that week. The sky was choked with dark clouds, spitting rain. I heard a vehicle skid into the driveway, tires grinding on wet dirt. The front door slammed. My dad collapsed in a chair.

"I hate him!"

I had never seen him so agitated.

"You would not believe what that arrogant motherfucker did today."

I didn't want to hear. I only wanted to help end his frustration. "Walk away, Dad. I don't think it's going to get any better."

"Do you think I should?"

He needed out. "Yes."

"I'm worried what you'll think of me if I quit."

He wrote a letter of resignation, made copies and sent them to the company's principal shareholders and subcontractors. He placed one in an envelope for the Captain. I drove with him to Lunenburg to deliver it. I asked him to park away from the ship's view, so I could stay out of it.

I waited. Rainwater spattered the windshield. My breath had barely begun to fog the glass when I saw my dad walk towards the truck, quick steps, head down—bullish. We drove home, silent.

The next day at work, mate Brian asked me to go for a walk.

"Is it OK that we're not at work?" I asked.

"Don't worry, man, you're with the mate. This is a mate-sanctioned walk." He attempted to lighten the air, though his face turned a little red when he tried to talk of my dad's resignation. "I don't think you should quit."

"Well, I don't want to, but what about Dad and his pride? Don't you think I owe it to him?"

"Look, I respect your intentions, but I just think you should keep going. You still want this, right?"

"Yeah, I do. More than anything."

"There you go."

CHAPTER 5

Breaking Away

Lunenburg, Nova Scotia
Early September to November 25, 1997

WITH MY FATHER AND THE CAPTAIN AT ODDS, I'LL KEEP
a low profile. I'll do my work. Time will pass. Wounds will
heal. November 1 will come and we'll slip our lines. I'll sail
away, bound round the world. I am on no side. I will finish
these lunch dishes and then turn to making ratlines—high up
in the rig where everything passes beneath and no one sees me.

As I washed dishes in the scullery, lost in thought, the
Captain must have sensed my distance. He said, "Rigel, talk
to me."

I dried my hands and followed him to the end of the
ship's long wooden pier and sat on the massive log that
crossed its end. It was the way I'd noticed he preferred to
talk to people—on a bench, both looking the same direction.

"So, your dad quit the ship."

"Yeah."

"I find it hard to express how angry I am at that fact."

"Well, you don't know how upset he—"

"Listen." He stopped me short. "No matter how angry I ever
was at any management, I would always give two weeks' notice."

Well, you've never had to work for you.

38

"I consider your dad quitting partly to be my failure. He played an important role in the company, especially at the start. He became less useful as time went on, but we don't need to talk about that now. What I want to know is, are you going to quit too?"

"No."

"I've had the urge to quit. People would be scared to know how close I've been. People don't realize that I could throw my sea bag over my shoulder and be gone today. I could work as a deckhand on a tug, three weeks on, three weeks off, making $150 a day. On my three weeks off I'd travel. I don't need this." He swept his hand across his ship as if he'd just created her that instant, by magic. "You know I'm not a really good captain."

I laughed, embarrassed by his modesty.

"Really, that's not as humble a remark as it sounds. I am a better ship maker than a ship captain, but I am a very good ship maker. I really think this is a good place for you in your career right now. I think that the *Picton Castle* is the best thing going in North America in terms of traditional ships, with the rigging and the circumnavigation to come. And we have a good crew." We watched them toil on deck, their clothes and skin smeared with rust, grease, tar and paint. "We have Luscious Claire, Jazzy Jesse, Buckeye Becky, Passionate Pasha, Terrible Tom and you, Wretched Rige." It was the nickname he'd given me when I was a kid working in his *Ernestina*.

I looked at the ship, and for the first time since I'd arrived I saw not what work remained but what we had accomplished. I spoke hesitantly. "I just don't want to get caught in the middle."

The Captain soon did two things for the crew. First, he gave every single one of us a spot on the world voyage, even though he'd reserved the right not to. No doubt, in months, when our new crew became better sailors, some of us would just be taking up space—a $32,500 bunk. Second, he allowed us to take vacations at staggered intervals.

I took my week and spent it with Ariel in Quebec City. It had been a strange summer apart. We'd stayed in touch with letters. I painted her a picture that was exuberant and life-affirming and filled with learning. I did not show much of the darker spots, the painful or the humiliating.

For those kinds of hurts, and the urge that comes with longing, I had another way to cope—chasing girls. With the attention of pretty women I didn't feel so lonely, so inadequate. Their attention made me feel like a man, and I'd rub it on like a salve.

Together in Quebec, Ariel and I camped and then stayed in the Old City. She was reluctant at first even to look at me in my eyes that were the same green as hers, or to sniff my earlobes, or to put her chin in the crook of my neck and let me stroke her long blonde hair. But she did, and we had a delirious week that we'd thought we would never have. And splitting again was twice as hard.

When I returned to the ship, the frenzy of preparation had reached another peak. It was late September, and the ship had an unanticipated fundraising event in Boston. In the week before this trip, we worked for about ninety hours, still for the rate of $100. It took us two days to steam to Boston.

After a three-day string of daytime tours and nighttime receptions, we moved the ship to a sprawling industrial site in East Boston. Here the Captain would fulfill the second stage of his mission to Massachusetts: get fifteen tons of coal to fuel our cooking stove for fifteen months.

We removed the hatch boards that covered the squash court–sized cargo hold. We set up scaffolding under the hatch and made a human chain. Then we lifted 600 fifty-pound bags of coal, moved them to the ship, slung them aboard and lowered them into the hold, where we stacked them in an orderly pile. The rocks of coal ground against each other and their dust filtered through the plastic mesh bags. Soon the air was thick with oily black powder that worked its way inside our clothes, ground into our skin, caused us to sneeze through our dust masks and made our snot run black.

Our return to Lunenburg was delayed because of bad weather. Finally we pushed home through a cold, rainy fog. There was little time remaining to finish the ship for the voyage. Winter was falling on us fast.

The day after our return, mate Brian was up for his vacation. Bo'sun Josh and I were in the hold, shifting bags of coal, when the mate entered and stood before each of us in turn, looked us in the eyes and said, "See you in a week. Don't quit."

During that week we worked like zombies, removing the coal from the cargo hold and placing it on the dock, knowing we'd just have to put it back a few weeks later, once the hold had been sandblasted, painted and ballasted. We sent down the sails that we'd bent on just a couple of weeks before so we'd look good for our trip to Boston. They had to be treated with canvas preservative before we could bend them on again. We painted. We made ratlines. And because, thankfully, the Captain fired spaghetti-cooking Zed, we deckhands took turns making meals.

Despite all our efforts, it felt like we were only undoing our work. The ship was nowhere near ready to go. By the time the mate returned, there were just a couple of days remaining before the fare-paying crew were to arrive. Their primary berthing compartment, the main salon, wasn't even constructed yet. The Captain was ready to take his vacation, and if our exhaustion was any measure, he desperately needed it. Before leaving, he reluctantly told all but the mate and Dr. Beth that because funds were short, he'd have to cut our pay in half.

For the first time since he'd joined the ship, mate Brian called the crew together in a muster. We collected around the cargo hatch on the main deck. Some of us who'd been working below and in the rigging loft blinked in the afternoon sunlight like we'd been awakened from a deep sleep. *A meeting?* It had the feel of a mutiny.

Brian Donnelly wore a black toque and wraparound sunglasses. Red stubble darkened his jaw. His bony fighter's knuckles were clenched and barely visible under frayed cuffs.

"The reason I've called you all here is because of morale. We've all been working so hard for the past six months that we've lost sight of what we're doing here. I want you to realize that you're a part of something great. Although you may have forgotten, because you think your tasks are menial or insignificant, you *are* part of something great. I want you to remember that even if what you do feels little, there's bigness in being little. We're at a difficult place in the road, but I don't want you to give up. I think that now, even though the amateur crew will arrive in a couple of days and we'll have no bunks for them, and the engine room is torn into a million pieces, and the sails aren't bent on and no systems are up, and the Captain won't arrive for a week, we must turn and face the gale. This is just a bad spot. You'll see. Soon we'll be dancing in the trade winds. Flying fish will land on the deck, having hit the sails trying to fly over *our* ship."

I stood beside second mate Karen. She was shivering, smiling. The last week had been difficult for her. Since my father had left, she'd been relegated to the ship's office, a job she didn't relish. She answered calls from some amateur crew asking if they could have more time to extricate themselves from their lives if the ship wasn't going to be ready on time. The Captain contended that the ship *would* be ready on time, so Karen told them to get here and begin their training. She was doubtful, however.

I looked away from the second mate back to Brian as he finished his speech: "Take the rest of the day off. Get drunk and fuck."

The three couples on board made love. I wrote a letter to Ariel.

Most of the twenty-three fare-paying crew arrived a couple of days later. Less than a third of the new crew were college age, a third were young career people and the rest were either established or retired. They'd signed on before the rig was up, so they must have had imagination. They'd put their money down, so they must have been risk-takers. They wanted to learn, so they must have been curious. They wanted a new lifestyle, so they must not have been conformists. They had some money, so they were hardworking and in demand, or had inherited, or both. They wanted to travel, so they must have been restless.

The Captain would eventually distinguish two groups: Searchers and Explorers. Searchers knew what they wanted to find; they would not find it. Explorers did not know what they wanted to find; they would find it.

Right away the Searchers noticed that they had no bunks, and that the formal training they thought they'd come to Lunenburg for was weeks away. We threw them all right into the maw, and most worked diligently alongside the pro crew and subcontractors. Their numbers and enthusiasm brought a new life to the project. Despite the fact that our work hours were reduced to ten or eleven a day, we got a lot done. Only a couple of the new crew put up a stink about having to sleep in different parts of the ship because their bunks weren't built. Even those who had to sleep in the tool and paint storage compartment kept a smile.

The Captain soon returned to a mostly green crew, a far from ready ship and a rapidly approaching departure deadline. There was a shade of the deadly in that deadline. November 1 was a carefully chosen departure date, allowing us to depart after the East Coast and Caribbean hurricanes. The Gulf Stream would have moved its foul current away from Nova Scotia's coast by that time, and the northeast winds would be strong and fair. Wait too long, however, and the weather would grow too bad for this ship, with its untried rig and green crew. We could miss the peak trade winds for the long passages in the western South Pacific. That delay might have us crossing the Indian Ocean in December, when cyclones start to hit from the middle of the Indian Ocean to Madagascar. But if the Captain cut too many corners to get the ship to sea before she was ready, he could set up a host of dangers on board. On top of those concerns, he had to establish himself as the ultimate backstop of the ship, the master.

We began having musters every morning at eight o'clock. Always they began in the same way: the Captain stepped into the crew's centre of focus. The mate followed, with a mug of tea gripped tightly for warmth. The Captain stood straight at these gatherings, his face stern as stone. The mate stood slightly behind him on his right. Though Brian exuded the same toughness and composure as the Captain, he looked more rugged.

"Brian," the Captain would say, "is everyone here?"

The mate would pull out a list and begin to count, his lips moving slightly until everyone was accounted for. Captain Moreland would then address the pressing issues, assuring crew we'd depart on time. And perhaps to assuage those who expected structured sail-training classes and day sails, he offered that readying a ship for a world voyage was, in fact, sail training. "You're learning the ship, learning to work with each other . . . We can train for safety at sea, but the most important thing is learning to use your heads."

He explained some pet peeves of a traditional seaman. "Repeat orders. You must repeat orders—verbatim. It's not some power thing—an officer needs to know that his orders have been heard. It's about safety."

"Don't conjugate," added the mate.

"Don't conjugate," agreed the Captain. "If an officer says haul away the upper topsail halyard, don't say 'hauling.' It's like nails on a blackboard to us."

Occasionally, one of the youngest fare-paying crew members, a tall and rotund college kid with an enthusiastic interest in ships, would wave his hand excitedly like he was in elementary school and interrupt these talks with a distracting question. The Captain would stop speaking, indignant. The mate would step in and deliver the discipline. "Shut the fuck up, Bill."

Day after day, Bill would interrupt the muster, and day after day he'd be put in his place, establishing the gulf between officer and deckhand and setting an example for anyone who might think of interrupting muster with a question. Work started then and would carry on into dusk, six days a week.

By the second week, a professional hand was training a selection of eight new crew in rowing each morning while the rest worked.

By the third week, we were squeezing in the sail training that most of the crew thought they'd come to Lunenburg for. Work ended at dusk, around 1700 to 1730 hours. Then, bundled up against the cold of nighttime, new crew were taught to brace yards, hauling on lines to rotate the yards about the mast. They were taught to climb aloft, haul together, coil, tie basic knots—all this in the dark.

A couple of weeks passed in this pattern of long work-days and training. Our planned departure date of November 1 came and went. The Captain set a new date for ten days later. That date also came and went. Some of the fare-paying crew who'd been told the ship was going to leave on time felt cheated. They'd arrived thinking they were clients, and now they felt like indentured servants—shovelling snow from the decks of their tropical voyager, applying rust inhibitor while it froze on the brush, hauling scrap steel into the bowels of the ship's old water-ballast compartments. To ease their concerns, the Captain offered each a bonus of $100 and a per diem of $25 with back pay to the original planned departure date. The voyage was undercapitalized at this time and it was doubtless more than he could afford.

Despite the crew's unrest, and the frost and snow that dusted the decks, the voyage gained the glow of inevitability. The main salon was built and painted in a few days. The hull received two coats of white paint for the tropics. We treated the sails with canvas preservative and bent them onto the yards. We reloaded coal. We ballasted the ship. Along with crews of contractors, we installed battery banks, fresh-water tanks, a water maker, pipes and three small freezers.

The chief engineer, a Brit named Nobby, hustled about the ship in his engineer boots, grimacing like a hunted man. His list of jobs was staggering. Toiling madly to get the ship's assortment of new and antiquated systems up to the task of a world voyage, he teetered on the edge of exhaustion. Our fourth cook since I'd joined the ship, Lee, a good-looking and free-spirited South African of Dutch descent, arrived in those weeks. She provisioned for the voyage and left the job of cooking to the crew. We loaded five small wooden boats aboard the ship: two skiffs for making runs ashore from anchor, one excellent nine-man surf boat, one flat-bottomed Dutch sailing craft and one Lunenburg dory.

That dory belonged to Kim Smith. Kim was the dory builder from across the wharf and joined the ship as her professional carpenter. He had wild blue eyes and hair like straw, a mixture of blond and grey. Kim, the funniest man I'd ever met, could tickle the underbelly of every dragon that loomed over those days. His modesty was so disarming and his jokes so persistent that it was hard to see the immense pride he took in his dories.

Aside from being ship's carpenter, Kim was the cargo master. The Captain charged him to research what items would fetch the most money on the voyage and to buy as many as he could. As we travelled, he hoped to exchange the items for handcrafts. Crew would be paid five dollars an hour for assisting, and the cargo would be a contribution to the places we visited, giving us a means to participate in local culture. Once back in Canada, the handcrafts would be sold for a handsome profit. A third of the money would go to the ship, a third to the cargo master and a third to investors. I believed in the cargo plan and threw in $100. On November 24, we loaded the cargo. We stacked a tangled heap of used bicycles, two hundred used tires, five tons of used clothing, black bras, cooking oil, Pringles potato chips, soap, mayonnaise, WWII army boots and out-of-fashion bifocal eyeglasses.

After the cargo, we loaded old paint and a plastic Frosty the Snowman, digging tools, a broken chair, a massive sewing-machine bench, scraps of wood and scraps of steel. Finally, we lowered in a gasoline-powered welder.

On the day we loaded the cargo hold, I presented Captain Moreland a gift from Lunenburg kite maker Marilyn Congdon. It was a homeward-bound pennant, to be flown at the top of the mainmast on the last leg of the voyage. I put the pennant on the cargo hatch and unrolled it for the Captain. That giant black ribbon extended thirty feet to its forked end. A dragon's head, spitting fire, was sewn on it in yellow, red and blue fabric. I imagined what the pennant would look like flying aloft as we sailed back into Lunenburg a year and a half from now. *What will that be like? What will we be like?*

The next day, we made last-minute preparations. We cleaned the dock, emptied the shops. Morning went by in an excited blur. My dad came by to see us off. He looked on with a kind of restrained longing to be a part of it again. Despite early plans, I was now the only Crockett to be voyaging. Soon our docklines were singled up and I could sense that departure time was near. I was on the ship looking up at my dad as he crouched on the dock. We were trying to say goodbye.

"Do you want to write a note to Ariel before you go?" he asked.

I'd been trying to push her memory away. The quick flash of her name gave my stomach a sour-milk feeling. "I'll be right back." I ran to the fo'c'sle, stood on my sea chest and leaned my torso into my upper bunk. I pulled out a sheet of blank paper and a black pen. My hand shaking, I scrawled her a letter:

> *Dear Ariel,*
> *25 days behind schedule, we leave today for Panama. I have been so busy working that I've been lax in my correspondence. We're casting off now. I've got to go.*
> *I love you a lot.*
> *Rigel*

I wrote her address on a separate piece of paper and handed the two pages to my father on the dock.

"GENERAL QUARTERS!" shouted the mate. It was time.

"Goodbye, Dad." He reached down to me on the ship. We hugged, then I hustled aft to my post at the helm.

Captain Moreland ordered the forward and midships docklines be cast off. The hawsers snaked aboard.

"SET AND BACK THE OUTER JIB!" ordered the Captain. A couple of crewmen hauled. I could hear the sail's hanks scrape rhythmically up a stay. The outer jib snapped in the crisp wind. Two crew sheeted it to windward. The ship strained on her stern line as she pulled clear of the dock and swung round towards the harbour mouth like a storm door blown open.

The Captain ordered our stern line be slipped, then turned to me at the wheel. "Shape up on the channel."

I unwound the turns in the helm, looked back to the pier and saw my father standing in the small crowd, his eyes round with sadness. A foghorn sounded, and then another. Soon all the moaning foghorns of that ancient fishing town bellowed goodbye in a low, dissonant concert. The sound echoed off Lunenburg's frozen banks and the town's tee-tering stack of many-coloured houses and shops. The crew leaned over the weathered teak rail of the quarterdeck, waving farewell, cheering to the small crowd gathered on the dock. Jesse and second engineer Claire hugged in cele-bration. "We did it!" she yelled.

The chugging bass of the engine's smokestack dropped down a note after the Captain ordered the engine be put into gear. I kicked the wheel over a half-turn, knowing the propeller always throws the ship off course. I heard the musical tinkling of the water it kicked to the surface. We motor-sailed past the evergreen trees at the harbour's mouth and the rusty deep-sea draggers tied up at the fish plant. We sailed past Battery Point, a jutting finger of boul-ders with a small lighthouse standing watch at its end.

Captain Moreland ordered the crew to set the upper top-sails. I heard the squeak of blocks and new manila lines as those square sails were hoisted by their yards, reaching up, up, until they were taut as animal skins stretched for tanning.

With upper and lower topsails set, wind behind us and engine running, we slipped easily past the rocky headland of Ovens Point, named for the thundering oven-like caves drilled in its face by the waves. We slid past Rose Bay, my childhood home, and the bluffs of Rose Head. Dark blue-green waves exploded into white on its cliffs. I looked up at our rigging and the two square sails set on each mast. They'd turned a deep red, the colour of the sun setting behind us. The crew stepped timidly onto the quarterdeck, the traditional domain of officers, where I steered. They carried cameras to snap photos of our beautiful red sails, despite the Captain's increasing irritation.

I thought of the sunset. *Red sky at night, sailors delight. Right?*

CHAPTER 6

Sea Legs

North Atlantic
November 26 to December 4

THE SMACK OF TALL WAVES AGAINST MY PORTHOLE
penetrated my dreams. The engine vibrated the fo'c'sle where
I slept. The sea churned beneath as we tossed in the waves off
Nova Scotia. Nearly two hours after I'd crawled into my rack,
the fo'c'sle lights flashed on. Shipmates sat bolt upright in
their bunks. Bo'sun Josh spoke in an urgent voice. "Everybody
turn to. Mildred's broken her ankle. We have to wear ship."

I should've slept with my boots on, I thought as I lowered
my feet into them from my bunk and pulled the straps of
my foul-weather pants over my shoulders.

We crowded out the fo'c'sle door into the cold air on
deck. Our eyes were not yet used to the dark. Pelted by rain,
we headed down the windward side of the ship. An officer
told me to stand by the forebraces, made fast on the lee rail
amidships. I was part of a small crew stationed there to
rotate the yards. I looked aft to the bridge. Captain
Moreland stood silhouetted against the red glow of the
charthouse windows. His hands gripped the rail.

The order came to haul. Our cold hands gripped prickly
manila lines that were stiff with absorbed sea water.

The ship rolled to our side. Frigid water tumbled down the deck. It banked up the bulwarks and spilled into our boots. The mate eased the lee braces. I grunted a rhythm to help sailors haul together: "Two. Six. Haul!" We threw our weight back. The yards barely budged. *This isn't right,* I thought. On the main braces they had the same problem.

"Two. Six. Haul!" We hauled again. Nothing. Hatch boards chattered as more sailors clambered in behind me.

"Two. Six. Haul!" The yard gave some inches. "Two. Six. Haul!" The yard gave some more. Sails reluctantly turned on fore- and mainmasts. The Captain gave the helmsman his orders and brought the ship around on her downwind U-turn, careful not to get ahead of the slowly turning yards.

"Two. Six. Haul! Two. Six. Haul!" The yards were square to the ship. She pitched hard in the following sea. "Two. Six. Haul! Two. Six. Haul!" Soon she was broadside to swells and wind, rolling forty-five degrees either way.

A big roll dipped our rail. It lopped off a good swell that rolled onto us and bowled across the deck. It sloshed around the coamings, slowly draining out the freeing ports. The helmsman got the ship on course, swells on the port bow, and the ship rode more at ease.

When the off-watch crew were stood down, I sat on the main fife rail that girded the mainmast and let my boots dangle in disappointment over the cold water rushing from side to side. I listened to it stream by, cursing our bad luck, and wondered how Mildred, the retired microbiologist, could have broken her foot.

I watched Tom, my friend and fellow AB, move carefully from his handhold on a ladder to a handhold on the sturdy fife rail where I sat. White water broke around his large boots, which looked out of proportion with his whip-like frame. "Are you all right, Rige?"

Tom's big blue eyes and lashes suggested the sensitivity he worked hard to hide. I was surprised by his concern. "Yeah, I'm good. Just thinking."

"Maybe you should head in. Get some sleep."

"You're probably right. Good night."

By breakfast, the seas had lain down and we were close to shore. The ship had retraced the hundred miles we'd made south of Lunenburg and was nearly in Halifax harbour. Despite the fact that we'd been turned back from the tropics, most of the crew seemed delighted to return to Nova Scotia.

Soon we entered the harbour, past the warehouses that lined the bay. On one of their walls was written *Welcome to Halifax* in tall signal flags. We passed the historic downtown, took in sail and readied the ship to come alongside. The Captain docked his ship off the Halifax Maritime Museum wharf opposite the 1913 Steamship *Acadia*. She was a little larger than the *Picton Castle*, and had a similar white hull, made of steel and studded with rivets, complete with graceful counter and the *Picton Castle*'s former plumb bow. A closer look showed that she was built less than one hundred miles north of our ship's birthplace in Selby, north England. And while our ship was fourteen years younger, she looked older, and could easily do duty next to the *Acadia* as a museum piece. But she wasn't; the *Picton Castle* was a living, working thing, and even as our lines hit the museum wharf, an ambulance and press photographers swarmed alongside the ship.

Two deckhands assisted Mildred up the ladder from the main salon. She wore sunglasses and a brave face as she hobbled to the coaming that blocked her from the deck. I joined the two hands and walked with her to the gangway. When we reached it, the Captain relieved me and walked Mildred to the paramedics through the flashing cameras of the press. "I'll be back in Tahiti!" Mildred shouted as she left.

That day, I learned what had happened to Mildred. She was on second mate Karen's twelve-to-four watch.

The night before on the quarterdeck, Karen, always safety-conscious, had told her watch to stay buddied up any time they left her sight. They could go below to the mess to keep warm, just so long as they stayed awake. Mildred Broome went to the mess to wait out her watch. She didn't feel that she'd be of much use and spent her first two hours sitting on the bench, probably flipping through magazines, bracing herself against the rolls, having no real sense how the ship was going to move next. The massive engines below made a low-grade vibration and the radiator under her table would have heated only one side of her foul-weather pants, making her feel clammy. She read through the constant noise of rattling dishes and the occasional crash of something falling from a shelf, but after two hours in the mess she was unable to focus on the vibrating magazine print. Later she wouldn't be able to focus on the pictures. She stood up. An unlit kerosene lamp swung crazily near her head. She decided to get some fresh air on the aloha deck and walked carefully to the high side of the bench that made a crescent around the ship's stern. A gale blew across her right side. She looked around. The ocean was dark and swells rose around her, but the dramatic sweep of the deck kept the stern pretty dry.

She saw Marcello Bezina sitting hunched over a bucket on a hatch cover by the superstructure. Before we'd set sail she'd known him as the charismatic and handsome Montreal Italian who'd sold his luxury pet hotel to raise money for his voyage fare. He'd had a healthy, tanned complexion, but now his face was wan. He shivered, hypothermic, bubbles of yellow-green vomit glistening at the corners of his mouth. The sight was too much for Mildred. She felt that telltale pinch at the back of her tongue and rose gently, grasping the rail, looking for her moment to move safely to the lee side. She balanced, took a long stride towards a stanchion halfway there, and held on. The ship rolled and then levelled. She stepped for the lee rail. The ship lurched, rolling to port. Off balance, she ran to catch up with her falling body. Mildred slammed into the steel lube oil barrels lashed to the rail. She wedged a foot between them and continued to fall. With a pop-pop-popping sound, she wrapped her ankle around a barrel.

Marcello put down his barf bucket and forced himself to get up. Mildred lay crumpled on the deck, her eyes wide. She placed her hand on her mouth, a signal that Marcello took to mean she needed to vomit. He placed his hands under her arms and lifted her to the rail. She vomited, then relaxed, placing weight on her ankle. With a shriek of pain she fell to the deck, then was silent. Marcello noticed that the toes of her left boot pointed not to the front but to the side.

Word quickly got to the quarterdeck that Mildred was injured. Second mate Karen immediately woke the Captain. Doctor Beth, one of Karen's ABs, descended a ladder just feet from the scene. Taking in the gruesome angle of Mildred's foot, she knew it was dislocated and likely fractured as well. She had to get Mildred someplace where she could medicate her, work on her ankle and leave her safely until the ship could get to shore. She decided to take Mildred to her bunk in the main salon. But to do that, Beth would have to transport her across the main deck, which was surging with near-freezing water. She got a team of strong watch members and an air splint from her medical kit. She opened the splint, attached the Velcro closures about Mildred's ankle, then inflated the device to stabilize the ankle. Five of them carried Mildred along the deck to the main salon hatch, icy water washing over their boots. They sat her on the coaming at the top of the ladder with her feet directed into the salon. She descended, supporting herself with her arms and her one good foot, sliding on her rear. Mildred didn't cry or show pain; her only concern now was that she'd lost her shot at circumnavigation.

The main salon was dark. Sea chests slid and slammed about. A flashlight rattled across a table and someone retched in a forward bunk. The team helped Mildred to the settee between her bunk and a table. They prevented her sliding off while the ship rolled. Once she was on her back, they removed her splint and pants. Doctor Beth examined the ankle closely. Grasping the lower leg with her left hand, she saw that the foot was not only rotated outward to a right angle but was shifted to the side, no longer in line with the lower leg. Beth manipulated the foot slightly and, like a shiver that travelled up her arm, felt the grinding of bone fragments. Far worse than a dislocation, this was also a serious fracture.

The Captain arrived in the main salon very soon after Mildred. Rainwater dripped from his sou'wester. He didn't waste time assessing Mildred's medical condition, asking, "Beth, do I need to turn the ship around?"

"Yes, definitely."

With that, the Captain hurried to the deck, the tails of his black raincoat billowing around his rubber, knee-high riding boots.

Doctor Beth knew that the fracture could seriously complicate putting the joint back in place. Even in a standard joint reduction without broken bones, there'd be a danger of pinching a nerve or an artery. Now, sharp bone fragments threatened these delicate structures as well as the joint itself. But if she didn't take the risk and reduce the fracture, swelling would soon compromise those very nerves and arteries. Beth decided to reduce. However, with only one joint reduction to her name, she wanted a second opinion. There was a brain surgeon in the amateur crew, but he was far too seasick to be of help. She decided to call her medical advisory on the satellite phone. And as she wanted Mildred to be ready for the painful reduction when she returned, Beth administered a dose of Valium and morphine before leaving.

Having discussed her game plan with the physician at the marine advisory service and with second mate Karen, a trained medical technician, Beth returned to Mildred. The pain relief had kicked in. Mildred was numb, though aware.

Beth positioned Mildred's lower leg horizontally in the air and held her foot with two hands, one on the heel and the other near the toes. A seaman had been awakened to hold Beth steady against the rocking of the ship. Marge, the sailmaker, provided counter-traction at the knee. Karen held Mildred in place from under the table. Almost everyone helping was partially seasick, and no one but Beth and Marge dared look at the deformed foot for fear it would make them vomit.

Beth held the foot gently. With her long blonde hair pulled back in a ponytail and her big eyes wide, she looked very young. She breathed in deeply, looked up, cleared her mind of fear. Then she pulled.

Beth pulled nearly as hard as she could, stretching connective tissues just past their former length. In her own spine Beth felt the shuddering grind of Mildred's bones. Aligning the foot, she eased back.

Under the table, holding Mildred steady, Karen heard the gritty sound of the ankle reduction. Aside from that, Mildred didn't make a noise. She squinched her eyes, squeezing out a stream of tears that ran along the creases of pain into her ears, soon overflowing onto the settee beneath her.

Stranded in Halifax by foul wind and storms at sea, we made refinements to the ship. Our shakedown in a North

Atlantic winter gale had revealed some improvements needed. We were set to work adding another part of purchase to the braces, which allowed the yards to be turned with less struggle. I led a rigging crew of new hands to help alter the blocks and line. I was taken aback at how well they responded to direction. They seemed to appreciate what I knew about rigging and worked with interest alongside me. In teaching, I surprised myself with what I'd learned of rigging: a collection of tricks, techniques and concepts that had synthesized over the years.

We installed safety lines on either side of the cargo hatch and quarterdeck. The mate organized the station bill, outlining what every crew member should do in case of man overboard, fire or abandon ship. The engineer was able to acquire some late orders that he had been forced to abandon in our rush to get to sea. He also repaired the heads and the drive shaft on our backup fire pump. A day was spent re-securing items in the cargo hold, and one day crew were sent aloft to break ice from the rig. At the Victoria General Hospital, the chief of orthopaedic surgery mended the seven fractures in Mildred's leg and ankle, inserting a metal plate and five screws.

During this period the Captain queried the coast guard for weather information, trying to find the soonest possible window that would permit another drive for Panama.

With the critical work done, we waited. The uncertainty was difficult. *Did we miss our best shot? It's December now. Will it be so cold that ice will form on the ship and rig? Could we smash it off before it destabilizes us?*

In the main salon they taped Baggies to the overhead to catch leaks from the deck. In the fo'c'sle our breath condensed into beads on the steel plate that lined our quarters. After sunset the beads froze in a layer of frost. Said Tom with characteristic dourness, "Ice inside, ice outside."

We rested. Our voyage time-off schedule was implemented; we were given two days off for every day on.

Eventually, the Captain told us we'd make another try on December 2, after five days in Halifax. But the opportunity was taken from him by more stormy weather. When all hands gathered on the ship that day, the officers led us through our emergency drills. We were told to go through the motions slowly, calmly, until we were accustomed to the procedures. After that, the crew not on duty were allowed to leave the ship.

On my days off I wandered aimlessly through the city. Cold rain and sleet penetrated my wool jacket. Laurel made a trip to Halifax to visit the Captain. Though she seemed delighted to see him again, the ice and snow on deck reinforced her decision that roughing it on the ship for eighteen months was not for her. She did, however, plan to join the ship for some warm weather in the Society Islands. My parents also made the trip into Halifax. My mother had been disconsolate that she couldn't see us off the dock in Lunenburg, and I was glad to have another chance to say goodbye. Mom's decision not to voyage had been made without difficulty. During the time leading up to departure she had been strong and silent, absorbing the family's turmoil the way mothers often do. Her object in voyaging had been only to hold the family together; with husband and daughter staying ashore, she knew what she would do.

On one of those days I wandered into a bar where some shipmates were hanging out. My favourite local musicians were playing their hearts out, so we danced and drank. Stumbling home to the ship that night, I felt we were a crew. The voyage had begun and we were excited for it. If we left the next day, it wouldn't be too soon.

As it turned out, we did leave the next day. At 1400 hours on December 4, after seven days ashore, we headed to sea under a cold blue sky rippled with high cirrus clouds. The ship pulsed through tall chop that gradually lay down, smoothing the way before us. By the time my night watch rolled around, the clouds had dissolved and white stars pierced the cold night. I was told to steer south, heading the ship for Orion once again.

CHAPTER 7

Chain of Command

North Atlantic
December 5

THE MORNING AFTER LEAVING HALIFAX, WE STEAMED
beneath low rolls of greasy-looking cloud. Confused swells
bowled around us. A light wind from behind kept diesel
exhaust hovering over the ship. With sufficient wind we
would have set sail to add thrust to the ever-running
engines, but in this light air they stayed furled.

It rained in fits that morning. The long underwear and
wool clothing under my foul-weather gear felt too hot.
When I reported for watch, bo'sun Josh assigned the work
detail: "Do a ship check."

I made the rounds with one of the new crew and reported
back.

"Done? OK. Get a bucket of water from over the side and
measure its temperature. There's a thermometer on the
chart table."

I dipped a bucket of water, measured the temperature
and reported it to the mate. He recorded it in the log. I
reported to the bo'sun.

"Done? Good. Check the coffee, please."

One of the Thermoses was empty. No problem. Just a

simple matter of walking the Thermos from the scullery, aft, to galley, midships. There we had a bottomless supply. Pour coffee into Thermos. Replenish kettle with water. Throw a couple of scoops of coal into the stove. I reported back to the bo'sun.

"Tighten the gripes on the boats. They're starting to get slack."

It was already clear that tightening the gripes that held the boats against the ship was going to be a daily job. Manila, though not stretchy like some synthetic fibres, tends to creep, slowly getting longer and thinner under loads. My friend Don and I waited for the ship to roll so the boat was pressed against its hull, then we tightened the lashings, one turn at a time. We moved on to the next boat. When we were done, I reported to the bo'sun.

"OK, good. Get another water temperature measurement."

I took another temperature measurement about an hour after the first and reported it to the mate. I stood next to him as he leaned over the chart, plotting our position. "The water temperature's six degrees Cels—" Just then I felt a nudge on my leg and jumped to the side, realizing I had blocked the officers' ladder to the charthouse, one of the Captain's pet peeves. He scowled at me as he ascended.

I retreated from the charthouse quickly and reported to the bo'sun. "Hey, Rigel, you done?"

"Yeah. The old man's in a bad mood."

"I know. Even Brian called him Captain Dark Cloud."

I smiled, enjoying the small conspiracy, but felt surprised. It was unusual for Brian to say anything disparaging about his master's mood, even to a fellow officer. So out of character.

"What do you want me to do next, Josh?"

"Why don't you clean the inside head."

In the head, I dipped my sponge into a bucket of cold Lysol solution and swabbed the walls. The pale yellow rivulets that ran to the floor reminded me of a story Brian had told me. Years before, in military school, he was in charge of a team ordered to clean the communal showers. Brian had the floors scrubbed with bleach and the walls wiped liberally with ammonia. When the ammonia ran from the walls into the bleach on the floor, the two chemicals reacted, forming a noxious gas that sent the cadets running and taught Brian his first practical lesson in chemical warfare.

Despite the mess he made of the showers that day, Brian moved up the ranks of his military school at an impressive rate. By his senior year he had been promoted to battalion commander and was the single highest-ranking cadet in the school. Brian had an advantage over many of his class-mates: he wanted to be in military school. He considered it his boot camp for a career in the Special Forces.

Brian didn't end up in the army. The summer before his senior year, he was hired as an apprentice shipwright aboard schooner *Spirit of Massachusetts*. It was his first time working aboard a ship, and the liberal-leaning crew encouraged him to rethink his views on war.

After his final year of military school, a solid achieve-ment behind him and a bright career in the armed forces ahead, he chose instead to be a traditional seaman. Though this marked a dramatic change in ideology, it was not such a big change in lifestyle. A ship's company, like any army company, is a tribal group organized under a recognized chief. Just like the army, ship life revolves around a central creed based on survival. Part of that creed is strict obedi-ence to the chain of command; orders are never questioned in public. Just as important, an order is passed down the chain as if it came from each link personally. Both lifestyles are rigorous and regimented, and require keen awareness to reduce the inherent risks of the trade. Attention to these risks and a common effort towards definite, tangible goals can lead to the formation of rewarding bonds in this community. Brian found a lifestyle aboard ship that provided the kind of organizational structure he most believed in: a strong chain of command in a challenging physical environment, yet without military objectives.

Having found the environment to which he was best suited, he achieved the rank of chief mate in nearly every vessel on which he served, making his maritime career just as intense as his military one, though not as sterling. Shore leave in the British Virgin Islands without the reins of the military kicked off a long descent into hard boozing and picking fights that no skinny kid has a right to pick. He won a lot of those fights, but those he lost, combined with the rum he drank, left him in poor shape afterwards, putting him at serious odds with his masters.

As the years went by, he matured as a leader and found himself striving to instill in his crews his own will to belong to an elite. This drive towards strictness and excellence in seamanship was a potent ingredient that made Dan Moreland and Brian Donnelly an outstanding team when they were respectively chief mate and bo'sun of the US Brig *Niagara.* I remember Captain Moreland once remarking, "Brian Donnelly is the best bo'sun in the United States, hands down."

At the time, I figured I knew what it was to be a bo'sun: it was the best job on a ship. The bo'sun's in charge of maintaining the rig and managing the fo'c'sle hands. He doesn't have to share the heavy responsibilities of the higher officers. He enjoys the perfect balance of fun, responsibility and privilege. I did not at the time know the qualities of a good bo'sun. Years later, Moreland would maintain that "The heart of a bo'sun is a janitor's. The soul of a bo'sun is a seaman's. And the mind of a bo'sun is his own."

Continuing to wash the walls of the *Picton Castle*'s head, I sponged above the bear-claw bathtub, cluttered with the crew's toiletries. I washed around the carved gilt mirror frame above the sink. Sweeping my sponge underneath, I accidentally knocked a toothbrush onto the lid of the cat's litter box. I picked it up, checked for witnesses and placed it back on the sink. A look inside the litter box showed it hadn't been cleaned in days. I realized that I'd have to scoop it out before cleaning the floor. It felt pathetic to clean the cat litter, because that had been my responsibility as *Ernestina*'s cabin boy ten years before.

Many years later, joining the *Niagara*, I'd hoped that Brian Donnelly, the bo'sun, would sense my eagerness to learn and take me under his wing, guiding me through the arts of the traditional sailor. He did sense my eagerness, but just about everyone was eager.

Brian fit me on his chain of merit. Those who were contributing most to the shipboard culture he desired were at the top. Until I could prove myself, I was "lower than whale shit on the bottom of the ocean." A big talker without the skills to back it up. That summer I was the one walking around the capstan while the other crew worked aloft to step topmasts and cross yards.

I saw a crewman be thrown into the water on his birthday and vowed that no one would ever get me in. Brian took the opportunity to have me thrown into Lake Erie nearly every day. Then he let me come up for air long enough to show me his nautical library. "A man can do anything if he knows how to read."

Working privately on my understanding of seamanship went a long way towards improving my situation with Brian. On the evening before I left the *Niagara*, nearly ready to pass out after boozing with my fellow fo'c'sle hands, Brian stopped me on the street.

"Get back in that bar!" he yelled. And as the ensuing fog of black rum began to close around me, he said, "You excelled this summer, Rigel. I look forward to sailing with you in the *Picton Castle*, with me as chief mate and Beth as medical officer." We drank the last shot down and I stumbled back to the ship.

I stumbled out of the head now, catching my balance during a lurching roll. Everything was clean—walls, mirror, tub, toilet, sink, cat litter, floor. I poured the brownish cleaning water overboard and stepped back under cloud and rain. I walked by bo'sun Josh, who talked with one of the new crew. Offhandedly he said, "Rigel, get a bucket of water and measure its temperature."

"Get your own goddamn bucket of water," I blurted as if by reflex.

He turned to look at me, squinting his eyes and sneering his bearded upper lip against his thrice-busted nose. "What did you say?"

The new crewman standing next to him, a former bull rider named Cowboy Brad, stepped back looking amused, twitching his big moustache.

Thinking that to back down now might make things worse, I replied, "Get your own bucket."

"Rigel, get the bucket of water."

"No."

"Go get the bucket of water." Josh didn't raise his voice, but a poisonous mixture of anger, disbelief and a bit of hurt had brewed in him. I realized that I'd overstepped my bounds, that I couldn't win, that I shouldn't win.

I grabbed a bucket with a rope spliced to its handle and walked to the rail. A green swell rolled along the hull, so close I could touch it. I thought about Josh. He was the man Brian had taken under his wing aboard the *Niagara* and subsequently had wanted more than anyone to be the *Picton Castle*'s bo'sun. Brian admired Josh's silent strength and leadership by example, his ability to bring out the best in

his crew and his constant expectation that they be account-
able for their work. Over the summer I had found myself
doing the best I possibly could for Josh, because I didn't
want to let him down, because I respected him for his fair
treatment, his attitude and his judicious skill. Talking back
at him made me realize how raw I'd let the last few months
chafe me. Hauling a bucket of sea water from the cold
Atlantic, I felt I'd let Josh down terribly.

CHAPTER 8

Rudder Unhinged

North Atlantic
December 5 to 8

WHEN I TALKED TO KIM, THE LUNENBURG DORY MAKER, about my confrontation with Josh, I described the whole situation: Josh's offhanded order, my snarkiness, my insubordination.

"Oh, I would've said the same thing, Rige."

Though I didn't know Kim well, I realized that I'd managed to confide in the one person who'd agree with me.

I'd known him only through the neighbourhood grapevine, as a rebel with a decidedly reckless streak. He was a native Ontarian who'd realized at nineteen years old that he belonged in Nova Scotia, surrounded by boats. From his dory shop, Kim watched the *Picton Castle* come to life. He couldn't stand to see her sail off without him, and the Captain gave him an unpaid position as ship's carpenter.

As we stood watch on the quarterdeck, dampness in the air blurred the stars and the setting half-moon. The mist gave me a chill and left a slick dew on the deck and superstructure. The ship surged on through the windless night.

Earlier in the day, a following wind arose and the Captain ordered that the upper and lower topsails be set, along with the large foresail. The ship made a little more speed while motorsailing, but it remained to be seen how she'd handle under sail alone. Now, all but the lower topsails had been taken in. The three remaining sails hung from their yards, folded in quarters by their gear. In the white glow of our masthead light, they swung forward and aft with the pitching of the ship.

Orion rose in the east at the beginning of my watch. He climbed the sky in an arc and now stood over the southern horizon ahead. Aft of the ship, the Big Dipper dragged its handle through the waves.

Rapidly, a line of dense cloud shoved in to cover the northern constellations. The mate's back stiffened as he saw the green wall of a dense squall line register on the radar. He woke the Captain. We were quiet on the quarter-deck, waiting for orders, when it hit.

A powerful squall beat down on the ship from the starboard side. It drove hard rain and impaired visibility. The ship heeled sharply in the powerful blast. Swaths of water hissed through scuppers and freeing ports. In cold torrents it tumbled across the main deck. "Rigel, wake three of the best fo'c'sle hands," the mate commanded.

Brian ordered the helmsman to head the ship off the wind. The deck drained as the ship levelled momentarily. She accelerated. I woke the fo'c'sle hands and we hurried to the foremast, where Josh dispatched crew to the yards.

The ship heeled hard. I pushed to the windward side of the deck. I swung up to the rail and climbed the ratlines as fast as I could. The squall pressed me to the shrouds. Cold cable bit my hands. Rain crackled on my sou'wester. Unfurled square sails throbbed and snapped in the gale. They clapped full, lifted and dumped their wind. The fore lower topsail was stretched drum-tight. I heard its chain sheets work in their sheaves, steel on steel.

I climbed up the shrouds. Up around the tops. Up the topmast shrouds. I stopped at the upper topsail yard, fifty-five feet above water. That sail kicked up overhead in the wind, gusting fifty miles an hour. I stepped across the void from shroud to footrope. I grasped for something solid and pulled myself onto the yard. At once, I bent my waist over the spar and swung an arm over a fold of sail. I jammed it under my gut and moved out on the yard, shuffling my feet along the footrope as a green sailor stepped on beside me, jerking the footrope up towards the yard. He was new, but he knew what to do: hold tight and gather sail. We slapped another fold and jammed it under our guts before it flew back and flogged us. Bunched it in. Formed a canvas skin. Tied it down with a gasket so no wind could lift it free. Moved to the next sail.

By the time we reached the foresail, another force ten squall had hit. Squalls often come in a series, each blast of wind and rain more fierce than the one before. It ripped dense swarms of foam and spray from the swells. Frothy crests glowed red and green in our sidelights, ploughing off the bow as we pitched. Beside me, Jesse, who'd spoken often of force ten conditions encountered crossing the Atlantic by tall ship, said soberly, "This is really crazy."

When I climbed down to the deck, I was sent to the wheel. Mate Brian ordered me to keep the ship on course between major gusts. When it really blew, he had me head her off the wind to keep the lee rail above water and protect the ship's boats, which dangled over the side in their davits.

Over the din of the squall I could hear Kim: "It's blowin' up my nostrils and out my ears!"

I pulled hard on the wheel's spokes, responding to Brian's measured helm orders. The worm gear that allowed our wheel to turn the rudder was very powerful. Still, the storm conditions were making it difficult it turn. The sea behind us pushed our stern from side to side and I heard the rudder post knock hard in the socket that turned it at the base of our steering gear.

The squalls passed after two hours and abated to a light rain. When mate Brian stood us down from watch, Kim said the wind was so strong it blew the hat off his head. He said it was so strong that all he had to do was reach up in the air and pull down a different one.

We settled into another heavy-rolling night. I braced myself in my bunk and fell into a fitful sleep, waking occasionally to see the fo'c'sle at some unnatural angle. I'd clutch the edges of my bunk just in time to keep from falling out.

On watch the next morning, the wind was returning to its strength of the previous night. Gusts whipped the tops of the swells into foamy meringues and smeared them in streaks across the waves. The sky was thick with white cloud moving fast. Even with our propeller enhancing the responsiveness of the rudder, it took careful helmsmanship to ride the swells without being thrown off course. We cleaned, steered, stood lookout. We woke the next watch. The cycle of duty and time off felt more natural each day.

After watch I lay in my bunk, amazed that if everything went right no one would ask me to do anything for the next eight hours. Eight hours of uninterrupted free time. *When was the last time any of us had that?* I let the long hours draw me into a book, and I read until my eyes hurt and I felt seasick. I realized that the ship rolled much more than before. Out my porthole I saw a low cover of knotted grey cloud. It rained heavily. A winter storm was brewing.

I needed to use the head. I stepped down from my bunk, dressed and walked aft down the deck, timing my movement to the motion of the ship and the deep, cold water that tumbled side to side. I closed myself into the head. The place was once again ripe with the smell of vomit. *It's no wonder everyone gets sick in here.* Leaving the head, I passed by Kim in the mess room.

I knew that Kim had sailed in Lunenburg scallop draggers and that he'd spent many a winter at sea in weather worse than most of us had ever seen. Still, I wondered how anyone could be so cavalier. He sat at the mess table, his blue eyes and long eyelashes strangely magnified by thick oval reading glasses, poring over a hardbound edition of *The Perfect Storm.*

"How can you read that?" I asked. The ship rolled heavily. He just looked at me.

"Kim, what do you think of this ship? How is she compared to the scallop draggers you've been in?"

"Oh, she's great," he said.

"Really?"

"Well, she's . . . you know, some ships are too tender and they just lay right over. That's scary. And some ships are so stiff, they're just like a wall. And the waves pummel them and that's even worse than the tender kind. This ship's just right. She just kind of rolls with it."

It was true. Only rarely did an ill-timed swell catch the ship off guard and leave her staggering. Her wooden decks were tightening up and the rig felt really strong—steel masts, heavy wire, black spruce, chain sheets. The *Picton Castle* seemed glad to be at sea again.

It was our food service that was inadequate for the North Atlantic winter. That night at supper, with swells two storeys high, one crewman brought a big pot of rice and another brought chicken soup down to the main salon. They say hunger is the best sauce, and because the food was an hour late, excitement had risen among those who could stomach it.

They had waited blissfully unaware that cook Lee in the galley had been crying with frustration as she struggled to stay balanced on her slippery floor in the turbulent sea. She raged into a Dictaphone about the weather and her fickle coal stove that wouldn't heat her broth. Finally her soup did boil, but with a hungry crew waiting below, she'd saved time by leaving in the chicken skeleton. Reaching for one of her kettles to thin the broth, she grabbed the wrong one and poured in a slug of her godawful coffee, then stirred it in with the big black dildo she kept on the counter.

Down below, the pots of soup and rice were placed on a non-skid mat at the base of the foremast and lashed in place. When the crew finally had their meal, they sat down on the sea chests and settees that surrounded the tables, holding their bowls like beggars to keep them from spilling. Soon the tables were swimming in soup and chicken vertebrae.

That night on watch, the gusts were storm force—strong enough to peel shingles off rooftops and rip trees out of the ground, wind that's rarely experienced on land. Wind Kim said was strong enough to blow the handles off the hatches. The gusts peeled pellets of water off the ocean, hurled them at the ship and heeled her so her boats, secured high on their davits, nearly touched the swells. Mate Brian ordered me to head the ship off the wind.

On through the night, the ship pounded through the storm.

And in the morning, after the daily corn flakes and warm powdered milk, I mustered with my watch. The storm had abated to a gale. The sky was dark grey, the swells reduced to around ten feet with peaks of foam that reared up like white horses. I was told to relieve the helmsman. As I approached him, he told me that the ship was cranky in the following sea and mentioned an unfamiliar squeak in the steering gear.

"Hear that? Yes . . . there it is."

I repeated the course ordered and took the wheel. Curious about the sound, I looked under the wheel box for its source. It grew louder. In the grey morning light I saw a crack running up a weld in the socket that transferred the wheel's torque to the rudder. When the ship moved side to side, pressure was forced on the rudder. That intermittent pressure twisted open the crack in the weld. The fracture seemed to breathe.

I got the Captain's attention and showed him the break. His eyes widened as he realized he was close to losing his prime steering mechanism. There was a backup nearby—a three-foot-long emergency tiller in a box next to the wheel—but in order to install it, we would have to completely remove the 400-pound steel worm-gear apparatus that drove the rudder. In the best of conditions it would be difficult; in a gale, with a slippery deck and the ship rolling heavily, it would be deadly dangerous. As well, using the emergency tiller would require two trained helmsmen at all times—one on each side of the tiller using a block and tackle to pull it side to side.

The Captain quickly decided he would do what he could to save the broken socket. He ordered me on a course more downwind that put less strain on the fractured socket. I tried to ride with the swells while he backed off the throttle and sent carpenter Kim to get some steel c-clamps he hoped would prevent the crack from spreading. He sent another shipmate to summon Nobby from his breakfast.

Moments later, Nobby, our British engineer, strode down the quarterdeck towards the wheel. His seaboots rolled heel to toe. An expression of concern showed through his reddish, unkempt beard, a rectangular grimace that exposed both rows of teeth.

He arrived to see the Captain and chief mate affixing clamps about the fractured socket. After the three discussed the repair, the Captain decided that Nobby must place lengths of thick steel flat bar on either side of the fracture and bolt it up tight, sandwiching it in place. Then he'd have to weld the hell out of it.

Nobby took some measurements and prepared his cutting torch while Josh found the flat bar in the hold, extricated the portable welder and had it moved to the quarterdeck.

On the main deck, with sea water rolling over his boots, Nobby fired up his welding torch and cut his sections of flat bar. His jury-rig would have to be a hell of a lot stronger than the c-clamps that were there. I heard a thud as one hit the deck, its back snapped like a breadstick. I steered as gently as I could.

Nobby arrived on the quarterdeck with the newly fashioned components and began to assemble them with his nimble fingers. He hoped the bolts would stabilize the fracture enough that he could weld it shut. His repair would have to be brutally strong. If it failed, it would do so when stress was greatest—during a squall or a storm at night. If it failed then, we would likely lie broadside to the waves, rolling on our beam ends with twenty-foot seas crashing over the side. Installing the emergency steering gear then was a thought he did not want to consider.

Nobby mumbled something about his *"spannah"* and went below. After being aboard ship in the U.S. and Canada for almost four years without another Brit for miles, Nobby still insisted on saying "spanner" and not "wrench." Constant dialect, delivered in the thickest accent. When challenged to use the vernacular, he defended the "Queen's English" vehemently; and the Queen too; and the House of Lords; and the whole caste system of his motherland that places them at the top by virtue of heredity. And though his nickname, Nobby, is British slang for "noble," he had a strong affinity to the working class. It was all tied to his instincts for humility and loyalty, ideals that had served him well aboard the *Picton Castle*. And in his eyes the ship served him well in return, providing a steady paycheque, three meals a day, a huge engine room full of challenges and now the circumnavigation he'd worked almost four years for. He was sure as hell not going to let it fall apart now.

Nobby emerged on the quarterdeck in a blue baseball hat, black foul-weather pants and a blinding red suede welding jacket. He carried his welder's face shield by a post that extended from its bottom. Though loyal, Nobby was not a conformist. He obstinately refused to use the conventional style of face shield that straps to the head. Instead, he insisted on holding the mask to his face like he was at a masquerade ball.

The portable welding machine roared louder than a lawn mower. With gloved hands Nobby tapped the broken joint with his electrode, trying to strike an arc. Nothing. The electrode briefly flashed blue light. The welding machine bogged down, labouring to push current through his electrode. The electrode had fused to the steel. Nobby unclamped the welding rod from its holder, pried the quill from his work and tried again. He inserted a new welding rod and tapped the steel again. A blue flash and again the engine bogged down. Another rod stuck to the project. Nobby pried it loose and chucked it into the sea.

Nobby was a trained welder with years of professional experience under his belt, but the sea's heavy roll made the task challenging even for him. He needed to maintain a steady ⅛-inch gap between his rod and the fracture for an electric arc to cross. If he couldn't maintain this critical gap, an arc wouldn't form to melt the fractured steel and carry filler metal to build it up.

Finally, he struck an arc and held it, running a whole rod down to a stub. He put down his mask and I could see that his glasses and shield were fogged by condensation and salt spray. He pitched the stub of his rod into the sea, chipped the slag off his bead and took a quick look at the weld. The quality wasn't good enough. The gale-force winds allowed impurities into the bead. Over the combined roar of welding machine and gale, he called for someone to make him a windbreak. Cowboy Brad arrived with a sheet of plywood to block the wind.

Nobby struck an arc and fused the rod to his work. The welder bogged down. Electricity hummed. He stopped, broke the rod from his work and began again. *Tap, tap, tap. Flash.* The engine bogged down. The rod stuck. He stopped. Broke the rod from his work, frustration in his eyes, and inserted another. *Tap, tap, tap. Flash.* The electric blue arc remained, hissing, crackling, smelling like sulphur.

On he went. *Tap. Flash. Hiss and burn. Tap. Flash. Hum. Splash.* A large swell rolled into the ship's quarter. So focused on his work, Nobby didn't expect it and was knocked into the rail five feet away. He got a harness from the sea chest next to the helm and secured himself in place. *Tap. Flash. Hiss and burn. Tap. Flash. Hum. Splash.*

He started swearing. The salt spray and rain had soaked his leather welding gloves, conducting shock after shock to his fists.

Hours passed in this way. The next watch came on deck and AB Tom Ward relieved me on the helm. After reporting to my watch, I looked around. Many miles away to the east, I saw a waterspout, the marine version of a tornado. To the west, in a distant patch of sun, I saw a rainbow. I wanted to take some pictures of the welding procedure. I looked at the Captain, showing him the camera that I wore at my belt to ask for permission.

"Go ahead," he said. "This is what you came for, isn't it?"

Through the camera lens I saw Nobby hunched over his work, kneeling to stay balanced, legs spread uncomfortably.

His entire body was tensed as he steadied himself to keep the narrow gap necessary to maintain his arc. He endured electric shocks, icy wind and water for over six hours straight, laying a profusion of beads to compensate for the weakness of the contaminated welds.

Claire, the second engineer, climbed the ladder to the quarterdeck. The wind whipped her short, glossy black hair to one side. She squinted her big brown eyes against the rain. Her face and hands, often smeared with engine oil, gave her the look of a tomboy that was balanced by a sweet smile and a laugh like a tree full of songbirds.

Claire steadied herself with one arm. With the other she carried a sandwich for Nobby, helping to hold him together while he laboured to do the same for the ship. Tucked under her arm she carried a coffee can—her barf bucket. She used it every time she passed in or out of the engine room.

After delivering Nobby's sandwich, Claire descended the ladder to the main deck and swung open the steel engine-room door. She took a last breath of the cold, damp wind and stepped inside. The odour hit her like a hot, smelly pillow—air thick with a fine mist of oil, blown from the main engine at high pressure. One of the engine's seven in-line cylinders puffed hot, smelly combustion gas from under its octagonal head. Massive and over thirty years old, that engine throbbed and churned at the bottom of its cavernous engine room. On its flanks, atop huge rectangular diesel tanks, surrounded by a convolution of many-coloured pipes and valves, sat two diesel generators. One of them roared, adding to the din, burning diesel and demanding massive volumes of air for its work. These engines were so determined to get the air they needed for combustion that when the doors were closed, they sometimes drew their air down the smokestack of the diesel furnace that heated the after quarters, sucking smoke and orange flame into the engine room.

With no visual reference to the outside world, the engine room moved like an amusement ride. In its bilge sloshed a mixture of oil, water, vomit and hot rubber. The smell wafted up in the heat of the engine's massive iron block.

Claire had been counting down each nauseous minute of her six-hour watches. She'd stand an extra watch during this crisis, working almost twenty consecutive hours to give Nobby time for his repair.

Tap. Flash. Hiss. Burn. Tap. Flash. Hum and splash. The watches changed. The helmsmen changed. The ship scudded down with the swells and cold rain. *Tap. Flash. Hum and splash. Tap. Flash. Hiss. Burn.* Finally, by hour ten of the repair, Nobby was satisfied. He surveyed the job: bead on top of bead. Rows of weld burned angry blue and black. He neared exhaustion from the constant torture of welding in the gale. Still, he couldn't be totally sure the job would hold. And no one wanted to face the prospect of pulling off the prime steering gear to install the emergency tiller. The solution was to weld the tiller to the rudderpost on the deck below. When Nobby arrived on the aloha deck where the rudderpost was exposed, he saw that bo'sun Josh and mate Brian had already shaped the end of the emergency tiller with a gas-cutting torch and ground it to fit snugly. In almost no time Nobby made the final welds, finishing the job.

Meanwhile, the Captain had decided to head the *Picton Castle* for Bermuda instead of Panama. Though it would cost him more time and interrupt his crew's adjustment to the ship, a stop in port would allow him to permanently repair the jury-rigged steering gear and rest his tired crew. He made for the island.

That night was one of the darkest since we'd set sail. On watch, bo'sun Josh and I stood next to each other at the forward end of the quarterdeck. Cold wind nipped at our ears as we stood silent, watching the sturdy lower topsails pull at their chain sheets in the near gale-force wind. Hardly a word had been spoken between us since the bucket incident. When I did apologize, he just looked away. In the two days since my outburst, this was the first time he'd stood near me. In our silence I heard the wind hum, the engine chug, the rain patter my canvas sou'wester. Water rushed on deck. Eventually, with eyes fixed on the straining canvas of the main lower topsail, Josh said, "The mate's thinking of having us set the upper topsails."

He was silent again. The sound of the sea rushed in to fill the space left by his voice, and I thought with trepidation of our broken rudder and the punishing squalls we'd weathered since we left Lunenburg nearly two weeks before.

Again Josh spoke. "I think he should set his own goddamn upper topsails."

The mate didn't have us set the upper topsails. Less than an hour after Josh and I spoke, a series of squalls hit—each one more fierce than the last. The final squall nailed us with a mass of driving rain and spray torn from the surface to glow white in our masthead light and curl around us like a shroud moving faster than thought. The wind grabbed at our breath and enveloped the ship. She heeled hard. Water piled over the lee rail, expelling the air below the quarterdeck in a *whoosh*. It rolled and tumbled between bulwarks and superstructure. The mate stood next to me, giving orders. His steady voice gave me reassurance.

"Head her off a point, Rige."

I leaned into the helm and caught biting wind and rain on my face. I pulled against the force driving the ship's head into the storm. I flashed for a second to Nobby's repair: we'd probably broach to if it failed now. The wind

screamed and built. The ship heeled harder. Water tumbled aboard, surged along the deck. A swell rose to meet
our lifeboat, swung out on its davits. It entered the ocean to
its waterline and made a rooster-tail wake, moving faster
through the water than it ever had. Any deeper and we were
going to rip it from its davits.

Brian tensed his grip on the binnacle. "Fall off another
two points."

I hauled one spoke at a time, trying to make her fall off.
She responded and soon was headed nearly straight downwind. She stood up again, her yards braced jauntily,
spilling much of the squall's power, strong enough to draw
another comment from Kim: "It's strong enough to blow
the cunt off a cow!"

CHAPTER 9

Training

Bermuda to Aruba
December 9 to 20

BERMUDA'S OLD ROOFTOPS WERE STEPPED ON ALL FOUR sides and whitewashed. Stripes of shadow and bone white played on their surface as the winter sun travelled across the sky. When it set behind the cedars of St. George, all down the banks to the harbour, those black and white rooftop stripes blended to grey. We motored away from town to the narrow cut that led to the Atlantic, past a half-sunken iron sailing ship lying rusted, gutted and utterly abandoned. I saw three empty holes where masts once stood in that derelict square-rigger's deck—a deck that was now so rotten, frames and beams lay visible like the ribs of a long-dead animal. An iron bowsprit, tapered and riveted in the old style, protruded over her clipper bow. If one looked past the decay and rust, she was a ship much like the *Picton Castle*.

"A touch left," the Captain ordered me at the wheel, heading his ship for the cut.

I aimed the ship by the planks that ran along her deck. Directly ahead, two fissured walls of rock came into view with a ribbon of water running between. The Captain gripped the quarterdeck rail, craning his head over the side for a look down the cut. Without looking away, he commanded minute steering corrections with his slender fingers. Once he looked aft to see me holding back the giggles. Second helmsman Lori, the only other crew member to have circumnavigated, albeit on a cruise ship, had been making her usual wry comments and we were giddy with nervous laughter. A tense moment passed. He looked back to the channel with suppressed exasperation. A touch right. Steady. A touch left. Steady.

In the dusk, beyond the cut, lights on channel buoys blinked red and green, leading us back to northwest gales. The sun had set and the ship pitched in unprotected water. I was suddenly cold, dressed more for Bermuda than the wintry ocean. And now we were smack in the middle of it.

I saw crew coiling lines and heading below for supper. Later, after some had been fed, a helmsman came to relieve me. I reported the ordered course, waited for him to repeat it and walked to the charthouse to report the course to the Captain. Knowing what was coming, I spoke quickly and scrambled down the ladder to the main deck.

"Rigel!" barked the Captain from above.

I snapped around, looked up and saw the white of his tall forehead and face. His beard was recently shaven and ponytail clipped so his hair flew in the breeze. He gripped the bridge rail and leaned over it like a pulpit.

"Captain."

"What am I going to do with you?" he asked in a stern monotone.

I hated that question and how it made me feel like a child. I was silent for a moment. The air was cold. Frigid water washed around my boots. "I don't know," I said finally.

"Why do you insist on joking while you're at the helm?"

I shifted my feet in the water rushing by. "I don't know," I said, tilting my head back uncomfortably to look at him on the bridge, knowing it was perfectly reasonable to expect a helmsman not to laugh while steering a ship through a narrow cut—knowing I'd already been warned.

"Rigel, you're my best helmsman, and you've done more to prepare for this voyage than most people can imagine. Yet you continue to take it lightly, like everything's a goddamned joke." He paused. "What I need to do is send you to work in a paramilitary square-rigger for four years."

He turned and entered the charthouse. I walked down to the main salon to see if there was any casserole left. The compliment on my steering wasn't lost on me, but I was fuming. His words echoed through my mind. *I assume you mean the* Danmark, *the paramilitary square-rigger you worked in for four years.*

I sat down with a bowl of cold, pasty casserole. Across the table, Don and Patrick, two good friends that I knew from college and had encouraged to voyage, lay in their curtained bunks. Don had been battling seasickness for our first week at sea and had hardly eaten. When he stuck his head out from behind his curtain, it looked like he'd already shed some baby fat from his handsome Black Irish face. "Happy birthday, Rige."

"Thanks, Don."

I walked to my bunk, took off my boots, climbed into the damp enclosure and drew the curtain. I thought about my run-in with the Captain and wondered how I'd let it happen again. I had made the same mistake six days before, on our approach to Bermuda.

As we neared the island, ice-cold gales had melted into sunshine. The sea had lain down, too. Wind scales, hard edges and leaden grey softened to smooth blue swells. The island itself seemed at the centre of this phenomenon—a green oasis, protected from storm. I watched the crew as the sun rose and the island neared. They shed wool hats, then rain jackets, foul-weather pants, long sleeves, long pants. Everyone smiled. We couldn't believe our good luck that the steering gear had broken.

The feeling went away, however, when we needed to clean the ship's rust streamers with dilute phosphoric acid, or, as it's commonly called by one of its brand names, OSPHO. Smiles faded into confusion as bo'sun Josh put me in charge of a team of cleaners and instructed us how to spray OSPHO on rust streamers that had formed from sea water washing over pinholes of exposed steel, let it sit, then rub it off with a sponge. A man on my team couldn't see why he should have to endure overspray in his eyes to do this, and his feelings would be twice as strong when we cleaned the ship before heading out to sea, where it would not be seen by anyone. The intent, of course, was to make the hull easier to clean the next time, when she really did have to look white. It came as a surprise to many that cleaning ship was the greater part of our working lives.

"It's maintenance, man." I tried to look like I was having fun.

Occasionally we made way for a team washing the deck with a fire hose and long-handled scrub brushes. The cleaner's effect was gratifying and the pleasant turn in the weather even made the work enjoyable, but I heard people grumble about scrubbing a deck that had been awash for a week.

It wasn't long before I was called to my station at the helm. From there, I could see the white-and-red tower of a lighthouse. Some houses came into view—pastels of blue, yellow and pink. The mate, looking out on the fo'c'sle head, mocked the government regulation requiring Bermudans to paint their houses those colours. "This place is fuckin' Candy Land," he said.

When we entered the buoyed channel, the narrow cut into St. George's came into view. Second helmsman Lori and I were already giddy—excited to get to Bermuda, nervous about steering through the cut and giddier still knowing shenanigans at the wheel were strictly forbidden. The Captain made hand signals as we neared the opening until, fed up, he stormed back to the wheel. He said he liked laughter and he liked fun, and there's a time for both, but not when you're steering through the goddamn cut to St. George's!

As we steamed between the cut's walls, the rock visible beneath the clear water was sobering. Soon we were alongside the pier at Ordinance Island. Docklines were doubled up and covered in chafe gear. All lines on deck were coiled. Climbing aloft, we cast the sails free of their gaskets to hang from the yards and dry.

In the muster that followed, the Captain welcomed us to the island and told us of some choice watering holes like the White Horse Tavern, just down the pier. He had dropped anchor here on respite from his delivery of the *Picton Castle* to New York.

The last time the *Picton Castle* was in St. George's, he told us, she had been much more likely to end up like that abandoned three-master lying in the harbour than the sailing ship she was now, swan white, sails loosed to dry in the sun. He told the story of the two oak barrels of Gosling's rum that he'd procured on his last visit. One was empty—gone into bottles, most of them distributed to friends and supporters while in New York. The other was held in bond by Canadian customs, to be returned before we left. "It's probably just reaching its prime," he said.

"When are we going to tap that?" asked Cowboy Brad.

"Pretty soon," the Captain volunteered, with a rare smile that showed his back teeth.

Our days on the island passed in a blur of laundry runs, haircuts, mopeds and rum. Patricia, the Boston lobbyist, was welcomed back aboard, having left the ship in Halifax to take a break from the cold part of the voyage. Marcello, the Montreal Italian pet hotel baron, bounced back immediately from his seasickness. Colour returned to his tanned face. He combed his curly black hair, put on some fresh clothes and walked straight to the White Horse, as cool and smooth as the ship's black cat, Mr. Ficky. Marcello fit in well with us younger guys, though I suspected he was a little older.

Eight of us rented mopeds that we drove in formation whenever we were near the ship. In Lunenburg we'd had our jackets embroidered with the ship's logo, designed by the Captain. We wore them now as biker colours. The logo was a castle tower emblazoned with an anchor below the turret. A serpentine dragon entwined the castle as if he had just flown down from the sky, his front claws outstretched.

With throttles wide open we cruised the coastal roads to deserted beaches that were shielded by rock outcroppings, shaped by eons in the belly of the Atlantic. In the off-season quiet we laughed and shouted as we swam. Then we rode to other beaches with sand in our shoes.

One night we camped under a full moon on Long Beach. We drank Gosling's and ginger beer, roasted hot dogs on a fire of driftwood that smelled like cherries when it burned.

Mid-meal, the cowboy showed up with cook Lee on the back of his moped. Her thin arms were wrapped affectionately around his barrel torso. Born in South Africa, she'd already travelled widely, had been a runway model and a topless waitress, and spoke many languages. The cook and cowboy didn't stick around long, just long enough for us to feel jealous that he'd hooked up already, yet also relieved that we hadn't.

Later, when the rum bottles were empty, we lay on the cool sand, wrapped in bedrolls and warmed by liquor.

Milk-white moonlight spilled towards us across the ocean. We talked late, and before falling asleep below the high-tide line, Patrick spoke: "Hey, guys . . . guys! I have an idea . . . Let's sail around the world."

Soon enough, the *Picton Castle* pulled off the dock, shot the cut and continued south for the Caribbean. Northwest gales and two days of pounding finally yielded to calmer water in the Sargasso Sea—so blue after the stormy green of Nova Scotia's waters. With wind blowing briskly behind us, we set upper and lower topsails and t'gallants. I watched the sails pull as I steered.

After a while I looked over the stern and saw mate Brian on the aloha deck, fastening steel leaders to deep-sea fishing lures that he'd troll through these fertile waters. I looked out over the sea. Great rows of sargasso marched alongside us, like legions of copper-coloured spiders organized in ranks. A flying fish broke the surface and glided crosswind, deftly banking off swells, sinking towards the surface. Then it skittered its tail for speed, soared and disappeared into chop some hundred feet from where it emerged. *Its wings are so skinny*.

I remembered Brian's speech in Lunenburg, when he said we'd be dancing in the trade winds and that flying fish would land on the deck, having hit our sails trying to fly over our ship. I'd imagined then that the fish had broad, colourful wings, like butterflies, and wrote it to Ariel in a letter. Still, with their hummingbird wings flying for hundreds of yards, they were more amazing than I'd imagined. Brian looked up from his fishing gear with a hunter's grin.

Later, I saw more flying fish from aloft while securing chafe gear to the rigging. This time they flew in schools, or flocks, rather. From aloft, the sun shimmered off their blue backs. Together they moved like the waves themselves.

A flying fish finally did land on the deck, having first collided with Pasha, a gentle giant of a man who dressed like a pirate. By tradition, the Captain claimed, he had the cook prepare and serve that hapless fish to him. No one else on the ship had ever heard of the tradition of a captain eating the first errant flying fish in order to secure the voyage's success. Our captain had a lot of arcane knowledge. In Lunenburg, before the voyage, he had pulled aside mate Brian, bo'sun Josh and me to hand down his knowledge of sea chest construction. I was about to build one for the voyage, and was very interested.

Captain Moreland showed us the merits of each chest in his possession. "They're all different. That's the way it ought to be. They had sea chests built for *Pride I,* but they were all the same. They just didn't look right, all lined up in the fo'c'sle, exactly the same. In the age of sail, seamen would have brought their own chests to the ship, and they would have all been different." He had a light in his eyes. "This one's made of six boards, tall enough to sit on, not too wide that it can't be carried easily. I've placed runners beneath all of my chests. If you don't, the box decays. It's happened to me." The three of us paid close attention.

The Captain swung open the lid of a smaller box. "This one has proper, bent, forged-iron strap hinges, dovetailed corners, and it's wider at the bottom than the top. This design gives the chest stability and stands it off a bulkhead so you can throw open the lid and lean it back. There's typically a small compartment inside, mortised into the sides. Perhaps a sailor would paint his favourite ship under the lid."

He lifted one of the shackle-shaped beckets used for lifting the chest. "The fancier ones take longer to make than the chest."

I asked about the core of the becket, which gives strength beneath the decorative ropework. "What's the core made of?"

"Often rope," he said. "But just imagine you're a sailor carrying your sea chest through the streets of Hamburg to a new ship. Do that a few times and the rope core of the becket will chafe, stretch and break. That's why the best cores are made of wire rope, built up with parcelling, and have a rope-decorated steel bolt holding the becket in place.

"Beckets should be placed on the sides, just high enough so they don't scrape the floor when hanging down. When they're used for lifting, they must clear the lid of the box."

Using the Captain's advice back in Lunenburg, I had built a sea chest of six wide mahogany boards my father had given me as a graduation gift. Working nights and days off, I finished the chest just before we shipped out.

Now that we were underway, I decided to begin the beckets. I intended to make them better than any beckets I'd ever seen. I decided to use the best of all the advice I'd ever heard or read. I decided to show the officer I was a craftsman—that I was capable of the important jobs aboard ship that somehow continued to elude me. I relished that no one could tell me how to do this one.

Ropework aboard ship had reached its height during the whaling voyages of the nineteenth century. These ships were relatively small for their large crews, much like the *Picton Castle*, which actually could run safely with much fewer hands. On whaling voyages, personnel were needed for short periods of intense labour and otherwise had a fair amount of downtime. Illiteracy, and the long duration of deepwater voyages of the time, also contributed to handcrafts like knotting and scrimshaw.

The art of fancy ropework declined in the mid-nineteenth century clipper ship era. Those ships were larger, and war and economics left fewer sailors to man them. By necessity there was little time for leisure. Clifford Ashley, in his definitive book on knots, said that a sailor was judged by his chest beckets. I wanted to be that sailor.

As we sailed south through the Sargasso Sea, I finished watch at noon, found some abandoned wire rope in the forepeak and spliced its ends into eyes. I stretched the new cores on a makeshift rack of scrap wood and built them up with strips torn from an old bedsheet. By late afternoon my work was interrupted by a training session.

Bo'sun Josh told me to retrieve the heavy one-inch manila rope under the main salon floor that had been liberated when we replaced the braces in Halifax. The rope was brown, loose jawed, scratchy and musty like burlap. Following the bo'sun's orders, I cut it in two-fathom lengths, one for each member of the crew. Then, at the beginning of the Captain's watch, the mate called the crew together: "MUSTER MIDSHIPS!"

We gathered around the cargo hatch, water washing around our boots. Training in seamanship was a big draw for many of the hands aboard. We looked with interest at the Captain as he held a length of the manila comfortably in his left hand.

"This is the closest thing we have to old rope on this ship. Ordinarily, a ship would have a rope rotation. But since all of our rigging is new and none of the lines are worn, we haven't needed to do this yet. In the old coastal schooners, they would replace a worn forepeak halyard with a worn mainsheet halyard. A worn throat halyard would be replaced with a worn forepeak halyard. When that parted, it would be long-spliced and used as a mainsheet."

The Captain introduced his ambitious lesson plan. "Today I will show you how to long-splice, short-splice and eye-splice. I will show you fast so you learn to do it fast."

He unwound the strands of rope with quick flicks of his wrist, describing its basic construction, which until the advent of synthetic fibres had remained unchanged for thousands of years: fibres are twisted to the right to form yarns. Yarns are twisted together to the left to form strands. And then three strands are twisted together to the right to form rope.

The Captain doubled the rope back and passed a loose strand through its body. Someone asked, "Is all rope right-hand lay?"

"Pretty much," he replied, and continued to splice.

Cowboy Brad raised his hand and the Captain addressed him, tucking another strand. Cowboy Brad spoke with a drawl. "I know a lasso maker down in Phoenix who makes left-laid rope."

The Captain perked his eyebrows. All heads turned to the cowboy, inscrutable behind his big moustache and neckerchief. "He makes tight-jawed ³⁄₈-inch Dacron rope, twisted to the left so it don't get all knotted up when a left-hander uses it."

"Really. I didn't know that," the Captain replied, absently making another tuck while recalling another use for left-laid rope. "You know, at the height of the age of sail, when no detail was spared in seamanship, a deadeye lanyard, which provides purchase at the base of a shroud"—he paused to think, tracing in the air with his finger the natural counter-clockwise tendencies of left-laid deadeye lanyards—"would be left-laid on the port side, so the Matthew Walker knot that holds it in place could be in the forward end of the inboard side of a deadeye, consistent with the starboard side, instead of the inboard side of the after hole, as it's done now."

The crew looked puzzled. They watched while the Captain demonstrated two more types of splice followed by the two seizings most commonly used aboard. When he finished, the mate divided the crew into groups so less experienced hands could go over their splices and seizings with a member of the pro crew. I helped a couple of new hands learn to eye-splice, and was pleased by what I'd picked up from the Captain myself.

On watch that night, I saw that the stars had changed. Orion had moved higher. In the space he once occupied, there were a host of stars I'd never seen before. If we'd stayed in Lunenburg, it would have taken a couple of months for the constellation to change position like that. With calmer water, foreign stars and cool wind pulling in our square sails, it felt like we'd travelled through time.

The gibbous moon drowned all but the brightest stars in its hazy glow. I showed some of my watchmates the six bright stars that form a hexagon around Betelgeuse, the red giant in Orion's shoulder. "Capella, Aldebaran, Rigel, Sirius, Procyon, Pollux. Just remember this: Captain, All-de Rigging Seems Properly Polished. See how they sound like the stars? Just go clockwise from that bright star at the top of the hexagon."

The cycle of steering, looking out for ships, running ship checks and watching stars passed quickly. In the morning, we continued to motorsail at a fast clip down the Sargasso Sea towards the Caribbean.

I'd been keeping an eye on the trawls that Brian had set soon after we'd left Bermuda. Now and then I'd think we had a fish and haul in one of the lines. Always the same— copper seaweed snagged on the hooks. Then, one bright day, the morning routine of cleaning below decks was broken by a woman's voice from the stern: "FISH ON!"

Crew ran aft to the aloha deck. Bare and sandalled feet splashed in the small river that washed back and forth amidships. Running aft myself, I yanked an iron belaying pin from the rail. I hefted it like a framing hammer, ready to put the beast out of its misery. Brian had the same idea, hefting his pin, running up the other side of the deck.

Over the stern in our frothy wake, a big yellow flattish fish skimmed the water on his side. "A mahi mahi. Pull him in! Pull him in!" Brian said, gritting his teeth. He lost patience while a crewman tried to gaff the dangling fish and slung the mahi aboard himself. It arced over the rail— a gleaming three-foot rainbow.

Slap. He hit the deck. He struggled, slamming his bull forehead against the wood. His canary scales and blue speckles blended into jade. From proud head to sickle tail stretched a cobalt fin, fully fanned by long delicate bones, shivering in the sunlight like a Sioux chief's headdress.

The mahi threw his hook. "Quick! Get that line back in the water!" Brian said, clubbing the mahi. "We might catch its mate!" A mahi mahi mates for life.

I brought my club down on the mahi's head and hit bone, just above its human-looking eye. Pulling back, I saw jade scales stuck to my galvanized iron club. Now the fish slapped more than before and Brian brought down his club again. The fish slapped, flipping and writhing, sliding in a trail of shimmering slime down the slope of the deck. Whack. Whack. Whack. Whack. Then I hit the fish just behind his eye. Soft tissue gave way and scarlet blood burst from his head, spraying Brian and the newly scrubbed superstructure behind him. He gave me a grudging look. When I looked back to the fish, from sickle tail to human-looking eye, the mahi mahi ran grey like a watercolour in the rain.

Brian saw me stare at the transformed fish. "Amazing, isn't it?" he said solemnly. "That's the spirit leaving his body."

CHAPTER 10

Christmas

Bermuda to Aruba
December 20 to 25

CATCHING THAT MAHI MAHI WAS GOOD FOR MORALE.
One of the amateur crew, formerly a sports-fishing captain,
showed me how to clean and freeze it. Already I could sense
possessiveness from the crew towards the fish. They weren't
ready to trust the cook with our hard-won fillets, not after
the bacon she'd cooked that was bristling with pig hair.

We were motorsailing south at a good rate, nearly two
hundred miles a day, and the weather continued to warm.
We were in the trade winds now, and the heavy clouds that
had blanketed the North Atlantic broke up and rolled
across blue sky like cotton balls.

One Sunday, our day off, cook Lee stopped wearing all
clothing but her red thong. She was a tall, lean woman. Her
feet had arches like cats' backs and she bounced while she
walked, causing her breasts to shiver—doubtless from her
training as a runway model. Unlike most of us, who'd put
on shorts for the warmer weather only to find we were
white as toothpaste, she was beautifully tanned.

A group had gathered on the cargo hatch. Its grainy canvas cover leaned towards the swells breaking over the lee

rail, making it feel like a beach. The spot had become a gathering place for those relaxing off-watch, and they talked, read and worked on projects. I took my beckets to the next step, trying to weave thirty-two strands of fine, flaxen, left-laid twine in a cross-hatch pattern around the wire rope cores I'd spliced and parcelled days before. I had the two cores stretched on a small rack, side by side, and though I'd stood them vertically, I couldn't organize the thirty-two strands into a cross-hatch pattern.

That was when I heard the cook's voice, warm with her South African accent. "Do you need some help with that? I love doing this kind of stuff," she said as she sat cross-legged in front of me, taking half of my strands and pulling them taut. Back and forth we passed them, alternating our way down the becket. We'd lean from side to side to keep from toppling over as the ship rolled, and the noontime shadows moved under her goosebumped breasts in time with the roll of the ship. Too soon I found the cross-hatching was completed and the cook left to work on lunch.

Jesse walked by me on the hatch. "When your grandkids ask about the beckets on your sea chest, tell them you made them with your topless helper while you sailed around the world on a square-rigger."

Moments later, as I picked up my work, careful not to dangle any loose bits of twine in the torrents of water that rushed across the deck, I saw Tom in his swim trunks run past lean and white. He jumped and slid on his stomach along the wet planks, apparently unconcerned about splinters. The powerful standing wave that crashed constantly across the deck caught him there and slid him along a scum of algae that the morning deck washes couldn't seem to keep ahead of. Tom rolled and splashed like flotsam in the surf.

Patrick, who'd been in a boundless good mood ever since we'd left Halifax, raced up after him, sprayed him with Joy dish soap and scrubbed him with a hard-bristled deck brush.

All around them the blue water was frothy with white-caps breaking on the frequent swells. By most standards this was rough weather, but after our first few weeks at sea it was nothing. Don and I spent an hour just drawing buckets from the swells and splashing them in each other's face, Three Stooges style. Soon everyone got the idea of taking a bath, taking turns hauling buckets of salt water from over the side and lathering with detergent.

All around, men and women soaped discreetly, reaching under their suits, pulling fabric from skin to pour in a bucket of salt water in to rinse. Bellies, breasts and chests, there was little privacy on this ship. You learned not to care too much.

In the evening, as we sailed through the Anegada Passage, the Captain tapped the rum keg, making good on his promise to Cowboy Brad. The Captain had a deckhand siphon the rum into his collection of old Gamel Dansk bottles, and in a couple of hours he stood before the crew in the tropical twilight wearing a loose white linen shirt and a black flowered sarong that hung just below his knees. He dangled a fourteen-inch marlinspike lazily from his hand and leaned back on the oak pinrail. Next to him, a tarnished copper tank of cool punch sweated in the tropical humidity. This was a special occasion; the cook was not usually allowed to make ice for beverages.

Captain Moreland announced our entry into the Caribbean. He said a few words about drinking underway, summing them up jocularly: "Just don't be an asshole." And beginning a ritual of Sunday cocktail parties inherited from the *Romance*, dubbed *marlinspikes*, he placed his marlinspike in the tank, gave the punch a stir and ladled full a plastic cup. After that, the crew each took a turn. If all went well, every Sunday we'd have a little party like this—a staff party at a job you never leave.

For three days the wind and course were constant as we made tracks for Aruba. The square sails remained set—a stack of three on each mast, pulling hard. With wind so steady, there was no need to adjust yards. Braces stayed untouched. The engine pushed. We would make Aruba by Christmas Eve, I'd heard.

At 1000 hours on the twenty-fourth, we pulled alongside in Aruba. By lunchtime: lines doubled, chafing gear secured, superstructure scrubbed with sponge and cleanser, deck rinsed, hoses drained, sails harbour furled, yards laboriously squared and levelled until the mate was satisfied they were correct to within a degree. Finally, a muster.

The Captain welcomed us to Aruba. He had spent a few Christmases here from ages four to ten, when his father was stationed on the island as a U.S. diplomat, beginning in 1958. His Creole nanny, Viola Jack, whom he'd described as a third parent, took him on her long errands to the Aruban docks. There, she'd catch up with friends and family aboard Caribbean trading schooners. Young Dan was allowed to climb in their rigging, breathe the wolf-den air of a working fo'c'sle, the sweet odour of fruit ripening on a hot deck, and take home the intoxicating smell of tar on his hands. He got a taste of ship life from those sun-burned ebony-skinned sailors living a life all but gone in the Caribbean Sea.

There was certainly no trace of it left in Aruba now. From the deck of our ship I saw a town that looked like the Magic Kingdom. Tall hotels, short palm trees and fast food restaurants were clustered down the beaches. Tied next to us, the graceful *QE2* towered to nearly twice our height, her docklines almost as big around as our yards. Her world circumnavigations went for eighty thousand dollars, not thirty-two, and they took less than half as long. Different ship—different crew. While the *QE2*'s complement returned quietly from the T-shirt shops and restaurants to their air-conditioned cabins, our crew stumbled home drunk, loud and stinky.

On Christmas Day, I headed away from the ship to try to make a phone call. There was only one public place allowing international calls. I bought a ten-dollar phone card and used up all my time leaving an awkward message on Ariel's machine, still owing the phone company a dollar.

I left the automated operator squawking on the phone. *Why do I hold on?* I berated myself for not making the most of the present, for spending a day's pay on a stammering message. I walked through the stifling heat of town, over-dressed in my only clean pants.

I decided not to blow the rest of my cash and time off on expensive food and useless souvenirs, and headed back to the ship to see if my friends had anything planned. In minutes we were walking towards the Jeep rental with a yellow surfboard that I'd stashed in the fo'c'sle next to the second engineer's cello.

As we arrived, the Captain pulled out of the lot in a blue Jeep. He looked at us. I waved hello. He looked away. It was one of the things the new crew were having the hardest time adjusting to: never knowing when to expect a discourtesy.

The rental man didn't speak much English, but in a flash of signatures and greenbacks we were driving down a dusty ribbon of asphalt, feeling the buzz of nubby tires and the hiss of the hot trade wind whipping through our open Jeep. It wasn't long before the beach resort scene was behind and the hotels turned to abandoned shacks, cactus and dry brush. Green parrots flew across our path, and then the path disappeared. On our left the shore was violent with breakers and long rocks reaching to the sea. Ages of detritus had been pummelled there, driven by the persistent trade winds. On our right stretched a desert flatland of red clay.

Patrick threw his head back and laughed maniacally, slamming his foot on the gas.

"Oh, shit!" I said, turning around in the back seat, groping between the cushions for a seat belt. Behind us a dust cloud rose like a red devil. He took the Jeep at breakneck speed into a rugged desert with no trails. We took turns driving, each one more daring than the last as we grew more certain we were invincible. I did donuts and fish hooks, pushing the limits of the Jeep's wide wheelbase. Tom jumped a crevasse, rode the edges of a washed-out road and took an off-camber turn that seemed sure to flip the Jeep. And Don slid in behind the wheel with a look so intense that his eyes might have been two pools of smouldering lava. Don terrified us without even touching the gas.

The red desert terrain turned to grey rock and shale. We passed army bunkers and a surfer's cove. From the Jeep we watched surfers ride waves towards jagged vertical rock, jumping off just in time to avoid bloody death. None of us but Tom had ever caught a wave before, so we thought better of our surfing adventure and decided instead to keep driving and take turns walking with the surfboard down the nude beach.

Later, driving back to the ship in the twilight past the rows of short palms, we decided we'd get our gear and return to the desert, cook over fire and sleep under stars. It would be a perfect Christmas night. But as we walked aboard, we saw a celebration underway. Lights were strung. That plastic Frosty the Snowman we'd packed in the hold had been tied to the mast. The smell of roast turkey, gravy and potatoes rose from the main salon. A ragged, fake Christmas tree that the Captain's family had first used in Aruba was propped up against the ceaseless trade wind by our largest shackles, surrounded by an expansive mound of newspaper-wrapped presents.

All wore their best clothing and smiles. Second mate Karen, in a light country dress, helped present the food she'd cooked. Her face glowed with the flush of a recent tan and praise for one of the few really tasty meals to come out of the galley since we'd left Lunenburg. Presents and rum punch were next. I left the crew in the humid main salon and poured myself a glass, not expecting any gifts. But soon I heard my name and turned around to receive a heavy package. I carefully unwrapped the paper and found a canvas carrying bag with a silkscreen of the ship's silhouette and, underneath that, a book. A thick, worn black book with an embossed leather cover and its title written in gold: *The Century Book of Facts.* Inside the cover I read an inscription: *For Rigel—Sailing around the world in the* Picton Castle— *Aruba, Christmas 1997—yours, Daniel Moreland.*

Looking around, I saw that everyone had received a gift from the Captain—each a wonderful, personal gift from his possessions—knife, palm, needles, fid. Amazed by his extravagant generosity, I looked him in the eyes and thanked him sincerely. "It's nothing," he said.

Everyone else was similarly amazed, and perhaps a little embarrassed that our only offering was a silver Zippo lighter that Cowboy Brad had taken a collection for and had engraved with the ship's profile and name. The Captain received the token graciously and gave the crew a ceremonious bow, holding the lighter to his chest.

As the party wound on, we abandoned our camping plans. I retrieved a coconut from the Jeep that I'd picked earlier from a leaning palm. With my slender rigging knife, dusted with rust from the salt air, I tried to carve away the dense husk that protects a coconut. I carved and cut and whittled at the husk. It was so tough and elastic, I could have just as easily carved open a bowling ball.

"Do you want some help with that?" the Captain offered.

"Sure," I said, handing him my knife and the coconut.

"No." He raised his hand and disappeared into his cabin, returning moments later with a two-foot-long machete in a wooden scabbard, tucked into the belt that supported his flowered sarong. With the sleeves of his white shirt rolled up past his tattooed forearm, he wrapped his fingers around the machete's wooden pistol grip and brandished the exotic-looking knife. It had the dull, authentic look of hand-forged carbon steel. The blade was very heavy, and round at the end. It had a fine white edge where it'd been recently whetted. Holding the coconut stem down in his left hand like a cognac glass, he attacked, swinging his knife sharply from its pistol grip.

Each swing buried deep into the coconut husk, chipping it away like broadaxe to balsa tree. In seconds he revealed the nut inside, which was nearly white. The Captain repositioned the coconut in his hand. Three sharp hits with the back of his machete and he had broken a fissure around the exposed nut and opened it like a soft-boiled egg. We passed it around. The water inside was sweet and nourishing.

"Where did you get that knife?" I asked.

"Indonesia," he replied matter-of-factly, as if he wanted to end the conversation there. But he'd got my imagination going. I imagined myself buying such a knife someday, maybe in a year, and becoming a coconut expert in my own right.

"We should put some rum in this," I said.

"Nah. I'd never ruin sweet coconut water with rum."

CHAPTER 11

Lunatic Smile

Aruba to the San Blas Archipelago, Panama
December 30, 1997, to January 7, 1998

ON THE THIRTIETH OF DECEMBER, THE SLEEK BLACK
topsail schooner *Pride of Baltimore II* was tied to the pier just
aft of us. We'd rafted against each other in Bermuda, then
met up again in Aruba.

Pride II was headed to Asia across the turbulent North
Pacific. The fast wooden 1812-era privateer with her raked
masts, and our stalwart steel merchant barque were nearly a
century apart in the evolution of sail. If you threw in a fifteenth-
century European exploration ship and a few of the remaining
nineteenth-century fishing schooners, you'd have a cross-
section of the modern-day traditional fleet, with its level of
variety unheard of at any one time during the age of sail.

Captain Moreland ordered us to set the fore topmast
staysail and cast off the docklines. The warm trade wind
that pummelled Aruba's northwestern shore floated over
the island and filled our sturdy headsail, pushing the *Picton
Castle*—engine off—bow first into the Caribbean Sea. From
the quarterdeck our captain waved to the captain of the
Pride II, then turned to receive the warm applause of his
crew, who were impressed by his engineless manoeuvre.

"It was you. You did it," he said, bowing and waving his hand theatrically across the crew. "It wasn't really that hard—we just set the fore topmast staysail and blew off the dock."

Shortly, he ordered that the square sails be set. Because the ship was not saturated with engine noise, the evolution unfolded with a new immediacy. Chain sheets rattled in their sheaves and new manila lines squeaked in their blocks. Braces were let slack to sag across the sky so as not to impede the slow labour of their yards bearing the canvas upward. The following breeze pushed the ship faster and I heard water ripple around the hull plating.

I couldn't allow myself to be distracted. Now that the *Picton Castle* was under sail alone, a strong weather helm drove her to head into the wind, making her difficult to steer. Worse, the wind was directly behind us. It filled the sails on the mainmast, which in turn blanketed the sails on the fore. Those sails flogged lazily, snapping full and spilling their wind, more with the motion of the ship pitching than the strength of the moderate breeze, still softened by the island of Aruba.

We pivoted in the wind as I tried to compensate with the rudder, turning the wheel too much, worsening our swing. I looked behind to our eel wake that meandered away from the shore, knowing that if I didn't get the ship under control, I'd soon attract the Captain's attention.

He climbed the quarterdeck ladder with a scowl and said, "Rigel, what's going on? You're oversteering. The engine's not on. She's not going to be as responsive."

"Yes, sir. I'll get it," I reassured him. But she continued to pivot, reluctant to settle on her downwind course. Our running with the wind reduced the breeze across the deck. The tropical sun climbed fast overhead, heating the oiled surface of the quarterdeck, burning the bottoms of my feet. I moved around uncomfortably, sweating in a navy blue polyester blend crew shirt, struggling to make the ship track straight. I attracted more recrimination, though eventually, steering with smaller corrections, I was able to judge the force pushing the ship off course and compensate with the correct amount of rudder.

Soon I was relieved at the wheel and reported to bo'sun Josh, who was readying the ship for passage to the San Blas Islands: lash the boarding ladder. Secure the hold. Tie chafe gear to the shrouds to protect them from flogging sails. Climb to each yard and overhaul the buntlines. Hang their slack over the sails so they don't chafe. Nip them in place with weak sisal yarns so they break free when we haul the buntlines to draw each sail to its yard.

In the galley, three crew set up for the midday meal. Dig for food buried among old bicycles in the hold. Haul a fifty-pound bag of coal to the cook in the galley. Sweep coal dust tracked through the main salon. Chop veggies. Make salad. Make drinks. Wash dishes. Begin again.

At night, Karen and her watch baked bread. As a result, off-duty crew had started waking for breakfast again, having something to look forward to other than increasingly stale and crumbled corn flakes with warm powdered milk. Food and morale were closely linked; we were starting to need a cook who really cared for us. It was a good thing an assistant cook was arriving in the San Blas. I imagined that when we arrived, we'd probably forget our manners and eat him alive.

At seven knots, we were making decent time. On the day of New Year's Eve, the wind blew strong on the quarter, kicking up close bullish swells that shoved the ship along and rocked her like a cradle. Amidships on the lee side, water spilled in the scuppers and flowed all around as if the *Picton Castle* were a loaded cargo ship. In this saltwater bath I disinfected the galley waste bins with Lysol, scrubbing them with the designated sponge.

Mate Brian walked behind me and stopped by my side, wearing his favourite blue surf shorts and white T-shirt, sleeves removed. I saw the pilot whale tooth that he'd worn about his neck on a leather thong for nearly a decade.

"Hey, Rige. How do you like the weather?"

"It's great," I said, smiling over my garbage bin. The mid-morning sun, cooling breeze and ocean spray felt good blowing across my sunburned shoulders and nappy hair.

"Really? There's three squalls on the horizon," he said, pointing them out with a hand-rolled cig pinched between thumb and forefinger.

I looked over the rust-streaked bulwarks and saw the squalls, rather close to each other, three grey smudges on the horizon.

"Whatever he's doing, a seaman should always be aware of the weather. When I was first sailing under Skipper in the *Romance,* he asked me the same question: 'Hey, Brian. How do you like the weather?'" Brian imitated Skipper's scratchy singsong voice. "I said, 'Oh, it's great!' Then he stormed away, yelling, 'Aww fuck, Brian!'"

"Well, thanks."

"No problem," said Brian as he walked back to the charthouse.

At 1600 hours on New Year's Eve, when the Captain's watch took the deck, work stopped early, *Wet Paint* signs went up and training began. Within moments all hands stood on the main deck, sea water coursing from side to side, colliding with bare and sandalled feet. The air had cooled and we once again wore T-shirts, covering the bare chests and sports bras of midday.

The Captain descended from his bench ahead of the charthouse, a perch he'd taken to in recent weeks where he could observe the rig, deck and crew with an eagle's vigilance. We gave full attention as he introduced the evening's training with the sureness of hammer striking anvil.

"Today we *heave to*." He explained how to stop a sailing ship from moving forward by opposing the square sails on each mast, and to have her move slowly sideways in case one needs to wait for daylight, ride out dangerous weather or launch boats for a man-overboard rescue. "First we'll take in the mainsail."

The mate took charge of the finer points, ensuring the correct lines were let go or hauled at the right time, pulling sail to yard like a window blind. The Captain gave the order to furl: "UP AND STOW."

Seasoned crew headed for the shrouds immediately, having anticipated the call. We swung around the turnbuckles and, in bare feet, pistoned our legs up the narrow cord of the ratlines, growing more used to its bite with each step. The slower but equally ambitious crew were left to scrabble at the bottom, hoping to get on the yard before becoming supernumerary. It might have been kind to let everyone have a try, but generally, if you couldn't climb to the yard first, you didn't deserve to secure the gasket at the yardarm.

There was grumbling among some of the new crew not willing to elbow in. I had heard complaints about the competition, the lack of help from the professionals aboard, our reluctance to defer responsibilities. Many were surprised to be reprimanded for laughing while they hauled braces in the morning, or for lying on the cargo hatch off watch while the on-duty crew hauled the braces unassisted.

Aloft, we shinnied out the main yard, sliding barefoot on footropes, releasing gaskets from their tight coils perched atop the spar. Those gaskets then streamed down, trying to lick the deck. Working together, ten of us folded the sail into itself and rolled it on top of the yard. We spiralled gaskets tightly from the yardarms in, and secured them with a hitch, teaching the new crew aloft by example. We climbed down to the deck, feet burning.

"HARD RIGHT," the Captain ordered, turning his head towards the wheel. The ship seemed to move slower as she turned and took the swells broadside, rocking heavily, loping like a giant beast.

"STAND BY TO HEAVE TO." A band of sailors ran to the main braces on the quarterdeck. I stayed on the main deck, helping assign crew to man the lines, so they could locate and cast off the unfamiliar lee gear, lifts, tacks and sheets.

"MAINSAIL HAUL." The upper yards turned, but the lower yard wouldn't move, despite the four strong crew who hauled in time on its brace. The ship turned to the wind. The square sails started to shiver and flog. The free clews of the foresail yanked at their tack and sheet like crazy horses.

We needed the main yard to come around; it was locked in place. Across the deck I saw a crew member assigned to cast off the tack. She held it with a turn around its heavy cleat, arresting the entire manoeuvre, a frozen expression on her face.

"CAST OFF THE MAIN TACK!" the Captain barked. I moved to assist. We released it slowly, and with the popping noise of a line eased under great strain, it wound around its cleat.

The ship slowed, stopped and then crept backwards, tracing a tight crescent. She spilled the wind in her mainsails and carved slowly forward. We hove to again for all watches that afternoon.

Our eight-to-midnight duty passed quickly. Those of us awake were eager to tick over the New Year in our floating home. At the turn of the hour, when Karen's watch had emerged into the cool night air to relieve us, Brian walked to the leeward quarter to launch some fireworks.

He held a lighter in his right hand and a black bucket in his left. Red and yellow rockets shot from it, low and blurry in the mist. The wind caught them, carrying coloured light away from the ship and over the sea. Mist blocked the moon and starlight, making the night air feel murky and close.

I talked to Kristin by the mizzen-mast as it flared yellow in the fireworks. She leaned against it, bare shoulder cocked forward, one knee bent, arms folded against the chilly mist so that she seemed just a little guarded, a touch nervous. The crew counted down to midnight and I felt we might kiss as we were silent for a nervous moment. She was playful and wise and artistic. She laughed at my jokes and I spent hours entertaining her. Many men in the crew were attracted to her, I knew that. *And this voyage is long.* I turned and watched the fireworks arc to the sky and be carried away by the wind.

The wind carried us through to morning, and in the light of late dawn I came on deck to see that we were among islands. I had never imagined that the Caribbean, so close to home, was another world. On white sand islands barely higher than the main deck of our ship, palm trees tall and bushy swayed and leaned willy-nilly over the faded thatched roofs of bamboo houses. Long dugout canoes sat on the shores. We glided among these idylls until 1400 hours, when the Captain ordered that the sails be furled and told the mate, "LET GO."

In a clatter of chain ripping through steel hawse pipe, we were anchored.

With the anchor on the bottom of this aqua blue water, a flotilla of canoe-borne Indians pushed away from their sand islands and paddled towards us. As they approached, I saw brown-skinned women wearing appliquéd blouses, printed sarongs and long cotton kerchiefs in primary colours. They sat in the bows and middles of their dugouts while the men, dressed in drab tank tops and shorts, pad-dled in the sterns.

Approaching us, the dugouts nosed up to our steel hull like suckling pigs. Our excited crew leaned over the side for a better look, and word was passed: Kuna Indians.

Their heads were tilted back to observe us, and I caught a marking on the women's faces, a thin black tattoo-scar that stretched from the forehead down the bridge of the nose. Each wore a gold hoop, bull-wise.

They plunged their slender arms into white five-gallon buckets and presented handmade wares for sale—splendid *molas*, layered patterns of fabric and embroidery. All around us these exotic women displayed their crafts, depicting the icons of their lives: parrot, crab, lobster, fish, hibiscus, snake. They spread them overhead with their forearms wrapped in beads nearly to the elbows, in intricate patterns of red, yellow and blue.

"Twenty dollars," said a Kuna woman.

One of the crew bit and ran to her bunk for some cash, not able to see the orgy of selling she'd begun. Sale followed sale. Another bid was made: "Fifteen. Fifteen." A crew member smiled holding his colourful *mola*.

The buyers shifted positions, more offers were made. "Two for ten. Two for ten." Kim, quickly changing his role from carpenter to cargo master, ran to the deck with a haggard expression, beads of sweat gleaming on his tanned forehead and sticking to his straw hair. He carried a tote of WWII army boots that he dropped next to a tote of soap and boxes of tools. He ran below again and hauled up a garbage bag of used clothing, pouring it onto the hatch.

We threw rope ladders over the side and stood on the rail helping the Kunas board the ship. Buying continued with a renewed frenzy. I went to my bunk to grab some goods I'd bought in Nova Scotia for trading. My C-cell batteries started a run and I picked up a selection of *molas*, one to decorate my bunk, the rest to be tucked away for family.

Kim, standing shirtless on the hatch, held some used clothing, shouting, "*Dos molas. Dos molas!*" Prices continued to drop.

Seanette, a former Vegas blackjack dealer, joined Kim in the fray. Standing on the hatch shouting, flinging her platinum hair and wearing nothing but short shorts and a sports bra, she was a powerful presence standing above the Kunas, so small and demure in their traditional full-length dresses. Seanette dealt her trade goods like she was running her $100,000-limit craps table back home. "Two *bien molas!* Two *bien molas!*" she shouted.

A couple of young Kuna women stood near me. One saw me admire the rectilinear patterns of beads on her forearms and calves. She pulled a string of multicoloured beads from her bucket and began wrapping them loosely about my arm. Turn after turn my bracelet broadened like her own, but without the distinct pattern. I could only wonder at the care it took to bead her bracelet, the series of beads on each turn aligning perfectly with the last. The Kunas' *molas* embodied the same craftsmanship. I imagined that a skilled seamstress might spend at least forty hours cutting the fabric and making each delicate stitch by hand.

Her brown hands raised goosebumps as they secured the bracelet, skimming lightly across the hairs on my arm. I tried to remember how long it was since I'd been touched like this. Privacy was in such demand aboard ship that we defended ourselves with invisible walls. She tied the last knot in the thread and said, "Ten dollars."

Ten dollars! Ten dollars was more than a day's pay. I offered her five and we settled on seven. I felt silly for thinking she'd give me the beads for free. Driven out of the mountains by the conquistadors, the Kunas learned to be tough and shrewd, preserving themselves and their culture

on these low sandy islands from more recent invaders:
pirates, Panamanians, Americans, Canadians.

As I handed my money to the woman, I asked to look at
more of her wares. She produced an elegant shell necklace.
Miniature grey-green cowries squiggled with dark green
lines were strung on three strands and twisted together like
rope. They were Ariel's favourite colour, so I gave the
woman a pack of batteries for the necklace. I clutched it in
my fist, keeping this link to Ariel a secret, guarding it like a
flame that might later help to nourish and warm.

The afternoon faded into a brief tropical twilight. Kim
and Seanette stood on the cargo hatch, radiant but exhaust-
ed after a day of bartering with the Kuna women. The last of
the Indians handed their buckets into the dugouts.

As night fell, the slender crescent moon brightened in
the western sky, seeming larger as it sank. I realized that
our ship's descent towards the equator had turned the
aspect of the moon so it looked like a *U*. It gleamed, a
lunatic smile, reflecting white on still water. The stars were
brilliant in the cloudless sky. And tall palms on the islands
were nearly still in the night breeze that pushed a sailing
cayuko to a neighbouring island. Minor chords and gentle
Latin rhythms danced from the catgut strings of Pat's and
Don's guitars.

I wished I could share the moment with someone back
home, and padded down the cool deck to my fo'c'sle bunk.
I flipped on the fifteen-watt light, grabbed a spiral-bound
notebook and began to write Ariel a letter, drawing first the
Cheshire cat moon and then the *cayuko* sailing beneath it.

Dear Ariel,

*The solar system is flat. The earth spins on an axis. That axis
nearly aligns with the one the solar system rotates on. The moon's
orbit nearly aligns with the earth's and the solar system's. A*

plane that cuts through the earth, the moon, the sun, the planets, and all the stars in the zodiac, would nearly align with the equator. That's why the planets march overhead down here, and the crescent moon looks like a smile.

Guess what else. Bananas grow like this:

I didn't know that.

~~So, we're at the western end of the C~~

~~From my bunk~~

~~So, why am I writing you this time? Hopefully not to fi~~

~~So, I almost sent you an e-mail from Aruba. It seemed like such a good idea until it occurred that it would disrupt the strange continuity of letter time—the delayed fragments of irrelevance. I wouldn't want to interrupt that with anything, save an awkward phone message on Christmas Day. This~~ ~~obsession~~ ~~drive to continuously write you seems strange. Almost desperate and a little obsessive, especially as our lives diverge.~~

~~I can't express~~

~~And it seem~~

~~And we wil~~

~~I feel drawn to this sailing life like I never have~~

~~And~~ ~~they~~ ~~I am~~ ~~thrilled by this way of life and the~~ ~~having the time of my life.~~

~~Tomorrow~~

I tried to sleep through the pre-dawn rooster crows, drifting in and out of dreams about shiny hatchets and butcher's blocks.

I awoke to a day off. After helping the rest of the crew brace the yards square so the ship looked pretty at anchor, Kristin and I took the second boat run ashore to a rickety wooden pier and walked through the chop that lapped at the shore's hard-packed white sand. We'd planned to charter a sail in a *cayuko*, or dugout. Down the shore a man stood up from his seat on a palm tree log as if he were expecting us, but he didn't smile. His straight black hair combed neatly down suggested he was a disciplined man.

He turned and walked between four slender posts that supported a thatched roof, which sheltered his boat. He grabbed the sides of his sixteen-foot-long *cayuko* and pushed it towards the water. I ducked under the thatched roof to help. My fingers curled around the boat's smooth gunwale and I realized I held a carefully carved ridge. Looking along the gunwale, I saw it was perfectly fair. The boat had a short keel at bow and stern, was light and very old. Someone had tacked a flattened Miller Highlife can over a small hole in the floor. A quick glance at the islands showed that there weren't a lot of three-foot-wide cedar trees to carve into boats, especially ones free of knots. Kuna families pass living trees down through generations for this purpose. We pulled the boat into the water until I was up to my knees.

Our *cayuko* skipper quickly stepped his mast, which was little more than a straight tree with branches and bark removed. His patchwork bedsheet sail snapped in the breeze. He ran back to the shelter, returning with a long pole that he used to push up the loose peak of the sail until taut, forming a lopsided quadrangle, a sprit rig. He set a tiny jib, turned the boat towards the sea and, still straight-faced, motioned for us to get in. Kristin and I laughed nervously as we climbed aboard, tipping jerkily side to side. Butterflies. Awkward pauses. We sat on the comfortable round floor of the dugout and it became surprisingly stable. The skipper shoved off, paddled a few beats, then hauled tight his sail, tying its sheet to a hole in the quarter with a couple of overhand knots.

The *cayuko* slipped like a knife through the water. I saw Jesse and Becky—the most recent of the four professional crew couples—sail by in another *cayuko*, framed by the *Picton Castle* at anchor. They smiled at us with an unmistakable complicity.

For an hour we sailed. We whipped over shallows in the perfectly balanced craft. Our skipper rarely corrected our course with his carved paddle. "May I steer?" I asked. He looked at me blankly. I gestured steering and pointed to myself.

"NO."

Kristin laughed. She had a good sense of humour, and most times could shrug off the difficulties of ship life, often helping others out of a funk. She's independent, and that helps. She knew I liked to spend time by myself ashore. This could work.

Kristin and I parted ways after beaching the *cayuko* and helping to pull it under shelter.

I headed back to the rickety pier to turn to the village. The sun was overhead, reflecting off the white sand and beating down hard. I squinted. All was dry. My bare feet squeaked through hot sand as I walked towards a bamboo storefront. There, Gustavio greeted me. Our first day in the islands he set up tours for our crew to visit ceremonies and gravesites, where they had to pay for every picture snapped. I smiled as I recognized the unctuous businessman by his short frame, big head and bangs that hung over his eyes.

He offered me a beer from his fridge. I accepted it gladly and poured back the cold drink, feeling its soothing bubbles in my nose. He had one himself, and as he drank, I noticed one of his eyelids drooping lazily. He'd been drinking already.

As part of their ceremonial life the Kunas celebrate the mysteries of female maturation. When a girl reaches fifteen, the village devotes a week to her, with much drinking and dancing. On the last day she receives the short haircut that will be her badge of womanhood. One such celebration was currently taking place, and I imagined that was why he was drunk.

"Checkers?" he asked.

"Sure."

"For money?"

"No. No, thanks."

"A bottle of rum?"

I could get one on the ship easily enough if I lose. And if I win . . .

I lost.

"I'll give it to you tomorrow, Gustavio."

"No *problema*. Call me Gusto."

"Gusto?"

"*Sí, Mucho Gusto.*" He handed me another beer.

We played another game, not for money, not for rum. I lost that one too. We drank another beer, and another. The sun crept past noon and the heat grew. I felt it rise in waves from the sand and pass through me on its way to the sky. Kids screamed and played outside the store, all smiles and wide eyes as they ran, unconcerned by the hot sand. I finished our game and my beer and thanked Gusto. I leaned out the door of his store and playfully chased the band of kids through the village.

We raced through closely packed huts of bamboo. Visions of the Kunas' lives flicked through the slats like motion picture film. A small woman bent over her appliqué *mola*. She was draped in flowing colours, brown eyes close to quick needle.

The children turned. Ducked around palms. Under macramé

hammocks. Kicked sand. Under thatch. They laughed as I chased them, turning their heads back to see the pale sheep-haired monster in pursuit.

I returned to Gustavio. We drank more beer and walked towards the pier. The ship sat at anchor, yards braced neatly. Ribbons of rust streaked her hull. Dalmatian splotches of black showed where paint had peeled. A boat crew wiped the hull clean for painting in an effort to make the ship presentable for our scheduled passage through the Panama Canal.

I looked down to my beer and bare feet, glad for a day away. A little distance from the pier, Gusto showed me a couple of square pools that had been dug in the sand, flooded and reinforced with wood. In one swam a sea turtle; in the other, a four-foot-long shark. I'd never seen one before. Some boys jumped in the water, splashed around and teased the intimidating fish. I looked at Gusto, surprised. He smirked.

A drunken man swaying next to Gusto handed me a drink. It tasted like tequila, but I wondered if it was their local brew instead—a deadly concoction made of fermented sugar cane and caffeine.

I heard the grind of an outboard motor and soon a contingent of friends from the ship piled onto the dock in the dusk of late afternoon. Lee, the nudist cook, was the first ashore, leading in a whimsical way. Becky and Jesse stepped ashore behind her, as did Kristin and Todd, a former professional drummer turned writer, who was also Cowboy Brad's brother. Gusto latched on to Lee immediately, and she danced around avoiding his advances like a featherweight boxer in round one. We all followed to the end of the island, passed through dense scrub onto pebbly sand. Lee handed money to a Kuna man with a large outboard-powered dugout and we rode to a neighbouring deserted island.

We stayed on its beach as the evening grew darker. I found a leaning coconut palm and climbed, too drunk to care about splinters in my feet. I placed a hand on the top of a coconut's smooth green husk and pulled it down to the sand. I pulled down another, hopped to the ground and carried them back to the group, feeling like a provider. With my slender rigging knife, I stabbed and hacked through the coconut's supple armour. Someone handed me a large joint. I pulled hard and held the smoke while passing it back, its paper wrapping sticking to the coconut water on my fingers. I exhaled and a euphoric rush slanted through my head. I stood and smacked my half-opened coconut against the log until a fissure opened. I poured the sweet water into my mouth and, wiping with one hand, passed the coconut to Kristin.

We seven played in the water, and when it was dark, Gusto led us darting through the trees—back to the landing—to the other shore—towards a house where we could eat. We walked down a path, crunching through soft leaves fallen on the sand, now cool in the evening. The crescent moon softly lit our path, washing all in a hazy glow. I felt the welcome touch of Kristin's hand sliding into mine.

We entered a house and saw other crew eating. Warm smiles and hellos. Too drunk to make conversation, I felt on the edge of consciousness. A stocky Kuna man placed a plate of fresh fish and rice before me. Soon full, I lay with Kristin holding hands in a hammock, and drifted to sleep.

Heat. Sunlight. Outboard engine noise. "Rigel-Man. Liar-Man. Rigel-Man."

"Uuh?" *I'm in my bunk. It's morning. My head.* I squinted to see out my porthole. The water was still and slick, reflecting the orange glow of sunrise. Gusto stood on the bow of a skiff. Two others were with him. He shouted at me.

I rolled out of my bunk and headed to the main salon to buy a bottle of rum from Don. I handed him a ten and grabbed the bottle. As I arrived back on deck, Gusto pulled up to the ship. He stopped yelling and smiled as I handed him the bottle. He was in a haze—still going strong.

The day's work was priming the hull's bare steel and rust streaks. Drink, eat, sweat and paint. In my hangover state the sunlight glare off white paint grew painful. That night I slept well, and in the morning we got underway.

"HANDS TO THE WINDLASS," commanded mate Brian. "Bars in."

At the wheel, I took steering orders from the Captain as he piloted from aloft on the mainmast. He guided us for seven miles through some of the three hundred pristine islands in the Lemon Cays, to a narrow cut between two deserted shores. When we arrived, the sun was still high and we were encouraged to snorkel while reef and fish were best illuminated.

Underwater, the visibility seemed to reach forever. I was unable to dive more than a few feet below surface because I had not yet learned to equalize my ears, but from above I watched second mate Karen and other skilled divers swim thirty feet below to touch the anchor or pick up shells.

Don and I snorkelled away from the playground of the ship to shallower water near the island. Ribbons of light shimmered on the ribs of sand that dusted the bones of an ancient reef. Here and there were pockets of green sea-grass, orange shells, corals of red, white and black. Crabs sidled by, and diving down to pick up a shell, I was suddenly surrounded by a passing school of silver fish the size of mackerel shimmering like rain in brightest sunlight. I felt disoriented. There was no bottom, no surface, no cardinal directions. The fish continued to pass, more and more. I did not want to come up for air.

That night, after rum and a delicious steak cookout on the beach, we retreated from the mosquitoes to the ship. I remained on deck late, talking and flirting with Kristin. I walked her to the main salon hatch, where we hovered by the door. I was prolonging this play, this excitement—everything still out of reach. Then, in a blurry second, we rolled towards each other on the balls of our feet and kissed. I felt the end of flirting games, of loneliness and longing. I was turned on.

I felt her hands let go of my face and gently push away from my shoulders. The gesture spoke to me powerfully, subliminally. It said, I am not a quickly won prize. It said, You are not in control. She turned lightly on her feet and went below to sleep. I crashed in my fo'c'sle rack, twenty feet away. With ritual certainty I closed the curtain and turned off the light, to prevent a silhouetted finger puppet show.

In the morning, on-duty crew painted the ship. They looked frustrated, splattered in white, grumbling that they didn't shell out their life's savings to sail within inches of paradise only to coat a steel ship with house paint. There was a growing belief, particularly among the older crowd, that their free labour was being exploited so the company could get away with supplying cheap materials that wouldn't last. With free labour the ship could always afford to do the job again.

Bob Kingman, a contractor from Tahoe, California, had made much of the money for his voyage fare by doing work that would hold up over time. Now, painting the hall, he was paying to do just the opposite. Despite all the things he loved about the voyage, this was becoming a sore point.

That evening, after the paintbrushes and rollers had been cleaned, and the sun had set, newly familiar stars appeared overhead. The crescent moon had waxed some.

Rebecca had taken her flute and Claire her cello to the fo'c'sle head, where they were tuning up for a duet.

There were a surprising number of bedrolls spread to reserve a space in the cool outdoors rather than the still, humid heat below decks. Many were paired up like marriage beds. I'd heard the Captain express concern about the turmoil created when crew leave one broken shipboard romance for a new one, as very many would; and describe how it's destructive for individuals to act as half a couple rather than as shipmates, confiding in their lovers rather than confronting problems outright. But he knew enough not to stand in the way. With twenty men and sixteen women in the prime of life living close together, romance aboard was less a choice than a force of nature. Still, it amazed me how many mattresses were doubled up on deck—eight pairs?

Claire and Rebecca began to play with a slow and steady tempo. I would sleep in my bunk that night, but first I wanted to hear the music and breathe the cool night air. Let me stand here, stars above, cool deck below, while no one knows where I am. Let me listen to Rebecca and Claire play Pachebel's *Canon*. Let the wooden hull of Claire's cello resonate with the deck. Now, before they play one wrong note, let me go to my bunk and finish my letter.

> *I had a painful feeling in my upper abdomen just now when I heard Pachebel's* Canon *played from the fo'c'sle head with cello and flute.*
>
> *That's why I write you now. Not to fill your life with astronomy, but to let you know I'm thinking of you.*
>
> *Love, Rigel*

CHAPTER 12

Heaven's Gate

The Panama Canal, Colón to Balboa
January 9 and 10

IN A CHILLY MORNING MIST WE CROWDED AROUND THE cargo hatch of our ship, anchored some miles north of the Panama Canal in Limón Bay. We were waiting for the ship's agent, supposed to deliver our first batch of mail. The crew's excitement was palpable. It felt like we'd been away from loved ones for a long time, especially now, just after Christmas. We cast longing looks towards the city where the mail was, hoping only for some morsel of affection from home—from that other life.

Our expectant mood was mirrored all around by freighters and tankers waiting to pass through the Canal. By the look of them—unlit decks, rusty hulls—some had been waiting a long time. A cool, misty wind caused the ships to tug at their anchor chains, and it shrouded them so that they looked like ghosts awaiting passage through heaven's gate.

There weren't any ships like the *Picton Castle* waiting to transit the Panama Canal. It could be said that the Canal was the last rival of the commercial square-rigger. Those last great sailing ships were named for the other route from

Atlantic to Pacific, around Cape Horn. The steel Cape Horners had two and a half to ten times the *Picton Castle*'s displacement. They carried cargo from Europe or Africa westward to South American or Australian ports around the Horn of South America, and returned eastward with grain, nitrates, guano or hides.

Cape Horn's persistent westerlies circled the globe unimpeded by land. The roaring winds were chilled over Antarctic ice. They kicked up enormous seas and fierce weather. When rounding from east to west, against the wind and current, Cape Horners charged close-hauled down the world, into shortening days, threat of ice and smash of seas, until they'd gone as far south as the fifty-ninth or sixtieth parallel. There, they'd take the wind on the port side and weather the lee shore of Chile on the way to Valparaíso or some such South American port. Cape Horn was the harshest route any commercial vessel had reason to take, and the character of that route went into the ships and the men who sailed it.

For a time, that route helped the Cape Horner compete with steam. Steamships could not round the Horn and turn a profit. Coal was too expensive there, water too scarce, and steamship crews were too large to justify the slim margins to be made on Cape Horn voyages. In such a climate, the design and construction of the steel square-rigger continued to improve into the first decade of the twentieth century, principally through the vision of the German shipowner Ferdinand Laeisz with his famous Flying "P" Line.

Opening the canal to the Pacific in 1914 was a serious blow to the commercial square-rigger. The Panama Canal was of little use to a commercial wind ship as the Pacific side opened into a wide belt of calms—a belt of calms that we would soon have to transit. The steamship now had a sturdier foothold in the world cargo market. Trade under sail was revived somewhat after WWI. Laeisz built two more Cape Horners for his Flying "P" Line, but mostly the Cape Horn trade was kept alive through a Finnish fleet run by Gustav Erikson on the backs of square-riggers bought at scrap value and sailed until they were no longer fit to carry insured cargo.

WWII saw most of these remaining ships sunk, captured or taken as war prizes. Experienced crews were scattered and depleted, traditional cargo markets were crippled and diesel ships were now plying the oceans, each year transiting the Panama Canal by the thousands.

Now, at the end of the twentieth century, a new square-rigger—rigged like a Cape Horner, her captain and mate trained by Cape Horn sailors, her hold carrying an improbable cargo of two hundred used tires, a haphazard stack of bicycles, black bras, soap and old glasses—awaited passage through the Panama Canal.

Our Colón agent soon arrived with a duffle bag of mail, two Canal officials and a large, unexpected shipment of educational materials about El Niño that we were supposed to distribute through the Pacific as part of the ship's varied and, at least to me, mysterious agenda. Once we had formed a chain and handed the booklets aboard in their cardboard boxes, Doctor Beth called the mail.

As the stack of envelopes and packages was winnowed away, and second helmsman Lori approached the mail pile an infuriating twenty-one times, I gave up hope. Finally, though, my name was called. Doctor Beth handed me what looked like a heavy book, wrapped in brown paper. I eagerly peeled back the wrapping: *A Geographical Dictionary.* I opened the front cover, looking for an inscription:

> *To Rigel, with love, Christmas 1997*
> *Hope this finds you in Panama, early in the year.*
> *Dad*

I thought of my father. *He would have loved to be here. How's he doing? It's deepest winter in Nova Scotia.*

Mate Brian startled me from my thoughts, piping up to his girlfriend, who had distributed all the mail, "Beth, did all my friends write?"

"Yup," she replied.

He hadn't received a single letter.

While we were focused on the mail call, the Panama Canal officials had inspected the ship, taken measurements and talked with our captain. Now, as those officials climbed back aboard their boat, the Captain addressed us: "I thought we'd be waiting longer to transit, but we've been inspected and approved for transit tomorrow at 0300." Then the Captain and a small contingent climbed down the rope ladder into one of our skiffs to finalize arrangements for our canal passage. The Captain, Doctor Beth, cook Lee, her assistant, a boat driver and Marcello headed for shore.

Marcello? I had to wonder why this seasick member of the amateur crew would be an envoy for the ship. I remembered how, while we sailed through the Caribbean, I'd given him a haircut at the lee rail. His curly black hair had grown past his thick eyebrows. He wanted it short because of the heat, so I cut away all but a comb's thickness from the sides and back of his head, leaving some curl on top—a style that better suited his athletic physique.

As tight black curls fell to the deck, I saw that the hair underneath was salt-and-pepper grey. He noticed my surprise at the sudden transformation and interrupted his story about how he'd overcome a city ordinance to start his luxury pet hotel. "Grey, isn't it? I had to dye it black for the movie." Marcello's looks and demeanour suggested someone in his late twenties, yet he was actually forty-two.

Later, as we hit the Caribbean islands, Marcello impressed us by speaking Spanish. Only after much prodding would he admit that he spoke three additional languages.

I'd hardly heard Marcello say a mean thing to anyone, in any language. He was the model shipmate. People just seemed to want to be around him—to share in his good luck and absorb his enthusiasm for travel and the mysteries of life; to watch his eyes light up when talking; or perhaps just to be listened to, to be looked in the eye, like you were sharing some great secret. It seemed that Marcello had joined the ship simply to be himself in a whole new environment—to see what it was like to be Marcello on a ship in twenty-two countries around the world.

In Bermuda, I had taken entries in a gambling pool. When would our transom pass the last lock leading to the Pacific? The closest guess would win the kitty. Most of the optimists, including me, guessed early, not anticipating our stay in Aruba. One hedged his bet against the voyage fare, guessing we'd never pass through the Canal at all. Marcello would be by far the closest, but when we were warned of the lengthy wait ships often endure to transit the Canal, I figured he'd under-guessed as well. Now, as he sped towards Colón as the Captain's envoy, I wasn't so sure.

Back aboard, much work was needed to prepare the ship for transit. As the sun climbed the sky, burning off the morning mist, the mate divided us into groups that would each tackle one of the day's many tasks. We placed the El Niño pamphlets in empty food totes and stowed them in the hold. We climbed the rig and secured tackles to the ends of the yards so they could be used as cranes to lift anchors and boats aboard. On the foredeck, the bo'sun and his group used the foreyard and capstan to hoist our awkward one-ton fisherman's anchor over the rail and place it securely on deck. We lowered our twenty-three-foot-long Monomoy surfboat from davits to water, then floated her amidships, where we hoisted her with tackles from the two yards and gently set her diagonally across the cargo hatch. Aloft, we judiciously released rigging to prepare the yards to be cockbilled, with one yardarm brought down to the deck, clear from the lock walls. We hoisted the upper yards, allowing them to be braced sharper than usual.

At 0230 hours, we were awakened to prepare for the pilot's arrival. This highly trained seaman would use his vast local knowledge to guide us through the Canal. I descended from my bunk onto my sea chest and threw on some shorts and a T-shirt. Outside, the cool air wicked the sweat off my neck.

A young canal pilot arrived at 0300 hours sharp. The mate called us immediately to the windlass and put me on the first shift, as I'd be called to the wheel before the anchor was pulled from the bottom. Within minutes, the cool of night was chased away by the sweat of hard work and the false energy of coffee. Astern, I heard the engine start with a phlegmy cough, like an aged smoker woken from his dreams.

The mate gave the forward bell two sharp rings, reporting to the Captain that two shots, or 180 feet, of chain were between windlass and anchor. When the anchor was aweigh, the Captain would relinquish control to the pilot. Though he'd remain on deck, looking over his ship for the entire transit, the Captain was required to hand over the ship's operation while in the Canal. The mate ordered fresh crew to the windlass and sent me to the wheel. The deck was smooth and cool as I walked aft and climbed the ladder to the quarterdeck.

Spinning the wheel to determine midships, I felt my arm quake with fatigue from the windlass. As he connected the binnacle hood that would light the compass, the Captain briefed me on the pilot's system of helm orders: degrees of

rudder angle, used in modern ships with rudder angle indi-
cators. He told me the degree equivalents to our system.

The windlass crew broke the anchor free of the mud.
Our pilot gave me a course to steer, and soon we were headed straight down the seven-mile channel to the first of
three locks that would elevate our ship to Gatun Lake,
the man-made freshwater lake that spans two-thirds of the
isthmus, eighty-five feet above sea level.

Shortly, two sets of locks side by side came into view.
Each set can elevate or lower a ship in three stages. A dense
smear of yellow halogen light illuminated the long concrete
pier that protruded between them. It bustled with men in
white hard hats and electric cars on tracks, called mules.
The locks were alive, a miniature city.

A few days before, I had been surprised to learn that the
Canal runs north-south, not east-west. I hadn't expected
such vivid proof: above the halogen glow, directly ahead,
the Southern Cross came into view like five diamonds set
in gold. On the concrete pier a glaring neon arrow pointed
to the left lock entrance. I saw it all as we steamed slowly
down the channel.

A couple of small fibreglass rowboats came alongside,
and from them swarmed eight Panamanian line handlers
wearing blue, buttoned T-shirts and hard hats. They carried cardboard sleeping pallets, and despite the Canal's
tension, they immediately lay on the deck for a snooze.

The pilot gave me a helm order of ten degrees left rudder to make for the locks. I calculated the number of turns
and spun the wheel twice. He wasn't satisfied with our rate
of turn and ordered twenty degrees. I spun the wheel twice
more. The ship responded suddenly.

"Midships," he ordered. I unwound the turns as fast as
I could, holding a spoke with one hand and whipping it
around with my whole body, but now the ship had overshot

her mark. We headed for the bank. The Southern Cross wandered elusively across our bow.

"Twenty degrees right rudder!" he ordered. I stood before the wheel and spun it four turns to the right as fast as I could and turned to face him for more orders. I panted from the effort.

"Midships," he ordered. But before I'd taken even half the turns out, we were aiming for the neon arrow. With an edge of concern, he upgraded his command to twenty degrees left. I had not realized just how different our ship was from the modern vessels he was used to.

"Midships! Ten degrees left! Hard left. Hard right! Hard left!" It was a full eighteen turns from side to side, and he changed his orders with such rapidity that I couldn't complete any one of them. I kept count of the turns left and right of midships so I could land on any degree of rudder angle he needed.

Ten. Eleven. Twelve. Thirteen turns.

"Twenty degrees left rudder!"

One. Two. Three . . . Thirteen—midships. One. Two. Three. Four. "Twenty deg—"

"Full right rudder!"

Five. Six. Seven . . . I felt like my arm was going to fall off. I turned for all I was worth.

"Full left rudder!"

One. Two. Three . . . Our own captain could easily have guided the ship into the lock. I suddenly realized the symbiosis possible between captain and helmsman. *Six. Seven—midships. One. Two. Three—Faster!*

The concrete lock approached. The lights on their tall poles grew higher, blotting out all stars. That neon arrow wandered crazily ahead as we approached the lock. Four heaving lines flew aboard from seawalls on either side. Quickly, the line handlers sprang up from their cardboard and pulled those lines aboard. Steel wires were attached to the heaving lines, and with gloved hands they passed them through chocks in our bulwarks, looped them over our sturdy deck cleats and took a respectful step back. A signal was given to the shore team and winches on the electric mules reeled in the slack. They aligned the ship with the seawall as they tightened. They tightened further, shifting our substantial cleats three inches along the deck.

With their job done, the line handlers lay down on their cardboard pallets and fell asleep. I wiped sweat from my eyes and caught my breath. Pilot and captain breathed sighs of relief.

The electric mules pulled us ahead. They climbed a roller-coaster incline and drew us into the first chamber. Riveted iron gates closed off the Atlantic astern.

The still water of our lock was disturbed by upwelling currents all around. For ten minutes our chamber filled with water draining from the lock above until both were at the same level. Then the doors opened ahead and the process repeated. Finally, at the last gate on the east side of Panama, Gatun Lake itself drained into our lock, elevating us to its level. Amazingly, no pumps are used to maintain the level of the lake; it is filled only by rain. Ahead, the doors opened. We were pulled a little farther and the wire ropes went slack. The line handlers cast them off and we headed across the lake.

In a few hours, sunrise illuminated the lush rain forest surrounding Gatun Lake. Looking ahead, I saw we were part of a train of ships headed over Panama. Around us, many ships lay at anchor, getting a freshwater cure. Barnacles and seaweed that clung to their bottoms could not survive long in fresh water. Much of it would die, falling off and saving shipowners the expense of dry-docking and scraping.

The air was dead still. The sky was clear and the sun high. Captain and pilot took a perch atop the charthouse, shaded by fabric strung overhead. One of the Panamanian line handlers wove a hammock by the fo'c'sle with a netting needle and many-coloured twine. Another played ukulele on the shady aloha deck. Crew went about maintenance— painting the ship's name on the boats while they were conveniently aboard. And, taking advantage of the lovely fresh water in Gatun Lake, a crewman was ordered to secure a fire hose to the lower shrouds and run it into the *power shower* bucket, which had holes in the bottom to make a giant showerhead. Soon, we had our own freshwater cure.

By mid-afternoon, a relief pilot arrived. He was a fair bit older and, judging by his decorations and the quality of his radio equipment, high in the pilot establishment. He guided us effortlessly through the long verdant canal that made up the last third of the passage, and eased us down the locks to the Pacific Ocean.

As we approached the final gate, I stood next to Marcello on the main deck. I held the piece of paper bearing his prediction that had been sealed in an envelope one day out of Bermuda. We ran aft and watched our transom ease past the last great iron doors, which were riveted just like our ship. I checked my wristwatch: thirty-seven seconds ahead of his guess. He won the kitty but didn't look surprised, as if it was in the bag the whole time.

We anchored off Isla Flamenco, a small naval base joined to the mainland by a two-and-a-half-mile causeway. South of us, the Gulf of Panama opened into the world's largest ocean, otherwise known as Paradise. I saw Kim looking hungrily, not to the ocean, but over the stony causeway at Panama City. In its streets and its towers of concrete and glass, he saw a marketplace for the bulky second-hand goods cluttering the hold. He was cargo rich and cash poor. With the dollars he might earn from tire and bicycle sales, he could take advantage of low Panamanian prices and buy tools and materials for resale where they were really needed, like Pitcairn Island, like Vanuatu. I was sure at that moment he was plotting how to get his goods to the beach. The causeway was quite close, but it was constructed of slippery barnacle-covered boulders, constantly washed by Pacific surge. There was a decent landing many miles away at the Balboa Yacht Club, but Balboa was many miles from Panama City. Not to mention the cumbersome question of proper importation . . . and that nearby naval base.

CHAPTER 13

Hit or Stick

Panama City and Balboa
January 10 to 21

T HE MATE'S WATCH—MY WATCH—WAS ON DUTY THE FIRST day and night in Panama. Brian mustered the entire crew and made preparations to square the yards and tidy ship.

While we started the work, he pulled aside my watchmate, Clyde. Normally I took little notice of their exchanges, but Clyde, who was always demure in receiving orders, stared at Brian through his John Lennon glasses with an expression of disbelief; and Brian, who always delivered orders with certainty and piercing authority, looked resigned. Clyde soon nodded his head and retired to the fo'c'sle.

Later, I saw Clyde tossing among the scattered personal effects that cluttered his rack—dirty clothes, books, a soccer ball. He was too hot, too wired and too annoyed by the clamour on deck for any decent sleep. He'd been up since 0200 hours. He opened his bleary eyes to look at me as I entered.

"What's up, Clyde?"

"Brian told me to get some sleep before watch tonight. They want me to stand all night."

"What?" As a rule we'd split anchor duty into two-hour chunks and rotate it through a portion of the crew.

"That's the new policy, man. ABs are up all night on anchor duty."

"What about the rest of our watch?"

"They're up for an hour a piece to assist."

"Assist with what?"

"Brian said I'd be able to sleep for the hour you're on."

Clyde closed his eyes. And when he woke, his all-night vigilance passed slowly. In the morning, while the rest of his watch went ashore for a day off, Clyde slept.

I took the bus to Panama City with a group of shipmates. The crew's mood was in decline, though they didn't seem sluggish or morose. Instead, they were edgy, defensive, their backs up. Lately I'd found that two or more crew together winnowed away their time off, orbiting their complaints about the ship, the Captain, other crew, the lack of time off.

We walked towards the downtown and passed under a billboard of a smiling cartoon chicken in a cowboy hat carrying a steaming tray of drumsticks. The city boiled with stimuli. Pigeons flooded the cobblestone streets, scavenging corn niblets tossed by tourists who purchased them in Baggies from children. Clothing stores, electronics stores, restaurants, music, pharmacies, dark bars, street cats, beggars. Lights blared. There were new second floors cobbled over old one-storeys. There were signs that covered signs that covered signs. The city had grown like oysters out of the mud on the dead husks of the oysters that came before. The quick rhythm of Latin music timed the energy of the city.

Our group fragmented as we each defined missions for ourselves: mall, hotel, cinema, fast food, ice cream, telephone, whorehouse. For most it was a little too early for sightseeing tours and local delicacies. Satisfying repressed desire for luxuries and tastes of home had overcome most else a traveller might look for.

That night, many rented air-conditioned rooms at the Hotel International on Plaza Cinco de Mayo for about twenty-five dollars. Some seemed prepared to set up camp permanently, returning to the ship only when absolutely necessary, if not because of the restless mood aboard then because of the conditions.

Of the four men living aft in the bat cave, three stayed in the hotel. When I heard them talk of their sleeping quarters, I was glad to be bunked in the relatively airy fo'c'sle. I'd heard one of my bunkmates say our place smelled like a mouldy asshole, but it couldn't compare to the bat cave on a still night underway.

The main air source was a small hatch aft of the superstructure, which did little to ventilate the place in anything but a following breeze. The guys said it approached 130 degrees Fahrenheit with tropical humidity. They complained it was too hot to use a sheet, but if they didn't, they were immediately attacked by a colony of fleas that had been thriving in the dark recesses ever since the cats brought them aboard in Aruba. The most hirsute of the three bat cave residents, Cowboy Brad, had an itchy fungal growth the colour of cooked beets among his matted chest hair.

The day of the watch change, many did not return to the ship to assume their share of the duties. While I was off wandering the streets, chasing pigeons and eating paella, I saw drummer Todd, one of the bat cave crowd, looking surly. Patricia, the Boston lobbyist, had also gone AWOL. Later, she told me what she'd done.

She'd woken up early in her hotel and had someone deliver a note to the Captain. She'd written it on elegant stationery, stating that she would not join the ship that day for her watch, that she was going to Taboga Island and not to worry about her. Patricia said she'd joined the ship with the understanding that she wouldn't be required to work aboard while we were in port. That was why she'd put up with the cold and arduous delays in Lunenburg. She desired a travel experience with meaningful time off. Going back to the ship after one day of liberty didn't suit her. She checked out of her comfortable hotel and flagged a cab.

At the ferry dock off Taboga Island she had an awkward exchange with the driver. He avowed his undying love to her, gave her a cassette of amorous songs and offered to wait at the docks until her ferry returned. She deterred his advances and, somewhat flustered, leaned against a rail at the pier, brushed her black hair out of mascaraed eyelashes, held a cigarette to her red lips and had a smoke.

Shortly, she realized there was no activity aboard the ferries. The boats sat tied to the pier, bobbing laconically. Patricia looked around for a possible explanation and saw a wizened old Panamanian man, neatly dressed. He told her that the ferries were closed in observance of Martyrs' Day.

In 1964, a group of about two hundred Panamanian students marched to Balboa High School in the Canal Zone, bearing a historically significant Panamanian flag. They'd wanted to fly it next to Old Glory in accordance with a bilateral agreement signed by President John F. Kennedy. The Canal Zone residents, noted for their patriotism, would have none of it and gathered around the flag singing "The Star-Spangled Banner." A scuffle broke out between them and the students, and the Panamanian flag was torn. As word of the flag desecration spread, the protest escalated to a riot, with students stoning the high school and surrounding cars. The Canal Zone police attempted to control the students with tear gas. The rioters threw rocks at the police and the police responded by opening fire.

The first death occurred shortly thereafter, when Ascanio Arosemena, captain of the soccer team, born of a prominent old Panamanian family, was hit from behind

while helping a wounded protestor from the area of con-
flict. His lung was punctured and aorta severed, making
him the first of the martyrs who would represent this clash
that lasted for three days, resulted in the burning and loot-
ing of many American businesses, and left twenty-three
dead, four hundred wounded and five hundred arrested,
mostly Panamanians.

Just this morning, in recognition of Martyrs' Day, the
old man explained that two thousand marched on the U.S.
embassy, burned an American soldier in effigy and threw
red paint balloons against the walls.

Patricia realized that the best way for her to travel the
countryside was with this knowledgeable old man. He'd
stave off further unwanted advances and inform her of local
political history. As a lobbyist with liberal leanings, political
activism was one of Patricia's deepest interests. As they
talked, Patricia learned that she and her guide had more in
common than she'd thought: he was the former president of
the taxi drivers' union, while Patricia had represented the
Boston pipefitters' union before the legislature.

They hit it off and agreed that if she paid for gas, the old
man would drive her on a tour in his beat-up Chevy. They
began with visits to the two most important sites of the U.S.
invasion of Panama, starting with the American military
base in Balboa and ending with the slums that were devas-
tated as U.S. forces routed and captured the dictator Noriega.
Again, she was surprised to learn of the great damage to the
civilian neighbourhood during the invasion. She knew from
the news that the civilian death count was about two
hundred, yet her driver told her that three thousand civilian
lives were lost, a figure backed up by U.S. Attorney General
Ramsey Clark's independent inquiry. She saw that an entire
district was rebuilt with American reparations—high-rise
slums of concrete with small glass windows.

After a day of immersion in Panama's resistance to foreign power, Patricia returned to the ship. She learned that Lee, our fourth cook, had quit, and that a number of other amateur crew had gone AWOL. The Captain was busy talking to the crew, hearing their wishes: larger chunks of time off, a more organized sail training regimen, a fan in the bat cave hatch.

Patricia perceived that many of them were coming round to the Captain's point of view about their duties on the ship. Patricia, however, had made up her mind not to be swayed, having worked to ready the ship for nearly a month and a half in Lunenburg when she thought she'd be sail training and provisioning. She believed that the Captain had an agreement to honour. She went to her bunk and resolved to tell him so the next day.

At 0700 hours, the freshly promoted head cook, Ian, already showing signs of burnout, dragged himself out of the sweltering bat cave to serve us a breakfast of cookies before heading back to his rack. At 0800, our watch turned to. The day was already hot. I opened the buttons of the thin white cotton shirt that Kim had given me from his cargo of used goods.

Long cool sunrises were things of higher latitudes. As we approached the equator, the sun traced an ever more direct route to top dead centre of the sky. There was little breeze, and in the growing heat my hair stuck to the beads of sweat on my forehead.

Becky, a young Halifax woman on the professional crew, mixed up a batch of white paint to touch up stains and bare steel primer that dappled the superstructure. There was less paint for her to mix that morning; two amateur crew were AWOL. I felt a profound heaviness aboard ship. Hanging over everyone's head was the unacknowledged truth that this voyage depended on the amateur crew and not just on the revenues of their fares. It depended on their continued confidence that we could pull this voyage off. Yet, since leaving Halifax, we'd only continued to fall further behind schedule. Our entire social structure depended on their embracing the rigours of ship life and the chain of command. If a middle ground could not be met, it would mean an end to all we'd worked for.

What scared me most was that I was beginning not to care. It made me sick to think of the rest of the voyage continuing like this. I secretly began to imagine how I'd backpack South America if the voyage folded. *Ahh. Sweet freedom.*

Turning to, I carefully laid paint on the superstructure, trying to keep my touch-ups in a rectangular shape. Dave, a Halifax brain surgeon, painted next to me, not saying a word. Mild mannered and poised, Dave was the hardest crew member to read. He sought solitude, and I'd often see him alone, immersed in journals of neurosurgery and news from abroad received on his shortwave radio.

Late in the morning, when the glare of sunlight was most intense, reflecting off the water and white paint, Dave handed me his container and his one-and-a-half-inch brush, saying, "I'm done painting for today, Rige. Could you take this, please?"

"Umm . . . sure," I replied, stunned by his polite, matter-of-fact mutiny. I watched him descend into the main salon. Then, walking by the salon hatch on my way to return his paint to the locker, I could see him lying atop a couple of sea chests in the shade beneath the hatch, soaking up the meagre breeze that funnelled through from aft to forward.

Becky was at the paint locker when I returned Dave's paint. She clenched her fists in anger as I told her of his strike. I placed a bit of plastic over the container to preserve it and headed back to the superstructure to continue my work. Just Becky and I painted now.

It'd been just over one month since we left Nova Scotia, but looking at the ship I would have guessed it had been many more. Rust streaked the superstructure's white paint. It bled from the rivets in the bulwarks. Oil wore away from the deck to reveal naked wood. Varnish had chipped and yellowed. Turnbuckle threads rusted. Marline chaffed and yellowed on the shrouds, starving from lack of tar. The ship was atrophying just as quickly as the crew's spirit. Becky and I applied spot after spot of paint to the superstructure, she on one side, me on the other.

In minutes, Brian stormed around the aft end of the ship. I turned to meet his eyes and saw deep anger. A vein protuded on his forehead among beads of sweat. His clenched jaw was visible through perpetual red stubble. "Stand down, Rigel. If they're going to quit, we are too. Let's just let her fucking rust."

I took my paint to the locker. Becky was there already, cleaning the day's brushes. I assumed she was the one who told Brian of Dave's strike, but I felt that a much deeper anger drove him to call us off work. I looked aft and saw Patricia leave the door nearest the Captain's cabin, and wondered if Brian had been present at their meeting. *Who was he more angry at?*

I looked back to Becky, washing her brushes in three different containers of diesel fuel. Her paint-speckled arms shook slightly, and I realized she was trying not to cry. "What's wrong, Becky?"

"I can't believe what's happening. We were the strongest watch."

I saw for the first time the pride that Becky took in our watch, and realized I'd sold short her hopes for this voyage. We cleaned our brushes and I retired to the fo'c'sle, waiting for things to cool off.

The day after the strike, I headed off alone. I just wanted

to drift . . . away from the divisiveness of the ship, and the complaints of the crew, to be ready for the day to follow. It was the first of two all-hands days. The goal was to move all the heavy stores aft and all the light stores forward, cleaning and organizing the ship in the process. The redistribution of weight would raise the bow four inches and sink the stern four, deepening the rudder and increasing its effect. Hopefully, this would reduce the ship's weatherhelm, its tendency to head into the wind rather than track a direct course.

The work got off to a late start. Much of the crew had arrived late to the yacht club, missed the boat and had to wait for the next one. Nonetheless, the mood on the ship was so sensitive that none of the officers said a thing to the latecomers, save a stern look in the direction of the oncoming boat. Even the Captain that day wore boots, shorts and a beat-up shirt with the sleeves removed, rather than his customary bare feet, sarong and clean linen shirt.

The ship seemed changed by the absence of Seanette Rowland, the high-stakes Vegas blackjack dealer who took the *mola* market by storm in the San Blas Islands and spent her spare time filming the crew with a handycam, narrating the whole time. She had left the ship just that morning. I knew she was on the edge of a decision when I saw her crying to the Captain at the yacht club bar. His stern demeanour melted as he comforted her, and for a second I felt she might stay.

But perhaps she'd believed things were beyond repair. Unlike the crew who had left in Lunenburg and been given a celebration, quite the opposite happened for Seanette and Lee. They left with little ceremony, their bags handed down to them in the boat to disappear with them back up the Panama Canal.

There were others missing too. I heard bo'sun Josh say, "Where the hell are the brothers?" Cowboy Brad and

Drummer Todd had yet to return to the ship. Don summed it up best: "How can you expect a cowboy and a rock star to conform to the rules?"

Starting with the hold, we lifted out seventy-five used bicycles. Extricating the tangled vehicles one at a time was like removing burdock from the fur of a skittery dog. We pulled out all two hundred tires and placed them on deck. We pulled out the tons of remaining used clothing and cans of old paint. Then, barefoot and shirtless, dripping sweat in the still, humid air of the hold, we moved over ten tons of coal aft, wedging it under the freezers, stacking it high against the one-storey battery box, rivulets of perspiration eroding the coal dust that stuck to our skin. An unused hydraulic capstan was hoisted above, carted to the aloha deck and lashed in place. Fifty-five-gallon kerosene, gasoline and engine-oil drums, waste and spare, were lashed aft to pad eyes that Nobby welded to the superstructure. All the way aft, in the bat cave, boxes of Weetabix and garbage bags of toilet paper were extricated and carried to the forward hatch of the main salon, where they'd join the used clothing and replace the numerous spare spools of rope, moved to the after part of the salon, chasing out huge quantities of canned goods, salt beef and exotic dried goods.

The workday wore on, and just before 1700 hours, when we replaced the hatch boards and cover, tucking away perishables, I looked at the day's accomplishments. The ship was completely transformed. Seventy-five bicycles stood in neat ranks on the quarterdeck. Totes of canned goods were stacked high on the deck. Rope, cleaning supplies, cargo, rigging, crates of scrap wood—the ship's holds had nearly been evacuated. When work was over, those not on watch returned to shore to make the most of their liberty.

The next morning, we began work with the benefit of the past day's momentum. But eventually, tropical heat took its toll on the crew. By lunch, crew were complaining that they hadn't been given a morning break. Well after sunset, as we lowered the last totes of food on a tackle to the hold below, and our efforts had risen the bow and lowered the stern four inches, I heard Cowboy Brad mumbling through his bristly moustache about the five dollars the crew was promised in Lunenburg for each hour of handling cargo. Marcello, his biceps criss-crossed by veins swollen from the day's labour, complained of the Captain, "I hate people who are cheap. I just spent the day moving his shit. Why can't he at least buy us a case of beer?"

Many crew were feeling like dupes, like they were getting screwed. It sent ripples of bad feeling to every corner of the ship, and in the days that followed, Patricia found disgruntled crew calling on her in her hotel room, hoping that because of her easy rapport with the Captain she would champion their concerns about ship life. Now that Seanette had thrown down her cards and left the table, I was afraid others would do the same, taking a share of the kitty and our confidence.

I looked at a map of the world and at our schedule, and realized that the Pacific Ocean would take us seven months to cross. *Seven months!* I had never done anything for seven months, not without a break, and I wondered how seriously people were questioning their will, or more precisely— because I thought they sought enjoyment—their desire, to go the whole way.

Just about everyone around my age seemed willing to follow the example of the officers and pro crew. After all, two days off for one day on in port was more time off than any of us pro crew had ever known. The fact that the time was in no more than two-day chunks . . . well, I hoped it would get better. Besides, two days was enough if all you wanted to do was drink beer, chase strippers and shop at the mall. For those of us on a tighter budget, the shorter liberty periods were not a hindrance to travel overland or to extended hotel accommodation, because we were sleeping on the ship anyway. And there were some who relished the grittier aspects of life aboard, who'd arrived wanting little more than to be treated like members of the pro crew, whatever that would entail.

Despite our doubts after a couple of failed departure dates, we all arrived on the ship on the morning of January 21 to the announcement that we'd finally be leaving Panama. Checks were run throughout the ship to ensure gear had been properly stowed and lashed in place. Crew were sent aloft, streaming up the rig to release gaskets from all square sails but the main. Another group climbed atop the galley house to unlash the main topmast staysail. Still others shimmied out the headrig, side-stepping along the footrope as they cast off the gaskets and coiled them neatly in place.

With the sails free, the Captain commanded that the foreyards be braced on the port. Then, "Heave away on the windlass!"

Brian engaged the windlass's clutch, released its brake and commanded, "Bars in!" He then set us on the iron contraption. Sweating in the sun, we hauled the chain slowly through the hawse pipe. Brian moved forward for a look at the chain's progress, reporting to the Captain how much remained to lift. Soon, Brian announced "Up and down!" meaning that the chain made a vertical line to the anchor and it was soon going to be pulled from the mud.

"Set the inner and outer jib! Back them to port!" the Captain responded.

Hauling in rhythm, hand over hand, we raised the two headsails. The wind pried on those sails to shift the ship's head away from Panama's shore towards the Pacific.

Turbulent water washed around the bow. Afternoon sunlight sparkled on the Pacific's mild chop.

The crew strained on the windlass, hoisting anchor to hawse pipe. Meanwhile, the Captain ordered that all the squares be set. Second mate Karen managed the sails while Brian saw to it that the anchor was properly housed. As things steadied out and the helmsman shaped up on a course, we set 'tweensails. Crew and ship had sailed *off the hook* for the first time ever, hopefully to leave disagreements behind on Panama's rocky shore.

CHAPTER 14

Neptune's Ghosts

Panama to Galapagos
January 21 to 31

IN THE FAILING LIGHT OF AFTERNOON, WHILE WE SAILED southwest, the Captain ordered the mate to muster the crew. "MUSTER MIDSHIPS!" he called into each compartment.

The Captain knelt on the cargo hatch, adjusted his sarong and folded open a pilot chart of the South Pacific. The Captain explained how the chart could illustrate seasonal variations in wind, current and wave height. He drew attention to the purple wind roses scattered over the chart. Each looked like a target with arrow shafts protruding to indicate the wind's most likely direction and strength. He showed how he'd used them to plan our course to the Galapagos.

"Welcome to the Pacific," he said. "This passage should take between a week and ten days. In the *Romance* we did it in eight, but we used the engine for a couple of days in the doldrums, or the Inter-Tropical Convergence Zone. I have chosen a different course for us. It will lead us south using a fair current to get us through the doldrums. There, we'll pick up the southeast trades and head west to the Galapagos."

We crew were silent, uncertain as we swayed on the rolling deck. The Captain's tone became persuasive. "Listen, I know that a lot of you are self-starters, independent people, and are finding it difficult to adjust to the more regimented aspects of ship life. A lot of the work is quite menial, I know. Washing dishes and scrubbing heads for forty is not, perhaps, what you're all used to. You see, sailing around the world is like climbing Mount Everest. Though there are elements of skill and physical ability required, climbing Everest is essentially putting one foot in front of the other through the snow. This is like that, only hotter, much hotter.

"I want you all to keep your spirits up. We may have been in Panama too long, but now you're all about to reap the rewards of your hard work. Soon we'll be in the Galapagos, then French Polynesia. Remember, the best is yet to come."

With that, the Captain ended his address. I felt elated. *I'm in an excellent steel barque, we're headed for the Galapagos and we're going to cross the line.* But as the assembly dispersed, few faces were content. I saw the fine line of angry lips barely visible between cynical ears. The crew escaped the pounding sun, disappearing below to bunks of sweaty sheets and dog-eared paperbacks.

At twenty to midnight, I was awoken for watch. Not my usual watch—I'd replaced Tom Ward as the lead AB of Karen's watch, the twelve-to-four. Tom had been moved to the Captain's watch. Rumour was, the Captain was grooming him for third mate. Some crew feared Tom's acerbic edge, which lined his voice when he shouted orders. Still, he craved the promotion. With so many in the professional crew, opportunities to advance were few. He'd worked full-time in traditional ships for nearly a decade, and by now he felt he'd be wasting his time to remain before the mast.

Everything was different the night I joined Karen's watch. The confident breeze that pushed us from Panama had slackened, and the sails from the lowers to the t'gallants slapped the masts and snapped full, repeating the cycle every eight seconds as the ship cranked lazily on long Pacific swells. The night was moonless. Second mate Karen, engineer Claire, Doctor Beth, Kristin and Becky were all on this watch.

Karen's watch took the deck when everyone else was asleep. I think Karen relished that fact. Her watch had the mood of an enclave, removed from the ship's hierarchy. Under the protection of the night, she vented her deepening frustration about our captain's ways. She smarted from his injuries to her pride, and at the same time felt unable to address her concerns with him, or to escape them. And she did not wish to leave, so frustration gave way to disdain as pent-up feelings festered. Not until the end of the voyage would the Captain fully understand how deep her anger for him ran. He would feel betrayed.

Karen strove to make the culture of her watch different from the others. I'd prepared myself for the formality of mate Brian's watch, getting a notebook and a timepiece, even reading *The Art of War*, paying close attention to the five qualities of a good leader: wisdom, sincerity, humanity, courage and strictness. Thus prepared, I was surprised at how comfortable Karen's style was. She reacted positively when I took the initiative, like setting up the watch duties with a forty-minute rotation instead of the standard hour. She didn't hesitate to grant me authority to make decisions and act on them. I felt good on this watch, and by passing down the same trust Karen gave me, I was amazed at how easily things ran.

That night, I established a system whereby the watch standers initiated their own rotation while I looked over the side, entranced by the eerie spectacle of the doldrums. An ocean of jellyfish luminesced in fleeting bubbles of yellow-green that boiled beneath the surface—a surface that was heavy and dark, like oil, rippled by the rolling of our plated hull. I held the weathered teak quarterdeck rail while the ship rocked us side to side through a clinging fog.

This seclusion demanded a sacrifice. The twelve-to-four was the only watch where one couldn't get seven hours of uninterrupted sleep if you ate three meals a day. Free time in daylight was reduced, too. Still, it was a more lenient schedule than bo'sun Josh's, who, instead of the optimum eight hours' work, eight hours' free time, eight hours' sleep, would have the burden of maintaining our decaying ship twelve hours a day, six days a week, the whole way around the earth.

He spoke to me about it one day as we scratched at the ship's maintenance. "Entropy," he said, revealing his scientific view of things, "is inevitable. As time goes by, entropy increases. All I can do is keep pouring on the energy." Ordinarily calm, the stocky bo'sun was wild-eyed, like the scientists who'd sought entropy by measuring the growth of disorder in a closed system.

I had sympathy for him, but I didn't want to make his burden my own. Like everyone else there, I jealously guarded my free time. Our culture began with a population that felt overtaxed. Now no one wanted to give their free time to maintain the ship. All around me I saw the decay in the castle that was Josh's inheritance: dings and rust streaks, like bullet holes and blood, greasy smears from the engineers' oily hands, the swatch of treacherous slime that grew on the deck beneath the ladders, irrigated by a permanent wave. Royal yards remained lashed to the deck rather than their perches high on the masts. Their iron hardware was rusted by the constant wash of the sea. Our once yellow, stiff and oily manila lines were giving in to wear, hanging limp as old hay. Josh was the custodian of fingerprints, of the ship's stores, of a rig not formalized, of ratlines to seize, of rust. He had no enthusiastic help, and the ship, with all the ceremony of an ailing spouse, was dying faster than he could restore her. The lower topsail yards had shrunk in the iron bands that connected them to the masts. Those iron bands were grinding away at the softwood of the lower topsail yards. The mate had once said, "The ship will be done when we get home." I doubted even Josh believed that.

When our watch was over, I was told to rouse all hands for a tacking drill. Moments later, I stood in a sleepy, sweaty semi-circle around our sarong-clad captain. He discussed tacking: "Some captains instruct with models. We don't need a model—we have a ship. This is good tacking weather, and I predict the *Picton Castle* will be a good tacking ship." He paused and gave us a hint of how encompassing and minutely planned his vision of the ship was: "Remember, the carpenter mans the headsail sheet and the cook casts off the foresheet with a heathenish glee. Mate, stick out the crew for a tacking drill."

Mate Brian manned the ship by watches, "Four-to-eight aft! Eight-to-twelve forward! Twelve-to-four midships! Carpenter, cook. Stand by to brace up, starboard tack!"

"Steer full and by! Prepare to come ABOUT!" ordered the Captain. "Hard a lee!"

We stood in silent anticipation as the wind moved steadily forward. It blew over the beam. It marched over the forward parts of the ship where I'd never seen it pass while we were under sail.

"Spanker MIDSHIPS! Let fly the foresheet! Let fly headsail SHEETS!" Carpenter Kim hadn't eased the sheets fast enough. "LET THEM FLY!" the Captain shouted. The sails began to shiver as they spilled their wind. Blocks, high aloft, chattered in the turbulence.

There were two decisive slaps of stiff canvas on greasy masts as the t'gallants went aback. The upper topsails slapped the topmasts, then the lower topsails. Now the foresail tugged at its windward tack and its clew slapped at the air in fits.

"Back the HEADsails! Ease the spanker SHEET!"

There was concern in the eyes of those who'd never seen the unnatural transformation of a square-rigger going aback, of a Captain's barks. "Pass the staysails! Mainsail HAUL!" Our watch pulled feverishly—out of rhythm.

Lines fed around their belaying pins, which rattled like a bag of bones. The wind pushed on the sails of the mainmast and they spun around fast. We took up the slack as quickly as we could. Finally catching up, we torqued them around hard and the sails shivered on the other tack, waiting for the wind to fill them.

"Pass the headSAILS!" Three triangular sails tugged their way across the headstays to the opposite tack. "Let go and HAUL!" With that final order from the Captain there was a clatter of hatch boards as crew scrambled to organize themselves in rows and pull together on the forebraces. Shirtless heavy haulers muscled past uncertain ones to the front of the line.

The ship had stopped pushing forward, but she was turning decisively now with an uneasy roll as swells began to catch her on the beam. Moments later, order was restored. All sails were full on the other tack. The Captain was grinning. He had proven his ship to be a good tacking ship.

Now he gave the mate a try. Brian headed the ship off the wind to build momentum that would drive her to the other tack. He gave his orders, yet she wouldn't pass through irons. As far as I could see, he'd made every order at the appropriate time, but the ship stalled, bow into the wind. She wouldn't *make stays*. The dying breeze wasn't enough to power her through the wandering Pacific swells. The ship stopped turning. She stopped moving.

"Back the headsails! Square the main yards! Shift the helm!" The sails on the mainmast, now square to the direction of the wind, filled with air. The ship moved backwards, accelerating, ploughing against the rudder hard over. I felt how badly he wanted that tack—how I wanted that tack—yet no amount of determination could bring her around.

The wind continued to decline. The next day's tacking drill was a bust as well. In this light air, the ship refused to make stays. The Captain made the best of it by announcing a swim call. We dove off the pinrail and, from the level of the water, saw the ship from a foreign perspective. The height of the masts seemed diminished from the water. The hull, near and rolling, looked bulbous. Rust streaked from freeing ports, dings, dents and rivets. A real old hooker.

I swam forward to the new clipper bow welded to the seventy-year-old hull, looking almost as if it had been there for the ship's whole life. Just aft of the new bow was a large + shape. It was all that remained of an A-frame that had once supported an acoustic hammer used to prematurely detonate hostile mines that lay waiting to be triggered by engine noise. Like many of the North Sea trawlers, the *Picton Castle* had been pressed into service as a minesweeper. Behind her she would have towed a wide sweep of serrated wire and cutters that released submerged mines from their moorings. Once on the surface, the mines could be destroyed at a distance by gunfire.

Seeing that plus-shaped weld, I was reminded that a mine explosion had once lifted the ship's bow from the water. It was a testament to the strength and versatility of this venerable steel ship. The bow climbed a swell and fell, cleaving the water like an axe.

I left the surface for a moment and dove down. I heard silence, opened my eyes and saw blue water go on forever.

That idea of infinite depth was terrifying—that I could sink forever, be swallowed by ocean or fish.

And that night, soon after we took the watch, the wind died completely. Kristin put the helm hard right, and there it stayed for the entire four hours.

The ship would not respond to her rudder, yet after the first hour Karen announced, "We're two miles closer to the Galapagos, guys." We abandoned the helm; lookout was the only essential position.

I leaned over the rail and again watched the luminous show. Balls of yellow-green light exploded at many depths. Pulses emanated from jellyfish, large and small. That night was different from the last. Cloud cover was thinner. The glow of stars brought out a dense haze smeared across the sky. I had that castaway feeling of deep space I'd felt underwater, but I felt better because I was rooted to the ship. And though it seemed that we were without a point of reference, and weird stars surrounded us in all directions, I knew our hull was there because it was embraced in a glowing green halo of bioluminescence.

The next morning, I was in the fo'c'sle with Jesse. He was jockeying for the third mate position alongside Tom. Jesse had something that appealed to his superiors, an innate ability to fit into the military scheme of things. His will to excel in this environment made me feel miscast by comparison. On any other ship, one not engaged on such a long voyage, Jesse could have advanced faster. He'd made the sacrifice because he wanted to work for Moreland, and to steel himself for a long career in sailing ships. Jesse was so focused that he usually refused to discuss the same topic twice. Many around him took this focus for arrogance. In the fo'c'sle this morning, I asked to borrow one of his seamanship manuals.

"Hey, Jess, can I borrow your *Masting and Rigging*?"

"Sure," he replied cautiously.

Published in 1946 as a reference for model builders, this was among the most authoritative rigging handbooks for traditional ships. The *Picton Castle*'s rig looked almost like it had been built directly from the book's drawings. *Masting and Rigging the Clipper Ship and Ocean Carrier* is kept close to the heart of a rigger.

Jesse handed me a copy that looked like an old library book. Plastic covered the dust jacket and its artwork, a painting of a ship much like ours. I opened the cover and read the inscription: *Happy Birthday Jesse, to our "Bo'sun."*

I imagined Jesse, still filled with the joy of his first passages on a big square-rigger, requesting the book for his birthday from his parents. I saw him at the kitchen table, anticipating the book that he'd study with more vigour than he'd ever studied anything during his years at Dartmouth. I imagined him picturing the heights to which his new knowledge, guided by powerful ambition, would take him, but felt a pit in my stomach when I saw that his parents had, quite innocently, put "Bo'sun" in quotation marks, as if it were dubious or diminutive or temporary—not worthy of his total passion. By now I figured they realized how well he fit the mould of a seaman.

"Thanks, Jess. I won't keep it too long."

"It's OK, I have another copy."

"You do?"

"Yeah, Dan gave it to me," he said, unusually demure.

"That old edition that he had?"

"Yeah," he nearly whispered.

"Let me see it." I had, of course, seen it before, on the bookshelf in the mess, but again what interested me was the inscription. The cover of that edition was army green, with the title in gold. It had no dust jacket, just a cared-for, genuine feel. I opened the cover to reveal the Captain's unmistakable black-inked scrawl: *To Jesse, the rigger of the Picton Castle. Christmas, Aruba 1997.*

Now that was more like it. I could imagine no greater affirmation for him than to receive the credit for rigging one of the most ambitious conversion projects on the North American continent from the man whom we believed to be the last word on seamanship. I felt jealous that the praise fell short for the rest of us who'd worked just as hard at less glorious tasks.

It seemed that all of us had both a distaste for the Captain's authority and a desire to please him at the same time. I wished that my relationship with the Captain were as simple as those of the other crew. It was strange that in the middle of my befuddlement the Captain told me to talk to him on the quarterdeck. He placed his forearms on the teak rail and leaned outward, hunching his shoulders. He stared into the velvet-black distance.

"Rigel, your sister and I have been discussing her joining us for a while. For a month, starting in Tahiti."

Things just weren't very simple.

The Captain's next plan was a ritual of initiation—his hope at bringing the crew together—set for our crossing of the equator. For the past few days I'd noticed the ship divide into two distinct groups, the Shellbacks and the Pollywogs. The term *shellback* used to refer to an old sailor who'd been to sea so long that barnacles had grown on his back. Originally, it was slightly derogatory, denoting an old-fashioned sailor who failed to move with the times. Clearly, aboard the *Picton Castle* the term had quite the opposite connotation. We used it in its common sense, to mean a sailor who'd crossed the equator and been initiated by another Shellback. Everyone else was a Pollywog.

Captain Moreland, Becky, second helmsman Lori and new guy Gil were conspiring to initiate us Pollywogs with thinly veiled secrecy. And even though everyone knew they did it to frighten us, it worked. While I helped varnish the seams of the quarterdeck that had opened under the equatorial sun, I heard powerful people talk—the mates and the ABs. "How come the Shellbacks happen to be the meanest people on the ship?"

I predicted a backlash. Mate Brian, who'd invested a lot of time growing his thinning hair into a ponytail, threatened to defend it forcefully should any Shellback take it for his initiation. Tom had shaved himself a mohawk days before, probably so no Shellback would get the satisfaction.

The days grew hotter as we neared the equator. I knew the initiation was upon us when bo'sun Josh grudgingly handed down an order for me to help remove Kim's dory from the top of the galley house and fill it with sea water. "To swell the planks," he said, rolling his eyes at the obvious excuse. Filling it up with buckets from over the side, I thought about the upcoming ceremony. I knew the initiations would take the form of trials for unresolved trespasses or character flaws. It didn't take me long to guess what I'd be punished for.

Back in Lunenburg, there'd been a late October gale when the ship was tied to the dock. All of the fare-paying hands had arrived. Heavy wind and horizontal rain forced us to knock off early. The Captain summoned us to the nearby sail loft. We sat around him in a tight semicircle. He was preparing to teach the new crew some knots. Over his shoulder, through the rattling window, we could see the ship straining at her docklines. Her impressive rig was now catching the wind, heeling the ship as if she were sailing that breeze under lower topsails.

"You know that many unballasted square-riggers have capsized at the dock in lighter breezes than this." The Captain motioned towards his ship. The *Picton Castle* was still standing.

Days later, the cement truck arrived with our ballast. My college friend Michael and I were to help a crew of subcontractors flood the ship's old bilge tanks with cement. After a day of mushing in the wet cement, making sure no air pockets formed, Michael and I went out for a drink.

We went to the local bar where the fishermen hung out and the stale smell of cigarette smoke and beer clung to the carpet. We each had a drink. We talked too long and had to run back to the ship to be on time for duty. Hopped up from rain and rum, I suggested to Michael that we put our butt prints in the wet cement. He simply said, "OK," and took off for the hold. We found a spot that we were sure no one would find until much, much later. Then we pulled down our pants and sat in the cold, chunky peanut-butter concrete.

The next morning, three local subcontractors were staring at the imprint of our butt cheeks and taking sideways glances at me. Later, when I waited for the Captain to get off of the gangplank so I could board, he stopped halfway, made eye contact and said, "I could count the pimples on your ass."

We crossed the equator just after noon.

Neptune arrived over the foredeck wearing a beard of rope yarns and a paper crown. He shouted, "Second mate Karen Balog, heave to the Barque *Picton Castle* and lash the helm!" Karen ordered the helm hard left and eased the starboard main braces as we hauled to port. The ship stopped going forward and began to drift slowly downwind.

We crowded around King Neptune and his court, presiding from a bench on the cargo hatch in front of the dory, under the burning sun nearly at the zenith. He bellowed and roared at us, and took a champion slug from a gallon bottle of black rum.

I was woken for my midnight watch—hungover and spattered with vomit. I had a lingering guilty feeling that I did not yet understand. The four hours slipped by like a dream. In the morning, I walked about the ship. Patrick's hair was missing. Hieroglyphics were inked on his head in marker. He had a new earring. So did Don. Tom's mohawk was gone. Instead, he sported four bald spots in the pattern of the Southern Cross.

An image flashed of King Neptune sliding his pistol-gripped coconut machete across a chef's steel. I saw him hold Tom's head like a running back cradles a football and shave the five stars of the Southern Cross into the fuzz growing alongside his mohawk.

I felt a pain in my leg and looked down to see a fresh lesion that stretched from shin to foot, looking like a strip of uncooked bacon.

Another crew member's nipples were bleeding.

Mate and bo'sun both had new earrings. I recalled their trial: the Mate had been found guilty of having a bad attitude about line-crossing ceremonies and the bo'sun was found to be obsessed with work. They were told to put on sarongs on the jib-boom and return to the court, where they were dolloped with slime and dunked in the dory. After that, mate Brian left and returned dressed as Davy Jones. Bo'sun Josh returned a pirate.

It seemed that the ceremony then became a festival of opposites, as if drifting to the other side of the world caused a fast descent to our dark other-selves.

Kristin was, ironically, chastised for being a slacker—a kind of oblique praise. And just before my punishment, a friend, stricken for months by tropical ennui, was given a platter-sized trophy for being The World's Most Productive Deckhand.

Then the four original Shellbacks gave me a pair of shorts with the cheeks removed. They ordered me to climb to the highest yard and put them on. After changing, I slid down a t'gallant backstay giving the crew a dramatic setting moon, using my foot and shin to control my descent, too preoccupied to notice the skin smear away. Then I got my bare ass painted with tar and thrown in the dory.

That's when I became a Shellback and the gallon of rum came my way—again and again—rum and no water under equatorial sun.

Visions passed by of men dressed as women and women dressed as men; brothers in Speedos and goggles kissed one another. A sailor arrived wearing nothing but three canvas oil bags tied about his waist. Nobby, white as a ghost from years in the engine room, danced by wearing nothing but the Union Jack.

I moved nearer to the mate, who leaned on the main fife rail. I caught myself peeking at Doctor Beth's coconut bra. He handed me a bottle of amber rum. It went down like water. The sun looked big as a dinner plate held at arm's length. I guess that was when I realized that the crew was going through a mystical transformation and got the bright idea to sit on top of the mainmast. I asked the Captain, "Dan, can I truck the mainmast?"

"No!" was his shocked reply.

I immediately realized I'd suggested something bad. "What did you say?" the mate asked.

"Nothing." I took another slug of rum.

I sat under the main fife rail and, totally drunk, leaned against Kristin and talked gobbledegook. Through my fog I heard the words "Force Ten Kenworthy," spoken by the Captain. Jesse knelt before him looking uncomfortable. The court challenged him to say the name of each person on his watch and offer each a bit of praise. Flustered, he stumbled on a couple of names and digging in his heels he offered only a sarcastic bit of praise for one. He wanted out. Becky, his girlfriend on the throne, wanted out. But Jesse was still a Pollywog and many of his watchmates were Shellbacks. They flung slime at him, jeered. Lashing out.

I went behind the court and bounced along the bulwark on my way to the fo'c'sle. I sat on a fire extinguisher and discharged it. *What's that noise?* I barfed out a porthole, barely feeling it, then poured myself into my bunk, puke and all.

"Rigel, the Captain wants to see you."

I walked to his bench on the bridge, where he sat.

"Sit down. What the fuck were you thinking?"

Silence.

"You got too shit-faced to do your duty. What did I say about drinking on the ship?"

"You said 'don't be an asshole.'"

"Why did you ever ask if you could truck the mast?"

"I don't know."

"You were shit-faced, Rigel. No one will ever truck the mast of the *Picton Castle*. I know I looked like I was drinking a lot, but that was all show, I was blowing bubbles into the bottle. I know better. I got drunk on duty *once*. It was not good."

His voice softened and I knew the chewing out was coming to an end. "You know, I'm going easy on you. You'd be in big trouble if you weren't my girlfriend's brother. Taking off your pants on the t'gallant yard—that wasn't punishment for you, that was fun."

He dismissed me casually and I hobbled to the fo'c'sle. My lesion was stinging. It hurt when I moved my leg, but not as much as the humiliation of having inflicted it on myself. That and the humiliation of inflicting my injured, drinking-on-duty self on my fellow crew.

I ignored the foot for days. Then, two days from the Galapagos, it had grown painful and swollen and red. I finally showed it to Doctor Beth. Her shock did not encourage.

She cleaned the wound, filled me up with antibiotics and marked the extent of the red infection with a pen, an area that stretched from my knee nearly to my toes. Amputation, she feared, had not been far away.

The mate arrived periodically to offer help. "You might need to debreed that. Should I get my wire brush?"

The next day we hove to with the island of San Cristóbal just beyond the horizon.

"MUSTER MIDSHIPS!"

The Captain announced that we'd arrive the next day in Wreck Bay, San Cristóbal. He explained the difficulty of getting visas for entry to the Galapagos. They'd tried—it was impossible. However, he told us, a disabled ship is allowed to make port in the Galapagos. Despite the scepticism of the crew, he asserted that we were in need of repair. "It's true. We have two yards that are in need of repair. We have a couple of communication issues. Our ship is slightly broken." He announced a swim call.

While the others swam, I lay down in my bunk, nursed my swollen foot and wrote a letter.

Dear Ariel,   *30 January 1998*

I didn't realize the overpowering personality of this ocean until I swam the other day while we were hove to. This water is deeper blue than the Caribbean—steely, denser. I went under and opened my eyes to profound depth, silence and the unfathomable antiquity that a space walker must feel. I wanted to scream out with fear.

At night, in the doldrums, near the equator, long swells lift us through the still air, so humid that stars look like distant street lights seen through a misty windshield. The jellyfish light up for a second at a time in yellow-green, imitating the stars and surrounding us with points of light. Little holes in the darkness.

The Pacific is strangely alive, or alive strangely. I don't know how to say it. Where the Atlantic is somehow accessible, this-worldly, green-young, dangerous but understandable, the Pacific seems mystical.

Swells roll by. Each has its own peculiar direction. The undulations interfere, then carry on, unaffected by their union, determined to reach their shores. It doesn't give a sense of confusion. It gives a sense of order that must lie beyond my reach.

Maybe it's the mournful halo of luminescence that surrounds our hull, or perhaps it's the languid apathy brought on by the equatorial sun, or the sense of time losing all context that gives me the feeling our ship is coinciding with other planes of existence. More than one person has confided in me that they have seen ghosts. I tell them to find comfort in what is familiar and not to be afraid. Pagan rituals have interrupted the steady routine of watch standing. It's all very strange.

The twenty-day passage to Pitcairn is going to be bizarre.

I hope the wind stays like it's been for the last couple of days. Best sailing I've ever done. Downwind, downwind, downwind.

CHAPTER 15

Wreck Bay

San Cristóbal, Galapagos Islands
January 31 to February 12

A MIDNIGHT GALE DROVE LEADEN RAIN. STEEP SWELLS barraged the ship, twisting her anchor from a tenuous hold in the sandy bottom. The engine chugged to keep us off the rocks. On deck lay a confusion of lines. Moments before, we'd cast them off and braced the yards up sharp, nearly pointing them into the gale to reduce our windage. It seemed fitting weather to witness the breakdown of our culture.

Our skiff, raised high on its davits, filled with rain. It strained at its manila lashings. I reached from the quarterdeck to bail it. We'd already lost one boat to the curling surf and volcanic rock of Wreck Bay. We didn't need to lose another.

A few days before, we'd had a full day of work sending down the lower topsail yards so we could rebuild the shrunken wood within the iron bands that supported them. The afternoon sun was low in the sky. It enhanced sapphire shades in the bay and the tall green hills that embraced it. El Niño that year had tripled the annual rainfall and plant life flourished, always glossy from heavy moisture in the air. Every imaginable cloud type was mounded high above the island of San Cristóbal. The low sun lined them in golden orange.

The island was breathtaking, yet it seemed Kim saw only the fifteen-foot-tall, world-class wave breaking in the middle of the bay. He'd talked all week about how dory bottoms are shaped like surfboards, and about the fortunate accident which showed him that dories perform well in waves. He told us of his experiences surfing dories on the beaches of Nova Scotia, or rowing down the whitewater of the LaHave River in springtime. Kim had brought his own brand new dory all the way from Lunenburg, so I suppose that's why he decided not to ask permission to take it. Besides, work was over and he was off duty.

Bob Kingman watched him as he rowed towards the waves, which looked smooth and oily in the still afternoon. They hadn't looked that big from the ship, and Kim's back was to them as he rowed. He may not have seen how thick and powerful those world-class right-hand breakers were, but as he approached, he must have felt their size in his gut as swells lifted him high and let him down. It was peak wave season in Wreck Bay, and surfers had travelled all the way from Australia to have those monsters fling them towards the shore.

Kim must have felt the spray off the back of a big breaker as he lined his stern up on the very next one. It came fast. Kim gave a pull with his oars. The wave jacked up high on the volcanic bottom and the dory now slid downhill. Kim hurried to ship his oars, get his hands on gunwales and brace himself for the ride. The wave hit and Kim knew it was too late, but still he tried to ship his oars. The dory's nose went down and Kim tumbled backwards off his seat. He hit hard in the pointed bow. The bow dug in and the stern sailed overhead. A white-lipped and distended wall of water curled over the stern, blocking the sky. It sent Kim ass over teakettle.

The tumbling surge pulled at his body. White foam. Black. White. Black. Kim tumbled, found up and swam for the surface.

Another wave crushed down. White foam and black. White. Black. Another wave. Choking on water and losing his breath, Kim struggled in the surge. White foam and black. White. Black.

I saw mate Brian hurry to the Captain, who sat on the bench of the aloha deck. "Kim took his dory into the surf. Bob says he saw him pitchpole. I'm sure he's all right. I'd like to launch the boat and check on him."

"Yes. Go!"

The boat splashed down. I jumped in with Brian and Karen. We raced towards the breakers. The growing swell lifted the boat and dropped her. Planks and frames flexed and shivered. Brian slowed the engine.

We found Kim, the colour of skim milk, eyes glazed, clinging to a surfboard next to a perplexed Galapagan surfer, who would henceforth know Kim as Carpintero Loco. Both were bobbing in the giant swells near the break point. The dory was gone.

"I'm not coming any closer, Kim." The mate manoeuvred the rickety boat's bow into the swells.

Kim left the surfboard and I tossed him a line. We hauled him aboard and laid him on his back. He couldn't speak.

Back on the ship, our captain admonished, "Kim, do you realize that it was stupid to take your dory into the waves? You could have gotten your ass killed!"

"Well, I do now realize the importance of air."

The Captain looked shocked. Kim's insolence was a sure sign of recovery and the Captain's expression was partly relief, but to let Kim get away with backtalk might set a dangerous precedent. Nevertheless, he let it pass. At that moment I realized that Kim, half dead, had managed to attain the autonomy that the rest of us only wished for. Kim's unusual capacity for saying whatever was on his mind would bring him closer to the Captain than any of us.

But on the shore, the crew's malaise continued to build. Whether in the thatched breakfast stands, drinking gorgeous cold fruit drinks, or on the guided tours among marine iguanas, blue-footed boobies and giant tortoises, factions of angry amateur crew vented about the Captain and ship life. It hardly mattered that a first concession had been made—amateur crew now worked only one day in six, while the pros worked one in three—it was as if no compromise could repair the loss of faith. Or perhaps the frustration was over something ineffable, a feeling that clung like hot sweat, the sense that we'd lost control over our lives. It seemed we needed to keep moving, to stay at sea where moods were more even, but delays continued to stymie our progress.

Days later, the mood aboard was still choking and toxic. At 0700 hours, the sun was well on its race to the zenith. It burned up the early morning coolness, forcing the crew out of bedrolls in a sweat.

The lower yards had been repaired, though only a dejected skeleton crew remained aboard to cross them. I remembered what an honour it had been to help cross yards in Lunenburg—to participate in the highest expression of seamanship—and how discouraging it now was that so many crew wanted nothing to do with it. I thought I'd help out on my day off.

Mate Brian mustered the crew by 0800 hours. "We're going to cross the lower topsail yards. If you stay on the ship, I will recruit you for work. We're short-handed as it is."

Off-duty crew quickly piled aboard the skiff. On-duty

crew crept into the last scraps of morning shade or ran below to slap on sunscreen.

I found mate Brian below in the forepeak, digging for tools he'd need to cross the yard. "Brian, I'm helping with the crossing today."

"Good. Get some tag lines."

On the quarterdeck sat the main lower topsail yard on a pair of sawhorses, lashed against the ship's heavy rolls. Hoisting that telephone-pole-sized yard would take a great deal of awareness.

Clyde and I worked to anticipate the mate's procedure. We prepared the rigging that would be affixed to the yard once it was aloft. We secured tag lines to the yard to control it as it was hoisted.

Mate Brian delegated tasks to the skeleton crew while I bent the mast rope to the centre of the yard. I double-checked to make sure I had not led it afoul. I followed its path aloft, where it made a turn through a massive wooden block and was directed down and forward to the capstan.

Brian had sent three amateur crew to the capstan bars under Clyde's direction. While they walked circles to turn this antique winch, Clyde crouched and maintained tension on the tail of the mast rope, causing it to bind around the black whelps of the capstan's barrel. Its pawls tinkled in a complex rhythm, and with the morning sun the yard rose into the sky. Mate Brian and I climbed the shrouds and followed its ascent.

Aloft, we connected braces and downhauls to the yard, angled vertically to clear stays and rigging. Now the mate gave a series of orders and manipulated it close to horizontal. It was delicate work, levelling a yard of that size sixty feet up on a rolling ship. I watched the golden curls gleam on his freckled hands as he eased the line that held the yard vertical.

"Ease the starboard tag line," he ordered to a hand below.

A woman on deck returned his order sarcastically, likely

wishing she had a task with higher stakes. Brian's face darkened with the breach. He stuck out his jaw and continued.

"That's well! Make fast your tag lines! Make fast the mast rope! Everyone take a break!" He looked at me. "Let's get this yard positioned." We hooked a tackle to the yard, which would help us rotate it into position.

The mate gestured toward the crew member who'd mouthed off to him. "Did she take her bitch pills today?" He spoke under his breath. "I don't get it. Five days off and one day on—is that too much work? A sailing ship needs yards. Why the hell is she complaining? She's been to sea before. She knows that ships are a lot of work."

There were beads of sweat on the chief mate's tanned face. His forehead vein started to pulse, tracing a line from the centre of his wraparound sunglasses to his white-and-black bandana. "People complain about the cost of the voyage. They're saying they should have more time off because they *paid* to be here. We all *paid* to be here. They have no idea how hard you guys worked in Lunenburg. The price doesn't even come close to the cost. Dan's losing his fuckin' shirt." The mate took a second to breathe. "Dan wants me to give them a celestial navigation class—sun sights. To just hand it to them on a platter. I struggled to learn that shit. I earned it. Am I just going to give it away?"

Mate Brian took a pull on the tackle. He wiped his forehead. "We needed diesel to get down here. Diesel costs money. Food—it costs money. People say they aren't getting the training they want. Well, *news flash!* We're crossing two yards from the deck of a rolling, anchored ship. Seamanship training doesn't get any better than this. They say the Captain's a prick. *News flash!* Everyone knew that! It makes me sick."

He took another pull on the tackle and the yard lurched towards us. "These negative people can get the fuck out of here. They're bringing everybody down. They can leave and take their goddamned negativity. You know, this could be so fuckin' good. We should be having the time of our lives. But we're at our first scheduled stop and people are burnt out, like it's the end of the goddamn voyage!"

The next day, I hiked up into the hills, directly away from the ship. The one time I looked back to see her made my stomach knot up. Everything was falling apart. I'd made love with Kristin in that soupy, hot air of the coast that left you in a permanent flush, but the letter I'd posted to Ariel was too strong a reminder of my insincerity, of my lack of will to commit—to Kristin, to Ariel, to the ship and this way of life I was supposed to love. Finally hitching a ride the last few miles, I sat beneath a swollen rain cloud on the peak of a dead volcano where wild horses run, and I wrote my family a letter.

El Junco, San Cristóbal, Galapagos Islands   12 Feb 1998
Dear Family,

Sometimes writing down the date is a comfort. It reminds me that my sentence is finite. It just goes to show that sometimes misery can permeate the adventure of a lifetime. It seems that I am obsessed with the future and that I don't care about the present. It's dumb, really.

I continue writing letters to Ariel. I see her as a part of my future. I have let my relationship with a wonderful woman on the ship disintegrate. My mind isn't really on the ship. I don't allow myself to focus on my work. Instead I dream, almost constantly, about tree houses.

Maybe I have a distaste for the military side of life aboard; being tied to another's agenda, the claustrophobia brought on by this incestuous community. It is even foolish to think that it gets better with rank. From what I see, it gets worse. More responsibility, though it has privileges, means less liberty. The Captain has it worst of all. He has to balance the wishes of the amateur crew, his own vision of ship life, and the fiscal needs of the company.

There are many good things about this voyage. I enjoy the cycle of watch, and love being on the ocean. Trying to understand the personalities of these oceans has fuelled much thought and writing for me.

Good seamanship is an ethic to which I aspire. I always want it to be a part of my life in some way. I believe that the Picton Castle is the best arena to learn these crafts, because of her conversion, and the uncompromising traditionalism and the knowledge of the Captain and crew. It's just that sometimes I feel like I need more than to follow in history's footsteps. I believe that tradition is good, but maybe that's because it provides a foundation for looking ahead. I can't linger in tradition forever.

The travel has been phenomenal. We've been given plenty of time off here in the Galapagos. More than any other ship I've been on. I've been spending my time hitchhiking and walking to every part of San Cristóbal. The island is so lush and wildlife is so unafraid of people that I feel like I'm at the beginning of time.

When I get home, I'm starting a tree house construction company—safe, custom, luxury tree houses. Robert Kingman (one of the amateur crew leaving here) and I have been discussing a partnership. He is a rock climber and a landscape contractor in Tahoe, California. He runs his own business. I can't wait!

Love, Rigel

CHAPTER 16

Boiling Point

San Cristóbal and Santa Cruz, Galapagos Islands
February 12 to 21

Hungry after a long day's work, we waited on the cargo hatch for someone to announce cook Ian's deep-fried potato slices.

"FIRE IN THE GALLEY! FIRE IN THE GALLEY! FIRE IN THE GALLEY!"

The announcement came sooner than expected.

We scattered for extinguishers. Nobby started the fire pump. Jesse ran out the hose. Captain and mate dove into the galley. Flames and choking smoke licked the overhead. They jetted two extinguishers into the pot. We piled replacements outside the door. Clyde stood by, handing new ones to mate and captain. One empty, grab another. Their faces contorted as they looked through rolls of smoke, emptying another extinguisher into the pot. They stopped. The fire appeared quenched.

It reignited. With faces red, dripping sweat, holding breath, captain and mate dumped more extinguishers into the flames. It smothered. Brian threw a lid on the pot. With gloved hands he pulled it from the stove. Finally, it could cool.

The only damage done was to our already demoralized cook. He'd burned his hand.

Still, I wondered if the physical challenge of the fire would be easier to overcome than the crew's discontent. A morose group was holed up in a hotel that Bill had taken to calling The Pit of Despair. There they fanned the flames of each other's anger that had been growing since Lunenburg.

Captain Moreland decided to host a ship meeting—an open forum for people to air their concerns. Word filtered to every member of the crew. A local priest would be there to mediate if necessary.

In the Hotel San Francisco, we were shaking off another hangover, waking up from the floor, soaking up the breeze from an off-balance ceiling fan and anticipating the meeting. Tom, the master of imitations, stood up. He placed the back of one wrist on his waist, held a make-believe cigarette with the other hand and gave his best version of Patricia, the hard-line union boss: "Fuck you, I'm leaving and I'm taking my money with me. I didn't come here for this Outward Bound shit." Intonation, modulation, posture—perfection.

I imagined the ship meeting. A daytime talk show came to mind; Jerry Springer, perhaps. The reality would be different.

When the crew was assembled, the Captain began with praise. "Here we are, all together, and we have a problem. I want to preface this meeting by telling you how proud I am of you, of how far we've come. This meeting is an opportunity for everyone to get things out in the open. This is not a muster."

A disappointing silence followed. *Come on. Here's your chance. Let's crank this thing up.*

Chief engineer Nobby spoke first. He talked of his long involvement with the ship. In the context of all his years earning less than he was worth, tinkering in the bowels of the *Picton Castle* while it was frozen in the bloody ice, just him and the cats for weeks at a time while Dan worked tug-boats for money to keep the ship alive, this dark period seemed quite worth pushing beyond.

Some crew clapped. Second engineer Claire cheered for him: "Way to go, Nobby." He was unusually emotional. The thought of the voyage folding was particularly hard on him.

Again, silence.

Tom spoke next. Some were reluctant to hear him, fearing his caustic and often pessimistic edge. He spoke firm sentences. "The voyage is not going to be easy. It is going to change you. You have to empty your cup and bend like a willow, because if you're not willing to forget what you know, and allow yourself to change, this voyage is going to be very difficult."

Silence again.

No one spoke up. Finally, Patricia mumbled a few words that left me wondering where the fire had gone. The meeting was over.

The Captain sat down next to second mate Karen and me. "Well, that really took the wind out of their sails."

Nine crew decided to jump ship in Santa Cruz. It was a planned fifty days until we would reach the next airstrip, and people were inclined to act now. Cowboy Brad and Drummer Todd were going to take a break from the voyage. Bob Kingman was leaving, as were Tom Baker and new guy Gil. Rebecca the flautist took a medical leave. The videographer and his wife, whom we had picked up in Aruba, were leaving the ship on hostile terms. Cook Ian was calling home a lot. "To see if any of his relatives have died," said the Captain.

Ten people were jumping ship. Twenty-eight were staying, half of them professionals. I wondered if this spelled the end of the voyage. Similar voyages by Irving Johnson in his *Yankee* had not experienced this level of attrition, so the Captain hadn't planned on handing out this many pro-rated refunds. The ship was so far away from affluent regions of the world that I was concerned we wouldn't find the replacement crew that could get her running in the black. I wondered how long we could make it on hope. I wondered how much hope was left.

The other malcontents—Jeannine the costume designer, Lynn the ex-navy officer and lobbyist Patricia—decided to stick out the fifty days to see if things would get better.

Meanwhile, a physicist named T. Gray Curtis, who'd helped back the *Picton Castle*'s conversion project, visited the ship here, hoping to use her as a platform to make precise measurements of El Niño's effect on water temperature change. He hoped his data would advance understanding of the effects of climate change on evolution.

Back in New England, the ship's supporters, including Ben, the vice-president of the ship's company, and her primary financial backer, were against Gray's venture. They feared Gray would overlook important details while his expansive intellect raced beyond present realities. Our captain shared their fears.

Unhindered by their doubts, Gray worked his way through the appropriate channels, securing a ship move-ment order from the rear admiral of the Ecuadorean navy. The *Picton Castle*, by that order, was now required to move from the island of San Cristóbal to Santa Cruz and perform measurements along the way.

However, the Galapagos National Parks Service doubted the ship had sincere scientific intentions. They also doubt-ed that we were disabled, regarding our crew as passengers who were touring the islands freely. They wanted $7,000 (U.S.) for each member of the crew to allow Gray's water temperature measurements. Nonetheless, Gray negotiated and soon understood that the fee would be waived if we fol-lowed a direct course between the islands.

When the Captain finally decided to transit to the island of Santa Cruz, he broke the short passage up into two sections, anchoring for a night off the island of Santa Fe. Gray fretted, seeing the stop as a violation of the ship movement order. When we launched a boat to make an expedition, Gray approached Carpintero Loco, about to pull the start cord on the outboard.

"Do you realize what you're doing is illegal?"

"That'll just make it more fun!" Loco started the engine.

That was when Gray threatened to blow the whistle. And the Captain, with an anger like a blown-out topsail, decided to weigh anchor and push on to Santa Cruz.

The whole crew was pissed off. Most were sent forward to the windlass to strain on the iron bars. The balance of us helped Loco Kim hoist and secure the skiff. Of all the crew, Kim seemed the least perturbed.

With the single-minded intensity that he had given to dory surfing, Loco Kim now focused on cargo trading. He'd got his first taste of his cargo's sales potential when the port authorities, who frequented the ship in the early days of our visit, began to solicit the cargo hold for single items. It was a pain in the ass for him to stop carpentry and search bulk cargo for single items, but it helped keep the authorities happy. It also gave Loco Kim a kind of oblique permission to trade his goods openly, without importing them, paying duty or getting a permit.

He'd enjoyed some financial success in Wreck Bay but was hampered because all his customers had to accommodate themselves to the schedule of the frightening boat runs to and from the ship. Things were going to be different when we dropped the hook in Santa Cruz. He'd arrange his own retail operation, and publicize it with the help of his growing notoriety as a daredevil dory surfer.

The next morning, in Santa Cruz, Carpintero Loco Kim woke me up so I could help him get ready. "Rigel, wake up. It's time."

I looked out my porthole and saw a deep blue smudge of sky over the eastern horizon. I stepped down from my bunk and pulled on some shorts. I made sure my slender sheath knife that hung from my belt was tucked into my back pocket, and met Loco by the cargo hatch. He and Jesse had already pulled away some of the thick hatch boards. Jesse, deep in the cargo hold, grabbed a bicycle and tried to pull it free. It didn't come, so he leaned back. He pulled hard and extracted a whole cluster.

By that time, the early-rising bo'sun had arrived. So had the *ponga*, an outboard-powered wooden barge crewed by two quiet Galapagans whom Loco Kim had hired. With their assistance we loaded about seventy-five used bicycles, a hundred used tires, four half-ton bags of used clothing, dozens of black bras, plastic-handled Brazilian kitchen knives, boxes of used tools, jugs of cooking oil, a case of soap, cases of mayonnaise, about fifty pairs of green-mouldy army boots from WWII and a mail tote of out-of-fashion bifocals and trifocals with cloudy lenses and the strongest prescriptions.

Feeling left out, I watched Loco and Jesse ride ashore in the rickety *ponga*. Only much later, when the furore settled, would Jesse tell me what had happened. Once ashore, Loco Kim and Jesse found the truck they'd hired. It took three overflowing loads to get all of Loco Kim's goods to Bar El Marinero, a new all-pink drinking establishment that Loco had rented to host his two-day sale. The day before, he'd primed the local bargain hunters with a radio ad on a Catholic station so everybody would know about the great deals at Carpintero Loco's General Store.

It was madness from the moment his goods hit the floor. Whole families tried on bad used eyeglasses and asked how they looked. Small children swung machetes twice their size. Women tore open half-ton bags of used clothing and tried things on in the store. Cabbies rolled away tires. No reasonable offer was refused on the bicycles.

Combine that with the locals' haggling instinct and Loco's propensity to confuse the Spanish words for *six* and *sixty*, and *seven* and *seventy*. Multiply the confusion by 4,500, because that was the exchange rate of the U.S. dollar to the Ecuadorean sucre. One woman interrupted Loco Kim's calculations to tell him about the crazy man who'd taken his rowboat into the surf of Wreck Bay.

He had to agree, "Yes, that man must have been crazy."

Loco Kim and Jesse were so busy that they felt they were going insane. When the heat of the noonday sun hit and all seventy-five bicycles had been sold, there was a lull in the crowd of customers. Loco Kim thrust a wad of sucres into Jesse's hands and told him to get lunch and then relieve him.

After a satisfying meal, Jesse returned to Loco Kim. Loco's sharp blue eyes would not meet his. His face was drawn and pale, not like the tycoon of Santa Cruz that Jesse had known before lunch. When Jesse was within five paces of Loco, he heard him speak, jaw barely moving. "Don't stop at the store. Keep moving, like you don't know me."

Jesse assumed a poker face and walked in the direction of the ship. When he rounded the corner of a building, Loco raced up to him and stuffed each of Jesse's four pockets with Ecuadorean cash. The remaining roll of bills, which was the size of a cannonball, Loco jammed into Jesse's backpack.

"Get word to Dan. The cops showed up and they weren't looking to buy anything."

Jesse thought quickly as Loco sped back to the store. *The ship should be doing a boat run about now; I'll head for the dock.*

Tom had just arrived when Jesse ran up to the dock. Breathless, he unloaded the copious wads of cash into the skiff. "Tell Dan that the store got busted and that Kim's probably with the police."

Tom slammed the outboard hard over and raced off to the ship.

Jesse headed back to the store. It was empty—no Loco, no customers.

He lay down on a bag of clothing in the shade and smoked a cigarette, hoping he'd get paid five dollars for every hour he spent guarding Loco Kim's merchandise. Afternoon turned to dusk. Dusk turned to night. Jesse grew impatient.

We stayed in the Galapagos for another two days. I visited one of the world's most extraordinary beaches, with sand so soft it was like walking on ice cream. I walked lava tunnels, deep and vaulting, and rode horseback through the jungle to see a tortoise that was almost as big as a Volkswagen.

Loco Kim, off the hook for the moment, purchased boards of the finest knot-free cedar that any of us had ever seen. They were milled from trees that had fallen naturally or had been thinned out of a two-hundred-year-old coffee farm that used them to filter the light for the plants.

We loaded the planks from a *ponga*, late at night.

Two days after Carpintero Loco's General Store got busted, our Galapagos sojourn had reached critical mass. The Ecuadorean police force was taking an unsettling interest in Loco Kim. Immigration was concerned by the large number of crew who'd arrived by ship but were departing by plane. Things were further complicated by our new Ecuadorean cook, who'd arrived in our galley through the enthusiastic recommendation of his ex-wife.

The recently appointed port captain was eager to prove himself a big man and was totally inflexible. And the short-wave radio repairman, probably because he was running on island time, did not make a single one of his three appoint-ments to fix our backup long-distance communication device, the single side band radio, or SSB.

Our affiliation with the United Nations, as flagship for their 1998 Year of the Oceans campaign, may have been the only reason the Parks Department showed mercy on us. They claimed we'd violated their order not to take water temperature measurements or visit Santa Cruz. They issued this ultimatum: You can stay tonight, but when the sun comes up in the morning, if you are still here, you are all going to jail.

The Captain hurried through the streets in his rubber jellies, holding a straw hat to his head, telling whomever he could find to get back to the ship. "We're leaving."

CHAPTER 17

Lost at Sea

Rose Bay, Nova Scotia, and Picton Castle,
bound for Pitcairn Island

From: Picton Castle Home Office
To: Bob Crockett (E-Mail List)
Subject: Captain's Report
Date: February 22, 1998
Daily Position: Depart Puerto Ayora, Santa Cruz,
Galapagos Islands
Captain's Report: Departed Santa Cruz at 0430 hours.
Crew had a great time in the Galapagos and is looking for-
ward to Pitcairn. We are motorsailing, steering southerly in
modest rain squalls. All hands are onboard. We are clean-
ing up the ship, getting back into seagoing mode. All is well
onboard.

My father, Bob, got his daily e-mail from the ship's office on
the day the *Picton Castle* left the Galapagos. My dog, a ten-
year-old golden retriever named Spencer, stood by his chair
and barked. He wanted a walk. Bob gave in and took Spencer
to the shore of Rose Bay behind his house. It was winter.

*Rigel's dog is getting old. He used to dart around us like a
paddle ball. Come here, buddy. You stay alive. Rigel wants you*

to be alive when he gets back. He pushed his cold fingers into Spencer's lion mane.

He looked out at Rose Bay, a rough expanse of ice cakes separated by blue veins. The skin of a strangled man. The ice cakes rose and fell as if the bay struggled to breathe under its frigid blanket. All around he saw dead grass, dormant trees, decrepit docks, dark sky.

Rigel's leaving the Galapagos. I hope he knows how rare this experience is. I bet there's no damn ice there.

From: Picton Castle Home Office
To: Bob Crockett (E-Mail List)
Subject: Captain's Report
Date: February 23, 1998
Daily Position: 03°13(S, 090°53(W
Captain's Report: We are steering southwesterly in light airs and rain squalls. We are still under power and expect to do this for another day or two. All is OK onboard.

Bob jotted the ship's coordinates on a piece of paper and walked to the dining room. His *National Geographic Map of the World* was spread on the table. He plotted a blue dot at the new coordinates. It was a habit formed over months of gazing out of his north windows at the horizon, where grey sky met whitecapped grey-green water.

Three months before, on the night she left Lunenburg, the *Picton Castle* slipped across this horizon with her sails red in the sunset. Bob watched her travel behind the jagged slate cliffs of Rose Head. Then he drove east to Hirtle's Beach and watched her hull and sails diminish to a fleck of white. When her sails dipped below the horizon, Bob figured he was the last person to see her leave Nova Scotia.

Bob maintained his connection to that cold evening by making a spidery blue trail on his map that traced the ship's path around the world—one-twelfth of the way, by latitude. He curled his fingers under the map's white border and held it off the table. He enjoyed the security of holding his son in his hands, protecting him. A thought occurred to him. *Someday you're going to sail off the edge of this map.*

February 24

> No New Message

No update? Bob was a little surprised at how he'd come to depend on daily updates from the Captain, via the ship's office. With this one missed message he felt cast adrift— not only from his son but also from the voyage. The feeling was disconcerting and oddly painful. He picked up the telephone and called the ship's office. "Hi, it's Bob Crockett . . ."

"Hi. Sorry to bother you, but I was wondering if I could get the daily position . . .

"No. Well, OK. Is everything all right?

"A brief EPIRB signal picked up in Halifax?" Bob wondered if the emergency position-signalling device could have been triggered accidentally.

"Can they be reached? . . .

"Maybe they're out of the Inmarsat Phone's range . . .

"The manufacturer said they're in range? . . .

"Maybe their phone's busted. Has anyone tried the single side band radio? . . .

"Oh, it's broken . . .

"What's the coast guard doing? . . .

"No planes, I guess . . .

"If 95 percent of these are false alarms, they couldn't send planes for every one. But no phone contact—that concerns me . . .

"No, I'll keep it under my hat. I'm sure you'll hear from them soon."

Bob got up from his desk. "Let's go, Spencer. We're going for a walk." Catching a glimpse of the dining-room table, Bob averted his eyes from the world map that lay there without the day's position, now finding it a threat rather than a comfort.

While he walked the shore, hunched up in his jacket, Bob let out long sighs that were white in the cold air. For a second he allowed himself to fear. *What if they sank? No. They're OK. I'll hear from them tomorrow. I won't tell Sue. There isn't any reason to worry her . . . A broken SSB.*

February 25

"Nothing? . . .

"The coast guard? An amber alert? What's that? . . .

"Oh, an AMVER alert? . . .

"So they notify registered vessels in the Pacific that the *Picton Castle* is missing? Is there much shipping where they are? . . .

"I didn't think so.

"OK, let me know if you hear anything."

Bob looked at his map. He imagined where the ship would be if she was safe. A smile came to his face as he pictured her scudding downwind under a full press of sail. Certainly she'd entered the trades. She'd be riding those long Pacific swells—swells that had travelled for thousands of miles.

Again, Bob thought of the vastness of the Pacific. *AMVER alert?* Bob got his world atlas. He saw only one rarely used shipping lane crossing the *Picton Castle*'s track. *Well, since there's relatively little shipping, they wouldn't stand much chance of getting in a collision. Then again, what else could cause such a short signal but a bad collision with a submerged container? For such a short EPIRB signal, the ship would have*

*had to go down quickly. The ship would have had to go down
quickly with the EPIRB caught in the rig. God, I hope the life rafts
didn't get caught too.*

February 26

"Hi. It's Bob . . .

"No, nothing? . . .

"Well, knowing the weather's excellent on their route
gives one less reason for concern. Sometimes I get thinking about El Niño—sudden violent storms. You know . . .

"Well, good. Call me if you hear anything . . .

"Take care, bye."

February 27

"Hi. It's Bob. How's it going? . . .

"No, nothing yet? Do you know if they're going to
search? . . .

"Really, Senator Judd Greg? Kerry and Kennedy and
Congressman Frank? . . .

"Oh, and one other? New York? . . .

"This is good . . .

"A couple of days? . . .

"Yes, I understand. Howard Air Force Base isn't what it
used to be . . .

"Commandeer planes? Good luck . . .

"You say I should talk to Ben Wellington? . . .

"Yes, the ship's company's vice-president . . .

"OK, got it. Thanks."

"Hi, Ben, this is Bob Crockett."

Bob walked with Spencer across dirty brown snow to the shore,
where he liked to think. *Ben says he's sure that everything's all
right. They got the senators involved because they feel they have a*

legal and moral responsibility to do anything possible. Ben has a son on board . . . Legal and moral, my ass. He's worried too.

Bob felt that familiar empty hole in his stomach, so he pictured the ship safe, with her sails bunted up neatly and her iron claw of an anchor speeding to the bottom in the lee of Pitcairn Island.

February 28

The next day, Bob called Ben Wellington. He learned that since four senators had taken an interest in the case, the Joint Search and Rescue Center at Howard Air Force Base, working with the Alameda coast guard, had been able to acquire the resources to elevate the search. But as an unintended consequence the State Department had been hounding Ben for every crew member's passport number.

The State Department wanted to notify the next of kin.

March 1

"Nothing, huh?" Bob exhaled loudly.

"Oh, really?" His voice brightened. "It was on its way to Puerto Rico, a P-3 Orion? What kind of plane is that? . . .

"Fourteen hours of flight time and a radar that can spot a periscope at 150 miles. Amazing . . . If they're going to fly over the rhumb line all the way to the dead reckoning position, then that means the coast guard is pretty confident they're out there . . .

"Great, I'm so glad they're finally doing something."

March 2

"They didn't find them?" Bob felt a terrible pit in his stomach.

"What? It gets worse? . . .

"You're saying that the Ecuadorean navy reported a distress call? . . .

"Was it around the time of the EPIRB signal? . . .

"Only an hour—and we're only finding out now? . . .

"Why don't you trust the Ecuadorean navy? . . .

"A long story, huh? . . .

"And the State Department? Have you told them? . . .

"I haven't told my wife." Bob exhaled.

"Are they sending out more planes? . . .

"A C-130 . . .

"A drift search from the LKP? . . .

"What's an LKP? . . .

"Last Known Position. Oh, my God . . ."

Later, on the shore, the old dog Spencer stood in the water. He barked until Bob half-heartedly tossed him a rock to fetch. The golden retriever stuck his head underwater and grabbed the rock. Bob didn't notice. He was lost in thought. *"Maybe they're in life rafts. Maybe they'll be all right.*

"Right, Spencer?"

Spencer barked demandingly. Bob threw another rock.

March 3

"Hi, Ben. Any luck? . . .

"Still searching." Bob's heart sank.

"They forced your hand. Where did they get the passport numbers? . . .

"Oh, of course, they're the State Department . . .

"So you're calling everyone tonight . . .

"Oh, Felicia and David at the office, they're calling everyone . . .

"Thanks, Ben."

March 4

The C-130 hadn't found a thing. Bob knew the paper would contain a story about the possible sinking. He counted the hours until it would be distributed that after-noon. *I've got to tell Susie. Soon I'll have to drive to Susie's work and tell her. I'll give it a couple more hours.*

Ring, ring

"Yes, this is he . . ."

"The *Chronicle-Herald* . . .

"No, I don't really want to talk right now." *Click.*

Hours slipped by. Bob felt paralyzed. Days before, he'd taken the map off of the dining-room table so Sue wouldn't see the absence of plots and suspect something was wrong. Tears came to his eyes. He looked at the greedy belly of his globe, as if through heavy rain.

Ring, ring

"Felicia, what's up? You sound happy."

Bob learned that the first search planes, the P-3 Orions, had flown within a few hundred miles of the ship but had to turn back for lack of fuel. Another hour south and they would have found her.

The coast guard had been trying to contact the *Picton Castle* by Inmarsat Telephone ever since they'd received the ship's distress signal. After eight anxious days a tenacious controller at Alameda Coast Guard Base, Quartermaster First Class Anneta Culver, located the ship. Anneta Culver had a reputation among her co-workers for following every lead to its bitter end. On day eight Anneta played back a recording of her attempts to telephone the ship. She believed she heard a faint tell-tale buzz which indicated that someone had just hung up at the *Picton Castle*'s end. She called repeatedly after this. For forty-five minutes she shouted for the ship's status and position. Broken bits of our coordinates fell into place.

As our EPIRB was triggered accidentally in a drill, we had sailed into an Inmarsat Telephone dead spot—a dead spot that their computer model predicted should not have existed.

March 12

It was after supper on the *Picton Castle*. The air was cool. Grey clouds sailed past the full moon. Mate Brian shouted a muster call.

It's kind of late for this.

The Captain explained the reason for our meeting. It seemed that sixteen days before, our EPIRB had been accidentally activated for a couple of seconds in an abandon ship drill. When that happened, we triggered a chain of events that led to search planes, newspaper cover stories and some very worried parents. "The most worried were Don's and Pat's moms," said the Captain, giving my friends a look of feigned gravity.

He offered everyone on the ship an opportunity to call home at the company's expense, some three dollars a minute. He strongly urged that Don and Pat call home first.

After the muster, standing in the light of the full moon with cool sea water washing around my bare feet, I tried to decide if I would call home. It seemed unnatural. While underway, I'd forget that there was a world beyond the horizon. If that world did trickle into my awareness, I'd deal with it by writing letters. There was no intrusion that way; the thoughts were all mine. And if I didn't like what my letters said, they'd fly out my porthole.

Don came down the ladder from the quarterdeck and stood in front of me, looking at the water splashing our ankles.

"Don, what happened? How's your mom?"

The flush of red that brought life to Don's sunburned cheeks was gone. Perhaps it was the full moon's milky light that made his face look so pained. He couldn't talk at first, looking down at the deck to my side. Then, looking at me, he said, "She was crying uncontrollably, Rige. She said she'd have searched the shore of South America the rest of her life if only to find my dead bones."

I stared at him dumbly.

Moments later, I was standing in line.

"Hi, Dad. Hi, Mom . . .

"Yeah, I feel good. We had a party last night to celebrate the crossing of the royal yards. We're a real barque now . . .

"Yeah, I hope you weren't too worried."

The ship took a heavy roll and their words became stretched out, like words from a fast-moving car, only eerie and digital.

"What? There's a delay. I'm sorry, I just spoke over you . . . I'm glad too . . .

"Well, you guys take care. I'll call you from the Marquesas."

Captain Moreland said at the end of his muster, "None of this could have happened before the invention of the radio." At that moment it seemed he thought the invention was more trouble than it was worth. In the age of sail it was common to be out of contact with land for months, even years at a time.

As I tried to sleep that night, a dual image came to me. It was of my parents, worried out of their skulls, and of us, on our rolling wooden deck, drinking Gosling's rum tapped moments before from a warped oak barrel. We were celebrating the long-overdue crossing of our highest yards, the royals.

Royals. The word brought to mind kings and queens, glory and crowns. *Crowns.* Royal yards were this square-rigger's crown. Two days before, we had completed our ship, crowning her in the middle of the rolling Pacific, in the belly of the southeast trades.

It was amazing. In Lunenburg we'd worn harnesses aloft. This time we wore no harnesses, just shorts and T-shirts. Having lost my only footwear while we were in Panama, I was barefoot. No longer did we have the security of a dock, a calm harbour or, God forbid, a nearby hospital.

The sky was grey and the sea rolled hard when we hoisted the fore royal yard from the deck. The boisterous trade wind kicked up an ocean of heady whitecaps.

Bo'sun Josh stood on the windward side of the ship, on the port rail at the base of the fore shrouds. He reached his right arm out and laid a hand on the top of the yard as it crept aloft beside him while he climbed the ratlines. Muscles like twisted steel cables cast shadows down his arm. The yard was twenty-six feet long, but Josh looked like he might throw it over his shoulder and carry it aloft himself.

The yard was hoisted by a mast rope, which was attached near the centre of the yard, with the yard nipped vertically against the rope. The mast rope ran up to the very top of the foremast. There, it turned on a sheave and ran down behind the mast, where it turned at a block and wrapped around the cherry red drum of the capstan. A crew of sailors powered that capstan by walking around it, pushing on its bars that reached out like the arms of a turnstile. Their progress was measured by the syncopated tapping of the capstan's pawls, locking in every few inches of gain.

Josh climbed the shrouds little by little, guiding the top end of the yard aloft. Jesse was ordered to ascend after him, to control the centre of the yard. Jesse swung his well-muscled torso around the rising yard and clamped a tattooed arm around its middle. As the ship rolled towards them, the riggers held the yard in place, keeping it from swinging out over the water like a wrecking ball. When the ship rolled the other way, the yard lay against the shrouds and was more controlled. The capstan crew then circled their winch and the yard climbed in stages.

Brian ordered me to join the two riggers on the shrouds. I placed a hand on the lower yardarm and climbed after them. As the yard ascended, we negotiated the overhanging crosstrees and tops. Eighty feet later, we were still support- ing the vertical yard, each of us clinging to different sec- tions of the t'gallant mast.

Josh stepped like a log-roller onto the highest installed yard, the t'gallant. He secured some rigging and then gave the signal to hoist.

As the royal yard ascended to its final position, Jesse joined Josh on the yard, the two of them standing on either side of it. Months of tropical sun and rain had turned the wooden spar grey and furry. Wide checks ran along its tapering length. As the wind bellowed into the sail sus- pended beneath, the yard flexed, causing those checks to yawn like tired old men.

Josh and Jesse affixed the rigging that allows the yard to be manipulated and supported. As I climbed up to their level, I was concerned that I was becoming extraneous.

"Rigel, why don't you lay up to the t'gallant hounds and get ready to level the yard," said bo'sun Josh.

I was elated. I glanced at Jesse, who looked a little amused. For every yard crossing we'd done in Lunenburg, Jesse had been given the honour of levelling the yard. Now, because he was busy securing some rigging, it was my turn.

I climbed the t'gallant shrouds, which flexed underfoot like a rope ladder. I climbed until I could just wedge my toes between the two converging shrouds that supported the last of the ratlines. I would have to go higher to ease the nipper that held the yard vertical. The yard was suspended several feet up. I leaned away from the dark grain of the greasy mast and grasped a royal backstay in each hand.

I looked from where they converged at the very top of the mast to where they attached on the rail, nearly one hundred feet below, and felt my fingers mesh with the lay of the wire rope and my fingerprints settle around its flecks of rust. I let go with my feet, swung around and curled my lower legs around the stays. Shinnying up a little higher, I could slide my bare feet through a couple of thin loops of rope that Jesse had tied to the royal backstays. Carefully, I applied my weight, allowing his knots to bind on the wire and the narrow cord to bite into the sides of my feet.

"Rigel, no shoes, man?" Josh asked.

"Haven't seen 'em for weeks. Besides, my feet are harder than shoes. ARBEEDARRR."

With an arm on either side of the royal mast, I untied the nipper. Slowly, I levelled the yard. I opened the parrel, the gate that forms a hoop around the mast, and shifted the yard into place.

That was when the squall hit.

A blast of dank air displaced the temperate breeze that had been blowing by us all day. Pellets of horizontal rain followed. The ship surged forward. We felt the motion amplified by our height in the rig.

When the squall passed, I shinnied out the yard to secure the footrope and saw four tiers of square sails angled at perfect increments. I watched them snap full then spill their air as the ship rolled. Looking towards the horizon, I felt as if I were flying. Whenever I made a new step in the rig, where supporting wires dwindle to an apex and the ship below looks small as a toy, the feeling of flight hit me. Side to side the masts rocked slow and long, like the arm of a metronome set on largo. I swung forward and back over ocean and deck.

Every passage has ups and downs. The other royal yard had gone aloft a few days before. I'd watched it ascend heavenward towards chief mate and bo'sun from the spot where I was helping to hoist on the quarterdeck. The work was hard, and that day there were no cooling clouds to shield us from the tropical sun. Jesse walked by on his way from the galley to the scullery, carrying an armload of dishes. All day he had been casting looks aloft, hoping to be included in the evolution.

I knew how he felt. For a long time I'd been feeling overlooked—that my drive to excel was being squandered on dishes and deck washes. I needed to prove that I was worth something. To do that I needed to see my work mirrored in the machine of the ship, or in its acres of canvas. I looked up at the chief mate, standing balanced atop the t'gallant yard, hands over his head, fingertips resting on the royal yard that had just been levelled above him. He looked to be walking a swaying tightrope

A couple of days before, in a funk, I'd stopped mate Brian to ask if he'd consider making me a dayman. I told him that I'd like to help make sails. From experience, I knew he wasn't particularly open to suggestions, but I had to ask. I wanted to lose my sense of this endless circle of watches that always seemed to leave me in the same place.

"I hear you, Rige. Your request is noted. I'm not saying I'll put you there, but it's noted." His eyes looked into mine. He cocked his head just slightly, as if trying for a better view. Something told me he'd heard me.

"Thanks, Brian."

I'd cornered the mate at a critical time. Captain Moreland and he were leading the ship through a cultural transition. Just a day before, at a muster, mate Brian had announced that some of the crew would become daymen. Daymen wouldn't stand watch, they wouldn't do any of the daily cleaning chores like washing decks, cleaning heads and scrubbing rust off the superstructure. "But we'll work them like hell all day," he said. For twelve hours a day, minus lunch hour, the daymen would get opportunities to do more physical, trade-style work. More rigging.

That night in the fo'c'sle, the excitement was palpable. Crew discussed going dayman like caterpillars might discuss going butterfly. I kept my aspirations to myself, secretly hoping to be a part of the new wave of good morale.

I wasn't.

Instead, I was to be the able-bodied seaman, the AB, the right-hand man, for Tom, who'd been promoted to third mate. I'd been overlooked again, and anger blew through me like a house fire. For that day and the next I couldn't hide my resentment from the mate and bo'sun.

I threw my energy into hitching an intricate web of knots around my beckets, showing the officers what I figured they'd refused to see, that I was a craftsman. Any time I wasn't on watch, eating or sleeping, I spent weaving two handles of spite.

Brian pulled me aside exactly where I'd stopped him a few days before. He fixed me with his penetrating eyes. "Rige, I couldn't make you a dayman." He said he needed me to be Tom's AB. He needed someone who was experienced. Jesse wouldn't have worked; he'd been jockeying for the third mate position as well. I realized there was a reason I'd been chosen to support the new third mate.

Tom, for his part, seemed to have dug up a new seriousness about life aboard ship. I worked hard to stay on the ball and help him succeed while we were on watch. He recognized that, and a new bond ran deep between us.

We were on the most appealing watch now, the four-to-eight. On duty from 4 a.m. to 8 a.m. and then again from 4 p.m. to 8 p.m., we watched the sun rise and set each day over an ocean of long swells. A stiff breeze on the quarter kept every sail full for days at a time. Our smooth wake showed that the *Picton Castle*'s hull moved through the water efficiently.

The ship's logbook showed an increase in the day's runs since we'd crossed the royals. We could see how the ship heeled more yet could carry all canvas in a fresh breeze. We trimmed sail, set sail, even bent on new sail, installing hal-yards, sheets and downhauls like it was second nature. The ship had become our greater body, and for eight hours a day we were her muscle and her mind.

CHAPTER 18

Roots

Pitcairn Island
March 17 to 28

ONE TIME I STOOD BEFORE A FRIEND'S BOOKSHELF AND
scanned his *National Geographics*—the great yellow horizon.
My eyes rested on the spine of October 1983, Pitcairn/
Norfolk. I pulled it down and opened to a two-page photo.

In the photograph I saw a simple window, framed by
weather-beaten dunnage that had washed up on the shore
of Pitcairn Island. Leaning on the sill, from her cluttered
kitchen, was a woman. The lines on her face spoke of a lifetime of struggle and self-reliance—weathered like those
dunnage boards. She wore the suggestion of a smile.

That woman had died by the time I stayed at her house,
though her picture haunted me still. She looked marooned.

There was something else that I recognized, something
that I heard through the rickety walls of her old house made
of driftwood. Something that I heard through the island's
dense forest and from the jagged cliffs. Something that I
heard from her husband, who was my host; who exhibited
her same melancholy when the conversation drifted near her
memory—the same longing for something.

Her husband and I sat at the very table in the photograph,

similarly cluttered with the dishes of a generous breakfast. We did not speak directly of his wife. Only one sad subject passed between us, that of his lineage. "My mother told me that I would never be accepted as a true Pitcairner, and she was right."

"Why?" I couldn't imagine a name more Pitcairn than Christian. Fletcher Christian was second-in-command of the HMS *Bounty*. He'd led the mutiny against his captain, Lieutenant William Bligh, in 1789 and settled this fertile little island with eight fellow mutineers and nineteen Polynesians. Charles Christian is a direct descendant of Fletcher.

"My father was from Pitcairn, but my mother was an American. I was born in San Francisco."

"And that matters?"

Something in his noble blue eyes said yes.

"Do you want some more bacon, Rigel?"

"No, thanks, I'm stuffed."

"Another couple eggs?"

"I couldn't."

"Coffee, then?"

"Sure."

Charles Christian smiled. He'd won the battle. He was so generous. In fact, the Pitcairners are the most generous people I have ever met.

I watched Charles walk across the rough-sawn floor of his house. His bare feet looked more like pads, callused and muscled from a lifetime of shoelessness. As he walked towards me with a kettle and a jar of instant coffee, it occurred to me how important lineage is on this island. And as we talked, I began to realize that I was also part of a lineage: the lineage of the voyage around the world by square-rigger, calling at Pitcairn Island.

The myth of the square-rigger captain is strong on this island. Irving and Exy Johnson visited this island on all

seven of their cost-shared circumnavigations in their brigantine *Yankee*, taking themselves on about a forty-day detour
off the trans-Pacific trunk route. I sometimes felt that
Captain Moreland had done it all to return to Pitcairn Island
in his own ship. His call to return seemed so strong that, if
the ship sank at her anchorage in the lee of that sea-swept
rock, I thought he might be happy to end his days here.

A kinship ran between the culture of our ship and the
culture of the island. Captain Moreland had said, "You will
find you have a lot in common with the islanders. Pitcairn
Island is a ship too. The only difference is that our ship
moves through the water—the water moves past theirs.
They depend on each other. They gossip and get angry at
each other."

Because Charles and I both lived on ships, and because
the world of the square-rigger had visited the world of
Pitcairn since day one, my experience and Charles
Christian's were linked.

I listened closely when he spoke of Captain Irving
Johnson. In his expressive blue eyes I saw the amazement
his younger self felt watching Johnson effortlessly lift an
enormous sea turtle from the arms of two struggling crew.
Charles spoke with a light in his eyes of the year 1957, when
Johnson had raised one of the *Bounty*'s anchors off the
floor of Bounty Bay with his *Yankee*. That anchor now sits in
front of the Pitcairn Island courthouse.

Charles had loved the show that Irving Johnson brought
to his island every three years for decades. He enjoyed
reading Johnson's accounts of his visits to Pitcairn in his
books and articles that had helped put Pitcairn on the cultural map before any of the famous mutiny on the *Bounty*
films had been made. Charles had a childlike admiration
for Johnson's celebrity.

But I wanted to hear about Skipper. He was the man

linked to the *Picton Castle*'s lineage. As master/owner of the brigantine *Romance*, his third circumnavigation took him to Pitcairn Island in 1977, with our captain as his twenty-two-year-old first mate. I pictured Skipper, his legendary temper, his one eye and leathery hands. I was sure he had made quite an impression.

"Oh, Skipper brought us clothes. Everything we requested. He always brought it." Charles seemed to view Skipper as a distant uncle who had drifted in and out of their lives. Perhaps it was because Skipper and his wife, Gloria, had less of a flair for self-promotion than the Johnsons did. Anyone who'd met Skipper would know he's as humble as salt. Our own captain said, "Even though Irving was Skipper's senior, Skipper is the last of the old turks and Irving was the first of the new turks." Perhaps Skipper preferred just to sail his ship like an ordinary commercial master in the age of sail rather than promote his voyages. Being poor, living rich—he sailed his *Romance* until she rotted beneath him. His family was the young men and women who sailed in her.

"Now, Tiger Timbs—there's a gentleman captain! A real Fletcher Christian, he is. Have you seen his ship, the *Eye of the Wind*? She was in that movie *White Squall*. Oh, she's a pretty ship. Well, she came to Pitcairn and I made the passage to Tahiti. I was steering by the wind, with my eyes on the sails, and the first mate, who was more like a Captain Bligh, told me to steer by the compass. Tiger set him straight. Poor lad. He just didn't know what he was talking about." Charles's island accent was faintly reminiscent of its British roots and was musical with the joy of this recollection.

After Charles and I finished breakfast, we drove on a four-wheeler to his banana patch and harvested a mature tree. He let me cut it down with his sharp machete that he

coated with bacon fat to protect it from Pitcairn's destructive salt air.

Later, I said goodbye to Charles, as I tore a few strawberry-
flavoured bananas from a bunch that hung near his door, and
headed off to find Don and Tom. We had agreed to explore
the island together—the geyser, the stone spires, the great
swimming at St. Paul's rock, the pre-mutiny hieroglyphics
and profusion of obsidian at Down Rope.

As Pitcairn had neared on the horizon a week before, Don
and I looked hungrily at the island sitting atop the waves.

"It looks like a scoop of ripe avocado, doesn't it, Rige?"

I couldn't think of a better description. The island glis-
tened, green and ripe, bursting with flavour and life.

And after our rusty iron claw of an anchor sped to the
sandy bottom of the lee side, the natives tied up to the ship
in their stout aluminum longboat. When the Pitcairners
boarded, they were shy and reserved. They brought baskets
overflowing with fruit, mostly watermelons, yellow on the
inside and so crisp and delicious that they must have been
picked that day. We cut them into hearty wedges and tore at
their sunny flesh. The green crescents of their rinds
danced about our chins in smiles.

Everywhere we went, there was food. One of our hostesses
showed us how to eat pineapple the Pitcairn way. You shave
off the skin with a knife and, holding the fruit by its spiny
head, eat it, core and all. Pitcairn pineapple is that tender.
We harvested and shared a papaya, which the Pitcairners call
pawpaw. Later, I found a passion fruit on our path and
slurped out the bitter juice and seeds. Tom stopped to tie a
pretzel-like carrick bend in the dangling vines of one of the
island's flourishing banyan trees. And while marching along
a path through a dense forest, we stopped so I could climb a
coconut palm. I pulled down three young jelly nuts, named
for the consistency of the meat inside.

Still inexpert at opening coconuts, I made a small cut in each thick husk with the saw blade of my Swiss Army knife and banged the nuts against a rock. Bang. Bang. *Blat*—the first nut opened. Aaaaaaaaaah! Coconut water sprayed all over Don. Still, there was enough for us to drink ourselves so full that we could hardly eat the sweet jelly-meat inside.

We threw the husks away and kept walking. Up, up, to Highest Point. This is the name of the island's highest point, where one can feel a cool, steady trade wind and watch it ripple the perfect disc of ocean.

We argued about how far across that disc we could see from Highest Point. Based on a height of about eight hundred feet, Tom figured it must be thirty miles or so. It seemed more like eighty to me. In any event, none of us could see the uninhabited neighbouring islands of Henderson, Ducie or Oeno. Just Pitcairn and the ocean. The ocean, completely empty except for the *Picton Castle*, pitching at her anchor. We didn't look at her for long, just a couple of seconds. We didn't comment on how pretty she looked, yards braced up, broad ribbons of rust down her white hull. The *Picton Castle* was a place we'd rather not be at that moment.

We turned our backs and headed for Other Side.

CHAPTER 19

New Moon

Pitcairn Island to Nuku Hiva, Marquesas
March 28 to April 16

THE WEATHER SOURED MORE EACH DAY AWAY FROM Pitcairn Island. Wind and sea built. Low grey cloud smeared the sky like wet grease. It rained. The ship, nearly beam-to the growing swells, had an unfamiliar and sickening motion after four months of downwind sailing.

Almost any other year the passage from Pitcairn to the Marquesas would have been nearly downwind and in clear weather. But El Niño had forced the southeast trade wind to blow unstable from the northeast. So, with all canvas flying but the royals, we sailed close-hauled, constantly set by wind and current towards the treacherous, low coral atolls of the Tuamotu Archipelago.

On the fourth morning, at the change of the watch, we combined the manpower of two watches to sharpen up the braces in an attempt to sail closer to the wind. It had shifted to press us ever closer to the Tuamotus. With our watch on the main deck and mate Brian's on the quarterdeck, we hauled. The yards torqued around in fits. The nearer halves touched the shrouds as they angled more fore and aft, stretching to catch the wind that lay just beyond our reach.

"Give me one haul on the port fore lower topsail," Tom ordered.

"Fore lower topsail," we repeated.

The mate's watch did the same on the mainmast. They took a decisive haul. A sharp snap followed high in the rig and we instinctively scattered from under the falling piece of steel rod that had supported the lower topsail yard. It dented the deck with a thud, and I rushed to grab the broken part before it could roll overboard. The yard, no longer attached to the mast, hung from the strong wire-rope leeches of the sail above, swinging gently fore and aft in the wind.

"Why does it always happen on my watch?" Lean Tom raised his big hands in the air, repeating his favourite refrain to the grey sky.

Josh and Jesse climbed aloft to lash the yard in place. Tom stood us down from watch and I descended to the main salon on my way to the fo'c'sle.

In the humid air of the salon, Patricia sat quietly on her settee, thoughtfully tucking a hairbrush in among the soft flannel sheets and pillows that lined her bunk. I sat down across from her and noticed the vaguely sweet smell of perfume emanating from her bunk.

"Do you want this, Rigel?" she asked, handing me a binder of loose leaf.

"Sure, thanks. No reason to take that home with you. Have you heard that we might go to the Tuamotus rather than the Marquesas?"

"Why?"

"Because of the wind direction."

"I hope not."

"How come?"

"Because the Marquesas has an airstrip."

It hadn't occurred to me how soon she wanted to leave.

Still, all the clues had been there. She had decided not to go ashore for her second period of time off on Pitcairn, opting to escape into a book. And it explained why, on the way to Pitcairn Island, she'd sponsored Spa Day. It seemed that Spa Day was a rebellion against the ship's military culture, against the directive to put the ship before oneself, against the pressure to step in line, to be a bucko. Spa Day was to be a celebration of comfort and relaxation. It was a departure from the dirt and inconvenience of living aboard a ship that was constantly under construction—an escape from the unpleasantness of our Galapagan cook's constant rice and beans, his raw bacon soaked in olive oil, served on delaminating plywood supported by rusting waste-oil barrels.

Spa Day was Patricia's final impact on our culture. She'd realized she was never going to accept the ship's military aspects. And the divisiveness she felt between captain and crew would continue to rob her of the joy of ship life. The Captain offered to take Patricia off the watch cycle for the Pacific crossing, but she didn't want to do the voyage on those terms. Though it was deeply against her nature to quit, Patricia and three other women had made the difficult decision to abandon the voyage in the Marquesas.

So, on that bright Sunday, Patricia dipped generously into her eighteen-month supply of anti-wrinkle, pro-hydrating cleansing creams and did facials on the cargo hatch. Second engineer and cellist Claire chose the classical music that would lend Spa Day an air of refinement. Captain Moreland embraced the idea and gave massages. Vicki Sullivan, an occupational therapist, massaged hands and feet; that is, after first soaking them in sea water scented with oils.

When it was time for our watch that day, Tom met me at our muster station. Patricia and Vicki weren't there. "Where the hell is everybody?" he asked, frustrated that his crew wasn't five minutes early like he'd ordered. He looked over at the cargo hatch. The two truants looked back at him.

Patricia was the first to speak. "I'm just waiting for my toes to dry. I'll be a few minutes," she laughed.

Vicki spoke next. "I'm giving Patrick a foot rub, but I just finished one and I'll only be ten minutes on the other."

Tom's face darkened.

Even among those of us who intended to stick it out, there was talk of what we'd do if the voyage folded for lack of money and enthusiasm. How would we get back home on a couple of hundred dollars? Would we put our gear on a freighter? Would we hitch a ride as crew on a yacht? Would we go east? Would we go west? Would we fly? Would we stay aboard the ship until she made it back to Lunenburg? Would we wait until there was no hope and abandon her to rust in some tropical port? Would we return to see her a decade later, stripped and half sunken like that ship in Bermuda?

The weather remained unstable on our way to the Marquesas and the Captain took to sleeping on the bench in the charthouse. It meant the watch on deck had to be especially careful of noise. He'd been as morose as the weather since I'd seen him talking to my sister on the satellite phone days before. I'd heard through the grapevine that she wouldn't be coming to Tahiti; it was over. I felt like the whole thing was none of my business, yet I was inextricably wound up in their relationship. Though I missed her very much, the fact that my sister wasn't coming lifted a burden off my shoulders. In the meantime, Dan and I could continue to be captain and crewman; and my parents would not feel that they'd lost both son and daughter.

The day that the main lower topsail crane fell to the deck, when I turned in at my usual 2030 hours, things still didn't feel quite right. I opened my porthole and a chilly, wet gust blew across me and fluttered my curtain. For the first time in three months the wind was blowing on the starboard side.

The ship heeled over as she lumbered across the swells, and I slept quite a bit higher than I was used to. The feeling was less secure. Outside, the night was dark as could be. Low cloud obscured the stars. The new moon was on the other side of the globe—all her light spent that month.

Things continued to fall apart the next morning towards the end of watch. With a bang like a door slammed shut, the starboard gans'l sheet parted. I spun around and looked aloft to see the starboard clew whipping in the breeze. I ran forward to the clewline that could pull it safely up to the yard, and Tom calmly gave the order over my shoulder. I felt good about how we worked together as I hauled the line home, feeling it jerk like a big fish on a hook.

With the sail clewed up, he ordered me to re-lead the broken sheet, cutting away the frayed end, whipping the end to prevent fraying and wrapping it with tape to slow down the inevitable chafe. The plan was to install chain sheets on the gans'l someday, but with the condition of the ship seeming to backslide, I wondered if it would ever get done. I hooked my leg around the t'gallant shrouds and worked on the sheet while this great tower of wood, canvas, steel and wire pitched against the foul wind.

Second helmsman Lori, one of my watchmates, had remembered in my absence to wake the oncoming crew for breakfast. The rest of our watch was happy that the sheet had parted because it meant we'd have to hurry to complete the deck wash, and there would be no time for the ship's daily scrubbing with sponge and cleanser. The only one upset was Tom, more convinced than ever that fate was making everything break while he was on duty.

Bad weather persisted. The winds were baffling, determined to keep us from the Marquesas. With sun hidden behind cloud and rain, day and night blended into one another. Only the temperature seemed to change, growing hotter and stuffier by the mile. The daymen were placed on watches because of the unstable weather and the great inconvenience of employing a large work crew in the rain.

Off watch, most of us took to hiding in our bunks with curtains closed. There, I was free to escape. I imagined myself in a Costa Rican mountain rain forest building my tree house resort. With my crew I thinned underbrush and discovered freshwater springs. We set aside plots for vegetable gardens and determined where footpaths would be. We had materials delivered to us by elephant and built a long stairway that spiralled up a two-hundred-foot mahogany trunk. At the top we encircled the trunk with a house: two floors with a bed, shower, bathroom and plumbing that spiralled down beneath the stairs. Cabinets, desks, a porch.

In one of the walls was a small porthole, a dock for an aerial trolley. The trolley of my imagination was as big as a mailbox and carried food to all the tenants. It was propelled by a steam engine, and the steam exhaust warmed the food within. The trolley system originated at the Casas Arboreales headquarters, an expansive one-floor A-frame structure with a kitchen, reservation desk, laundry room, dining hall and dance floor which flexed with the rhythmic strumming and drumbeats of a Latin band that played into the night while we danced in the sturdy branches of a giant banyan tree.

Covered with a sheen of sweat, I'd write all this down for friends on the paper given to me by Patricia. I'd add sketches and rewrite numerous drafts, pitching the old pages out my porthole, watching them bob on swells past the ship, reminding me of Nova Scotia's big seagulls.

Occasionally I'd hear some action on deck as crew sharpened up braces or adjusted sails. Like the others hiding out in the fo'c'sle, I made sure my curtain was closed and pretended to sleep.

Sometimes I did sleep. But sleep when you don't really need it is a strange thing. Hot and sweaty, you drift in and out of dreams. You want to get up and do something. You start to read, but the details of the book become too strange to be plausible and you realize you're dreaming. You want to leave your bunk, but the draw to slumber is too strong.

The only thing that could force me out of bed was lying on my back and placing my arms overhead. Then the sour smell of my own armpits drove me to the main deck, where I washed with salt water and dish soap.

The wind, still unstable, changed its direction against the hands of a clock. The mates were forced to head the ship still farther away from the Marquesas to keep wind in the sails. Soon we were headed southwest, sailing farther from our goal each minute. One night a powerful squall heeled the ship over nearly as hard as the North Atlantic had on our passage south.

In the morning, the weather had changed yet again. The wind shift brought a stifling humidity. We wore ship, reversing our course by making a downwind U-turn. I worked in the shade of the fo'c'sle head by the foremast while the heat forced linseed oil to leach from footropes and shrouds. As the day wore on, the wind became calmer and remained that way overnight. We moved at walking speed.

I wrote in my journal:

There is no doubt that this voyage is a hard one. Oblivion is the sense I have most often. The idea that I'm doing something great is so distant and unreal. Like climbing Mt. Everest is putting one foot in front of the other in the snow, sailing around the world in the Picton Castle *is putting one sponge in front of one toilet brush in front of one deck brush in front of another sponge.*

I see nothing of challenge or growth or risk. I feel like a 23-year-old flunkey. And all work seems the same. We're still just maintaining the ship with the same half-measure lipstick applications and I just get closer to the resolve that I will not spend much more of my life actualizing the Captain's thoughts and trying to live up to his expectations.

Soon the Captain ordered the main engine to be fired up and that we on the four-to-eight watch take in and furl all sail. Steaming north caused a light breeze to wash over the deck, a saving grace as we once again approached the equator. Still, the effects of El Niño were strong. The intertropical convergence zone that usually sits between two and five degrees south was as far south as twenty degrees. The associated low pressure meant a low density of air molecules. That meant less oxygen inhaled with each breath. That meant lethargy, somnolence, bad moods.

One evening a friend confessed that he thought all the women had become synchronized in their menstrual cycles. I asked Vicki in the fo'c'sle if it was true.

"Definitely," she said in her Georgia accent. "It used to happen to all the girls in my volleyball team."

Four days later, in late morning, the horizon was broken by the Marquesas. All day we steamed through the chain of sharply peaked islands towards Nuku Hiva, near the northwestern end.

We loosed all squares that morning, not to set but to dry in the hot sun. There was no wind.

As it approached 2200 hours, and the sky was black and clear, and the air was cooling off, I lay in my fo'c'sle bunk and felt the engine slow to an idle chug.

"Let go." The Captain's words punctuated the engine's rhythm.

"Let go." The mate's words sounded through the fo'c'sle's deckhead. He unscrewed the brake on the windlass and let loose the anchor chain, which tore through the hawse pipe with a loud clatter that for a few seconds woke every hand. We had finally dropped the hook at Nuku Hiva.

Picton Castle at dock in Lunenburg, Nova Scotia, November 1997.

North Atlantic. Engineer Nobby welds steering gear. Captain Dan Moreland observes. AB Tom Ward steers.

Rigel Crockett and Kuna Indian women. Cook Lee Kotze.

Pacific Ocean. Hoisting the main royal yard. Bo'sun Josh Weissman pins the main royal yard to the shrouds against the ship's rolls.

Picton Castle at anchor in Nuku Hiva, Marquesas.

Takaroa, Tuamotu Archipelago. Children play in the headrig while crew paint the hull.

Marcello Bezina and Rigel Crockett in the Monomoy longboat, sailing around Bora-Bora with five others not in view.

Pacific Ocean. On the quarterdeck, Marge Mower sews a boltrope to a sail.

Pentecost, Vanuatu. Second mate Karen Balog entertains local children.

Torres Strait. Chief mate Brian gaffs a tuna. Third mate Tom Ward slings it aboard. Rigel Crockett holds the fish tote.

Mail call, Darwin, Australia. Clockwise from upper left: Becky Keen, Jesse Kenworthy; In entrance to main salon sit Rigel Crockett and Pat Houston; bo'sun Josh Weissman chuckles over letter; Mildred Broome, Jean Burke, Peter "Pasha" Greathead, Unknown, Bill Wellington, Marcello Bezina, chief mate Brian Donnelly, Doctor Beth, Clyde Sundeberg, Lori Moyer, Cowboy Brad Jarrell, Drummer Todd Jarrell.

Darwin, Australia. Kim Smith looks out of the cargo hold.

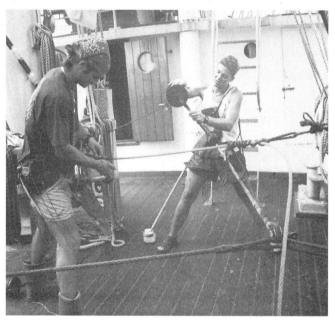

Indian Ocean. Jesse Kenworthy serves a wire splice. Vicki Sullivan serves a footrope with a serving mallet. Foremast and fo'c'sle in view.

Pacific Ocean. Climbing the main lower shrouds.

Indian Ocean. Cowboy Brad and others shoot the sun.

Indian Ocean. Captain Moreland lectures on the evolution of square rig. From left to right: Third mate Tom Ward, Captain Dan Moreland, Rigel Crockett, Paul Brand, Kristin Ellison, Becky Keen, Susannah Clark, bo'sun Josh Weissman, Drummer Todd Jarrell, Clyde Sundeberg, Jesse Kenworthy, Harry Taylor.

CHAPTER 20

New Skin

Taiohae Bay, Nuku Hiva, Marquesas
April 8 to 16

I PUSHED MY FACE AGAINST MY PORTHOLE, TRYING FOR
a better look at Nuku Hiva.

We were nestled in a large bay, the sides of which shot
out of the water to Gothic heights. It seemed that the volcanic island had erupted in vegetation rather than lava, and
trees and shrubs cascaded down and rooted happily all
along the mountain. Waterfalls spewed from those steep
walls and tumbled white to the black rocks that lined the
shore. Looking from shoreline to jagged skyline, it
occurred to me that we were anchored right in the caldera
of an extinct volcano, one side of which had crumbled into
the ocean. A few modest storefronts and a compound of
thatch huts lined the shore. *Paradise.*

When I went on deck and walked aft for chow, I saw
other crew members transfixed by the sight of land. There
was always a collective longing to be ashore as soon as we
dropped the hook, but I had never seen, or felt, the draw so
strong.

It started to rain. Brian walked aft to the aloha deck.
"Any of you not eating should slack the lines."

Manila rope shrinks in the rain and, aside from extra wear on lines, such shrinkage has been known to break the thinner upper yards. Most of us looked to our bowls of bulgur wheat porridge made by our emergency replacement cook, Pasha. Some looked towards the shore. Bo'sun Josh put away his plate to slack lines in the rain. I took a few more bites and grudgingly joined him.

After breakfast, we were warned that it would be a while before customs arrived. In the meantime we would get some work done. Brian told the bo'sun to organize the work parties.

First order of business was to give shelter from the rain. One group rigged an awning. Another cleaned every compartment from the main salon to the heads. Another organized the cargo hold. Another, with sponge and cleanser, cleaned rails and bulwarks, taking advantage of the rain. My group launched the skiff to scrub away algae and grass that grew in the pitted steel up to a foot above the waterline.

On the ship were a few copies of Herman Melville's *Typee*, a mostly factual account of the month he'd spent on this very island. I learned that he'd arrived in the whaling ship *Acushnet* after eighteen months of a voyage that was far from completion. But rather than endure the cracked paint on her sides, *burnt up by the scorching sun,* or *the weeds she trails along with her,* he longed for *the refreshing glimpse of one blade of grass—for a snuff at the fragrance of a handful of the loamy earth.* Like our crew members who had also made the decision to leave here, he was filled with strong misgivings, the feeling that he would be welshing on a contract. For Melville, though, it was more than a feeling. Before joining the *Acushnet*, he had signed his ship's articles, binding him to the term of her voyage. For our own crew, the contract was an agreement with themselves to finish what they'd set out to do. Melville justified his act by saying he had not signed up for tyranny, scanty provisions and unreasonably protracted cruises, so instead he tried his luck with the cannibalistic Marquesans.

In the skiff, three of us struggled to gain purchase on the hull. Each swipe of green scrubby or wire brush pushed us farther away, leaving slick algae in the pits of steel. Three months of hard travel with no hull maintenance had left her orange as a pumpkin. The rain chilled. Our bare feet slipped and sloshed in the skiff's bilge water. Paradise beckoned a few hundred feet away.

A thick tropical downpour started.

When the rain stopped, the flies came. They swarmed in like the rain droplets themselves. They alighted on the coamings, on the lunch being placed on the aloha deck, on our legs, our arms, our faces.

By noon, the shore party went to clear the ship through customs. By mid-afternoon, they returned. Customs inspected and approved the ship, and we were called to muster. Having finished scouring most of the waterline, we climbed to the deck.

The Captain addressed the remaining crew of twenty-five. He described how the authorities had agreed to waive their obligatory one-thousand-dollar deposit for every person entering French Polynesia—their insurance that we'd leave. They knew it was paradise and wanted to keep it that way. Most compellingly, he talked of the tattoos. Beautiful tattoos. There had been no tattoos when he was last here in the *Romance*. The Christian missionaries had long since outlawed the practice, but the Marquesans had begun to rediscover their traditions. The Marquesas had once again become the centre of Polynesian tattoo art.

With a smile the Captain reminded us that the tattoo clause was in effect, and coaxed a round of laughter from the crew at the irony that the only way we could miss watch was under the needle.

The Captain asked Marcello if he wanted to say a few words about his experience on the shore party. Marcello's voice was soft and slow, as if he consciously held back feelings of excitement and wonder. He spoke of the smells: tropical blossoms and fresh baguettes. Huge ripe grapefruit hanging from trees, tall stone idols, and unusual and beautiful tattoos. "I'm going to get one," he said.

That night, our watch and the mate's went ashore. It had been nearly fifty days since any of us had had a beer. It was already dark, so we walked straight to the patio of the Muana Nua, a brick-oven pizza and beer joint with a boarding house upstairs.

Our crew soon filled the place, as was the case with the nearest pub everywhere we went. The first round arrived. I took a sip and admired the white label, glistening with condensation. Hinano. A Polynesian woman sat cross-legged in profile, a red *pareau* wrapped around her full-figured body, her olive skin. She'd tucked a red hibiscus blossom behind her ear and wore a crown of white flowers in her long black hair. I looked closely at the beach and palm trees that formed her background and realized that she looked out to sea, probably towards some sailor off to the next port.

Effective advertising. I thought of Melville's description of the Marquesan women who'd swum out to his ship and invaded by way of the chains that secured the shrouds to the hull or by pulling their naked selves up the bobstays. Within minutes they were on deck panting from their exertions, but not too tired to rub each other's nubile bodies in fragrant oil and make savage love to every homesick man aboard. I took another drink.

Conversation started easily—several rounds of laughter at our wayward cook's expense. Turns out, upon arriving ashore, he went straight to the liquor store, got pissed to the eyeballs and climbed a tall tree. As the Captain, Patrick and Doctor Beth rounded the corner, walking into town, they saw Simone picking himself up from the dusty road. He was badly scraped, having fallen from the tree and hit just about every branch on the way down.

All three, more than fed up with his refusal to cook and his leering eyes, would not let him tag along. We all laughed at the thought of his eyes welling up with tears as they passed by. "Good old Knucklehead." We'd been calling him Knucklehead for weeks, assuming he couldn't speak a word of English.

Locals shuffled in and out, taking sidelong notice of us, careful not to engage us in conversation. A Melville-style orgy was not even a distant possibility, and I began to wonder if that was one of the made-up parts of his narrative. Given the locals' shyness, we felt free to gawk. As the Captain had told us before we landed, the Marquesans are beautiful people, the men more striking, like the male in a pair of cardinal mates. By comparison, the women seemed reserved.

Men rode by shirtless on horseback. Solid, symmetrical tattoos covered their torsos. Long black hair flowed down their backs. Almond-shaped eyes showed not the slightest concern or guile. With a hint of jealousy I had earlier watched a couple of female shipmates swoon shamelessly at the sight of a bare-chested young Marquesan man on the dock.

Now a tall, broad Marquesan stepped into the pizza joint. He pushed his hair back from his forehead and the motion caused his light quilted jacket to open, revealing a necklace of boar's tusks, six ivory crescents hung to face each other, three to each side on a chiselled torso. His hand had revealed a large diamond-shaped tattoo on the middle of his forehead. It was a tiki face, a male figure in Polynesian myth, sometimes identified as the first man. This face-on-face tattoo frightened me a bit, and I looked away.

Marcello spoke to Tattoo Head in French. Though he seemed interested in talking, he didn't relax. His eyes were wide and forbidding.

Rounds of beer timed the night. In the comfortably humid air, beer went down easily, and I barely noticed I was becoming drunk. I was wide awake from the morning's extra sleep, and the alcohol gave me a feeling of relaxed lucidity.

Marcello, handing me another beer, leaned his head close and said that Tattoo Head had invited us boar hunting. That he had dogs and spears. I turned to look at him. He was completely serious. I looked to the Marquesan. He was completely serious.

"Let's do it," I said.

"You're on."

I imagined myself running with Marcello and our guide into the mountains on this moonless night. A pack of dogs would run before us, lusty for the taste of blood. Barking, they'd corner a wild boar in a thicket. Desperate, he'd charge me. I'd root the butt of my spear in the ground, mutter a short prayer and skewer it through the head. The boar would charge the full length of my spear and collapse. In the watery light of dawn, Marcello and I would saunter back to the ship with the boar carried over our shoulders, its feet lashed to our spear.

Over another beer, Marcello and I discussed the logistics of our adventure. The plan grew complex. We were timing our provisioning with the boat runs and planning to meet Tattoo Head back on the wharf.

Soon other crew heard about our plans and began casting nearsighted doubts and negativity. "He doesn't seem trustworthy. I think he's on something. Are you sure this is a good idea?"

"Yeah. He's a good guy. I can tell."

"What if he's a psycho?"

"Well, Marcello has a black belt in tae kwon do."

All the while, Tattoo Head was drinking beer. We were all drinking beer. Though I couldn't understand much of what he said, I sensed he was growing irritated by the persistent questioning of his character. Occasionally he stood up to his full height of six foot four and spoke French in short, loud, hostile bursts.

No one protested our adventure more than mate Brian. "I don't think you should go."

"It's all right. Don't worry," I assured him.

"You're not going."

I took a hard swallow of beer as I heard his protest move from concern to order. *We're not on the ship. You can't order me around.* "Yeah, I'm going."

Brian took a sip of his rum and Coke, turned to me and said, "No, you're not. I'm not letting you go."

This could be my one chance to experience Marquesan life like a local. Frustrated, I took a stand. "I *am* going."

Brian didn't seem as perturbed as I thought he'd be. Crew were watching us silently. "Rigel, I promised your father that you'd come back alive. Letting you go into the woods with that guy would break that promise."

I looked away, locked my jaw. It was a slap in the face. I felt like a child, sent to my room, having tried to run away from home.

It wasn't long before eleven o'clock rolled around and we had to catch the last boat to the ship. Marcello and I walked back to the skiff side by side, some crew ahead, some behind.

"I can't believe they stopped us," he said.

"I know. It's bullshit."

"I came here to experience cultures, not to be a tourist," he said.

"Me, too."

"I want to collect experiences, not goddamn coffee cups."

Back on the ship, I went to my bunk and fell into an angry, drunken sleep.

I spent the next morning with Tom. We'd seen some guys surfing the small break at the centre of the bay and thought we'd give it a try. While I dug out my board and got ready to go ashore, the on-duty watch made boat runs. Patricia and Lynn arrived back on the ship to get their bags. They seemed slightly self-conscious walking aboard in their good clothes, hair soft and fluffy from a fresh washing. No longer members of the crew, they seemed more like defectors. As if eager to attain closure, they retrieved their heavy bags and left the ship for the last time.

When the boat returned, Tom and I discreetly placed the surfboard inside it. Cynically, I was concerned that crew might stop me if they saw me about to attempt a dangerous activity like surfing over volcanic rock. I cringed with the thought of the last night's confrontation.

Once ashore, Tom and I walked to the surf break. A group of deeply tanned Marquesans with long hair were taking turns riding a beat-up old surfboard. It was covered in peeling swatches of fibreglass and the red, green and gold colours of the Jamaican flag. Without a leash, a surfer paddled to the break and waited. He let one wave pass him and watched it reflect off the black volcanic boulders lining the shore. The reflected wave combined with the incoming wave to send a larger wave parallel to the shore rather than directly towards the jagged, porous rocks.

Though my board was twenty years old—thick at the bow and bright yellow, with a long sweeping curve rather like a banana—it was in better shape than theirs. I'd never caught a wave before and felt bad for having such a prize stick. Standing on the edge of a boulder, I jumped to the water, board under me, and paddled.

As the water drained off the wax on my board, I noticed it was thick with black volcanic sand. As it tumbled around me in waves, it seemed viscous and shimmery, like motor oil.

Once I'd paddled through the waves to the break, I took a minute to look at the shore. I was lower than the rocks. The street was invisible. The verdant mountain with its modest houses came into view. I scanned the water. The surfers were eyeing me. Tom raised his fist.

The waves aren't that big after all. The water is shallow. I held station, waiting for what I thought was the correct combination of waves. I let smaller waves pass under, feeling the cooling spray that whipped off their backs, enjoying a sight never seen from the beach. Finally a wave crested about me, lifting my feet over my head. I paddled. Not fast enough. I pitchpoled and, in my surprise, inhaled salt water, tumbling with the wave through white froth and black water, white and black. I came to the surface coughing and turned my face to the sea, not wanting to show embarrassment and at the same time wondering if I would have black sand at the bottoms of my lungs.

I waited at the break and heard Tom offer words of advice. "Paddle sooner. Lift your feet."

On the very next set, a wave reflected off the shore and I watched as it met the incoming wave to my left, closing on my position like scissors, kicking up a rooster tail of water where they intersected. I paddled and raised my feet. The board lifted. It slid down the wave. I shifted forward. The board stiffened. With a hand clutching each rail, I kneeled and then stood in a low crouch, skimming across the water. I jumped into the water just before meeting the rocks.

Tom and I hung out in the warm water with the surfers a while longer. I let them use my board. They loved its buoyancy that made it well suited to the small surf in the bay. Then we waded through the water along the beach. I paddled on the surfboard across the shallow water.

From the low profile of my board I saw Brian in the white skiff, taking a solitary retreat from his duty aboard. I paddled towards him, thinking about the night before, about the position he'd been in. I knew he felt he was acting in my best interest. *It's too bad it came to a confrontation.*

I approached Brian in his boat. He was looking over at Tom some distance behind me. "Hi, Brian."

He looked at me noncommittally. "Hi, Rige."

I paddled closer to his boat. "Hey, I wanted to apologize for last night."

He smiled. "It's all right. I can't count the number of times people have pulled me out of a bad situation." That's when it hit me that it really was a bad situation.

Neither of us ever said another word about boar hunting.

The next day, I explored the town with Marcello. We snacked on baguettes and buttery Camembert. We watched locals play ball, more impressed than ever by the solid geometry of tattoos that covered torsos, legs and arms. The images and symbols were simpler and more distinct than the intricate lines and sharp points of North American tattoos. Each tattoo seemed to contain meaning beyond the elegance of the shapes, bound together as much by the space between the images as by the images themselves. I'd never really wanted a tattoo before.

Walking past some ancient carved stone *tikis* with enormous alien eyes, we saw Simone sitting on the side of the street. He caught our glance and we immediately looked away, but it was too late. Muttering in Spanish, he hobbled in behind us, still injured from his tree fall, or perhaps faking. Completely ignoring him, we walked all the way to the other end of the bay, towards the colony of thatch huts where the four defectors were waiting for their flight. Marcello told me he'd heard that Simone tried to mooch a ride with them as they were driven to the hotel on the first day here. They'd rolled up the windows as his eyes swelled with tears. Thankfully, we ran into mate Brian and Doctor Beth.

The four of us walked into the Muana Nua for a beer. There, looking through the heavy-laden branches of a grapefruit tree, we saw the ship swinging on her anchor. The third of the crew on duty was making good progress renewing the hull. They were washing rust off the old paint job in preparation for another coat. It was slow work, but one side was completely done. As she swung on her anchor, she went from pumpkin orange to bone white with black splotches. We commented on the difference between the two sides and how good it was to see such progress. With the latest departure of four crew, I realized that the professionals now outnumbered the amateurs thirteen to twelve. Still, there was hope.

Later, Beth and Brian invited Marcello and me to ride with them in the back of a hired pickup to check out some local tattoo artists.

"You going to get inked, Rige?" Brian asked.

"Thinking about it."

By dark, I was back on the ship to get some sleep for Easter Sunday, spent cleaning the hull, chipping rust, sanding and priming bare steel. On Monday, all hands turned to, preparing the ship for a lasting paint job.

The next day, I followed my curiosity up a steep, winding road past the dwellings of Taiohae Bay to where I'd heard some crew were getting tattooed. On either side were modest one-storey houses with neat lawns, close together, almost as if they were on a suburban street. Their owners had taken such care to leave the shady foliage standing that I hadn't noticed them from the bay.

Andrew, a shipmate who'd really seized ship life, led me down a driveway that ended at the back door of a house. Brian sat in a chair in the middle of the drive, with his foot on a stump and his sun-browned calve under the buzzing tattoo needle of a rotund Marquesan man. The others sat on the gleaming black rocks that lined the driveway.

I stepped closer for a look at the tattoo. A blood-speckled outline of a gecko gleamed black in its swollen furrow, driven into Brian's skin by an ink-dipped sewing needle. That needle was lashed to the reciprocating arms of an electric razor with blades removed. On the gecko's two-dimensional body the artist had penned in traditional island symbols of fishnets, a crescent moon, Marquesan swastikas, iconic men.

Brian sat back meditatively puffing on a cigarette as if he relished the sensation of being tattooed. I noticed his older tattoo below the gecko, a tribal-style ankle band. I'd heard how painful it is to receive tattoos on the sensitive ankle. On Brian's back was a sun-faded tattoo of the *Romance*'s emblem, a trident branded on a heart. Brian had had the artist entwine that heart in a sea serpent.

With a meaty thumb, the artist shut off his razor. His arms, from knuckles to shoulder, were covered in Marquesan design. The most striking images were checkerboards and *tiki* faces, some with eyes open, some with eyes closed. The tattooist turned to look at me, a ciga-rette in his smiling mouth.

"This is Raphael," said Brian, introducing the artist.

"*Bon après-midi*, Raphael."

I looked around Raphael's yard. Over big glossy green leaves he had a glorious view of the Pacific. His young chil-dren played in the driveway, excited by their father's guests.

Their toys were a number of downtrodden orange house cats. They picked them up by their front legs, stretching the skinny creatures to nearly their own height, swinging them around or playing wheelbarrow. The cats' only protest was to slink away pathetically whenever a child approached.

Beth and Marcello had decided on ankle bands, and when I asked the Captain, he said he was going to get a tattoo on his shoulder and arm. What the tattoo would be, he'd let the artist decide.

"What are you getting, Rigel?" he asked.

"I'm not sure I'm getting a tattoo."

"What? Your body is your temple, right?" he teased.

"No. I'm just not sure."

"What else could you want? This is the Marquesas. It doesn't get any more right than this."

One of Raphael's children towed a forlorn cat past us. The razor buzzed on the mate's calf. The afternoon light cast everything in a deep glow. In the distance, down in the bay, I heard drums pounding.

"I know—I'm getting one."

"Well, good. What of?"

"I've been thinking of a sea turtle or a sun. I'll probably go with a sun." I made my decision quickly, before he would have a chance to influence it. A tattoo choice seemed the most personal of decisions, and I'd drawn round suns with geometric rays ever since I was a small child.

"Sun is good," the Captain replied, and began to draw a few samples that I might try on a pad of paper.

Soon, Brian stood with his tattoo complete. The gecko covered nearly his entire calf and shin, red from the trauma of the needle. I noticed how clean and black the lines looked, even though they were made with a sewing needle.

"A tattoo never looks as good as on the day you get it," Brian said.

Doctor Beth was next. Ever concerned about the sterility of medical instruments, she watched carefully as Raphael unwound the string that lashed the used stitching needle to the exposed arms of his battery-powered razor and threw it away. She watched Raphael pull a fresh needle from a plastic case and carefully wind thread about the tip to absorb ink stolen from the broken reservoir of a black pen refill.

To ensure he could comfortably tattoo around her entire ankle, Raphael had Beth recline on a table. While he and Marcello spoke in French, we anglophones discussed the painfulness of a tattoo on bony flesh.

Getting down to business, working against the failing light of late afternoon, Raphael took a firm hold of Beth's lower leg and pressed the vibrating needle to her ankle. I watched Beth's expression change from one of resolve to confusion and then pain. It looked as if it was with the greatest will that she resisted jerking away. Raphael stopped his operation.

People from the ship passed into and away from the scene, interested in the drama.

Raphael presented her with a flat piece of fragrant sandalwood from his carving stock. He indicated that she could bite it to help suppress the pain. She did. And for one long, torturous hour Raphael embedded a traditional feminine motif: blocks of symbols joined at the centre by a *tiki*. The simplicity of form and the strength of meaning that lived beneath the surface of the linked icons gave the tattoo a powerful, almost magical quality.

Marcello was next. Because the sun had now set, Raphael turned on an overhead light. I wondered if Marcello's tae kwon do training would help him ignore the pain of his tattoo. Raphael put needle to skin. Marcello's face contorted in surprise. He sat up and straightened his leg as if to back away from the source of pain. But he said the pain became more bearable as the tattoo progressed. His ankle band looked similar to Beth's, though comparing them, I was impressed at how Raphael had manipulated his symbols to complement their personalities. Beth's had a joyful, elfish quality and seemed to dance around her ankle. Marcello's were powerful, yet they suggested his sense of mystery.

Brian and Beth paid Raphael, surprised that he asked no more than thirty-five dollars each. Marcello gave him a pair of sunglasses, which Raphael immediately put on before walking into the house.

When Raphael was gone, Brian gave Marcello a look. "I thought you didn't like those."

"I don't. I can barely see through them."

"Well, what does he think they're worth?" Brian asked, a little tension in his voice.

"He likes them," Marcello replied.

I talked to Raphael in my broken French, agreeing to meet the next day after he'd finished the Captain's tattoo. The Captain was returning later that evening to start his own, but it was to be extensive and detailed, probably running into the next day.

The next morning we planned to leave the Marquesas. All hands were required aboard mid-morning, but I invoked the tattoo clause and met up with the Captain by the boat. Once ashore, we walked up the hill to Raphael's house.

Dan put aside his authoritarian demeanour and we talked easily. He joked about how I walked too fast like my sister. Dan's partly completed tattoo was very promising and bold, with large *tiki* profiles, eyes open and closed, traditional swirling swastikas and the semicircle of a sun rising over the horizon with small pennants flying from the its rays.

When we arrived, Raphael greeted us warmly and very quickly offered us seats in the shade of his workshop. He went to work on the Captain's arm and shoulder. The

Captain seemed barely aware of the needle's poke and scrape, staring into the distance, speaking calmly and measuredly about the voyage, his feeling that it was hanging in the balance.

I told him I thought that everyone who was on the fence about the voyage was gone—that I didn't think anyone else would leave.

"I'm not so sure," he said, mentioning a number of more solitary people who were taking their time integrating with the ship's community. People who held their cards close to their chests.

It was true. Some people didn't care how things were done aboard. The hull painting dragged on for six days when it should have taken half that. And the ship still needed a second coat.

Complaining was so rampant, crew didn't even hear each other any more. One would simply wait impatiently while his confidant vomited up grievances, then begin his own litany—you think your life sucks? Evenings at the bar, where crew normally bitched about the ship or the Captain, complaints flew like shrapnel. He was right: things might come to an end.

Soon the Captain's tattoo was finished. He was delighted with the art. Kind Raphael was flustered with the Captain's praise, honoured to have inked the chief of our tribe. The Captain pulled out a wad of South Pacific francs and looked at Raphael questioningly. He shrugged and suggested twenty-five dollars. The Captain motioned for him to increase his amount and continued until his price was doubled. Gratefully, Raphael accepted and the Captain hurried back to his ship.

I was the only crew member from the *Picton Castle* still on the island. Everyone else was heaving away on the anchor, preparing to go to the fuel dock. I felt like a truant watching the school bus go by, or like Melville must have felt watching the *Acushnet* weigh anchor in 1842. He must have been filled with a strange mix of relief and regret.

For a second my thoughts went to Patricia and the others leaving the ship. I felt Raphael's pen on my shoulder as he sketched a circle. I realized that I was committed. I would let the ship lead me.

"C'est bon. Commence, si tu veux. Un soleil avec le visage d'un tiki."

"Le tiki?" he replied in a sincere voice. *"Qu'est-ce que tu veux, les yeux overts ou fermés?"* He pointed at tattoos on his arms, to profiles and direct faces, all mystical, alien, peaceful. Some had round eyes, some had almond eyes and some had closed eyes. The closed eyes were beautiful, with a curving sleepy look. They were mysterious and suggested inner vision. I was pointing towards that one when it occurred to me, *No, I want to see. I want to be awake.* I chose round eyes.

I heard the buzz of his razor needle. Felt its deep sting. And went to the place I'd found as a child, exchanging Indian burns with friends.

The tattoo was done faster than I'd expected. I gave Raphael more money than he'd asked for. Smiling, he disappeared into his shop, returning with a bag of cream-coloured sandalwood dust and a pendant. The centrepiece was a *tiki* on one knee, staring ahead, enormous eyes, straight mouth. The necklace was wide and manly, tapered at the ends, woven of a fine vine. No metal anywhere.

"Merci," I said. *"C'n'est pas nécessaire."*

He smiled and handed me a third gift—a sea turtle, carved of bone—and insisted I take it.

"Merci, Raphael. Au revoir."

"Au revoir."

I hitched on the necklace and ran down the hill to the main road. As I got into the open, I saw the ship tied stern-to at a fuel dock farther away from town. I turned on the main road and ran towards her, enjoying the sensation of sun and wind on my fresh tattoo, feeling I could run forever.

As I turned onto a dirt road, my path merged with another. I saw a group of young men, perhaps from a running team, torsos tattooed with bold collars and arm bands, long black hair tied back. They motioned for me to join them and at a furious rate led me off the road and through the woods. Trees whipped past and I felt the sandalwood *tiki* rise and fall on my chest, like my heart that was pounding inside. We ran to the commercial dock and I peeled off towards the ship.

While the fuel was bunkered, the Captain had gone ashore and Brian stole a moment to address the crew on his own terms. He called all crew to the cargo hatch. It reminded me of that day in Lunenburg when he gave us the gift of perspective.

"Listen, we have to do some sucking-up here. OK? Though it may not seem like it in the day-to-day grind, this voyage is something great. You are doing something great. But I've got news for you: You don't always gotta love it. Travelling is going to get boring. Your relationships are going to get boring. Life aboard is going to get boring. And we all have to fuckin' tolerate ridiculous behaviour. That's all part of the payment to be here.

"You don't have a lot of power, sailing before the mast in a square-rigger. But you do have this: You chose to be here. You can choose to be here. The one thing we have power over is how we look at things. We have power over how we react to things. How we see the good in events. How we get involved. We have power. We are not jailed here. We can *decide* to stay.

"When you're feeling stress or anger, focus on the ship. She's the one constant. She keeps us alive. She keeps us happy. Remember, there's bigness in being little."

With his final business taken care of ashore, the Captain mustered us crew for a final announcement of destination—Takaroa in the Tuamotus; and the estimated length of the passage—three days. He handed the floor to Brian.

"When we get to Takaroa, we're still going to do some painting. She still needs another coat, and I for one am not going to Tahiti without a fresh coat of paint."

It seemed he was committing political suicide, but he wasn't. There was an undeniable surge of enthusiasm from the crew. The Captain gave him a pleased, somewhat mystified look, and walked to the quarterdeck. "Nobby, fire up when ready!"

CHAPTER 21

The Reef of Time

Nuku Hiva, Marquesas, to Takaroa, Tuamotu Archipelago
April 16 to 24

THE JAGGED RIDGES OF NUKU HIVA AND NEIGHBOURING
Ua Pou serrated the afternoon sky. A great vein of quartz
bolted through the near bluff of Taiohae Bay. We set all sail
from royals to spanker, and in variable wind drifted and
rolled through the night and all the next day. Every hour for
thirty hours, a helmsman was relieved to enter the charthouse and pencil in our position on a white plotting sheet.
For the position, she'd look at the GPS precisely on the
hour, log the coordinates to the nearest hundredth of a
mile, then plot a dot, write in the corresponding time, and
draw a triangle around the dot to show it had been deduced
electronically. The last thirty hours' marks combined to
make a short fat grey worm across the sheet.

Standing outside the charthouse and looking beyond the
limp spanker, the weathered teak taffrail and our mean-
dering wake, one could still see Nuku Hiva resting large on
the horizon.

We stowed sail and steamed, setting sail again the next
morning to be pushed by a light southeast trade. Over the
week-long passage the ship seemed eerily quiet and sleepy

with so few bodies aboard. Duties like steering, lookout and galley came around more often, and time seemed to pass faster. I wrote in my journal:

It's crazy how much I'm enjoying myself. The South Pacific is so enticing. We crossed just under half the ocean in what really doesn't seem like three months. Despite the fickle trades, I feel like the next four months will pass faster than any period in my life. The islands are so dense on this half of the ocean that we shouldn't be more than two days between most of them. People are going to start to get into the sailing and the travel. I am going to experience as much as I can.

It occurred to me how great this voyage is. We converted this old steamer into a first-class square-rigger, one of the very best in North America, and as if that wasn't enough, we're sailing it around the world. Work work work like you've never worked before. Next day: sail around the World! No wonder I was burnt out. Until perhaps a month ago, I was sure that I would be perfectly able to fit back into normal society again. Now I hope I never do.

But, these days, following the departure of five more people, we are left with a solid core crew and I'm worried for the first time that our voyage might not be completed. The fuel that we bought in the Marquesas costs $40 an hour to burn. As long as the trades are light, this is an extremely expensive voyage. I want to sail home on this Ship!

Four times during the passage we took in sail, and four times we set sail. After the last time we set sail, the Captain gathered us for a muster.

He spoke of the Tuamotus, the Dangerous Archipelago. The island chain stretches over a thousand miles from northwest to southeast, and it's riddled with unpredictable currents and capricious squalls. The islands themselves are barely above sea level and their tallest features are coconut palms, making them hard to observe at a distance. Our destination was Takaroa, a low coral atoll that forms an oblong ring of sand surrounding a shallow coral lagoon. The lagoon has a few narrow openings to the ocean, only one of which is navigable.

The Captain said that as the tide drops around the atoll, water rushes out of the lagoon through the narrow coral-walled cut. One of his navigational publications said it could run twenty knots at max ebb, another said nine. *Nine knots.* I remembered that nine knots was near our maximum speed, and chuckled as I imagined us charging full bore up a raging river and barely moving. That, of course, would not be the preferred method of approach, as the slightest steering error would send us onto the reef. Instead, we were to enter the cut just as the current gently ebbed from the lagoon. The extra water flowing past the rudder would improve steerage and make it easier to lay the ship against the dock.

One of the best features of the island, the Captain told us, is a wonderfully preserved wreck of the *County of Roxburgh*, a 2,000-ton, four-masted, full-rigged ship nearly three hundred feet long, tossed high and dry on the beach by the seventy-foot-high breakers of a 1906 cyclone. We'd be able to walk all around her. Climb inside her.

Takaroa Island was close on our port bow when the mate called me to the helm. There was no wind. The water was glassy and rolling with swells that reflected the intense morning sun. The island appeared to be a line of palms interrupted by the rusting wreck that hulked above the tops of the highest trees.

We steamed past the wreck, turned and passed by closer, then turned and passed by again. As we passed, the crew lined the rail to see the jaunty sweep of her great deck. She was many times larger than the *Picton Castle.* It was hard to believe that even a cyclone could have launched her so far onto the beach.

We steamed about three miles along the shore. There was not a single dwelling until we approached the cut to the lagoon. The tide was still on the rise and water rushed in, making it unfavourable for an entrance. The Captain needed to kill a couple of hours, so he ordered the mate to let go the anchor on the outer reef. There we snorkelled in the brilliant light of noon that illuminated the colourful fishes, small reef sharks and corals. The underwater terrain was shallow and pounded nearly as smooth as concrete, except in the cut leading past the town dock to inside the atoll. There, it was eroded deep and narrow by the water that had torn in and out twice a day for eternity.

When the tide changed, it was time for swimmers to return. Brian discreetly called me as I rinsed off my fins. He pointed away from the shore and said, "I think Jean's having trouble. Let's go."

We motored the skiff over to her. She had been too far from the ship when the current changed. It grew stronger by the minute, pulling her away from the island. The water had made the single grey braid that she hadn't cut since childhood thin like a wet cat's tail. She climbed aboard, embarrassed that she hadn't made it back under her own steam, but from the ripples forming on the water we knew it could have happened to anyone, and told her so. Jean was an exceptionally fit sixty-three-year-old with a bicyclist's physique. It hurt to see her demoralized. With so many crew leaving, her cheerful and silent determination to continue was a growing inspiration for us.

Aboard ship, we prepared docklines and fenders to tie up alongside the town dock. But during our work the growing current dragged the ship and anchor off the island's smooth coral ledge. It happened fast. I had no idea we were dragging until we were sent to the windlass.

Two hundred and seventy feet of chain—three tons—hung straight down. A one-ton anchor dangled on its end. It was early afternoon, the hottest part of the day. The dark, oiled decks radiated heat. Harsh sunlight glared off the mirror of the sea. No breeze to wick away the heat. Brian ordered crew to pump the windlass bars.

"Heave along," he said.

Ten strong crew strained together. The bars flexed. Brian sent more crew to the windlass bars—six per side. We strained. The chain did not budge. One side up. One side down. Switch. Up. Down. Up. Down.

Nothing.

The Captain came to the fo'c'sle head to confer with Brian. They looked over the bow into the water.

They ordered a hand to retrieve one of the heavy white hawsers that lay on the well deck. She dragged the shiny synthetic rope to the Captain, who tied it to the chain with a series of hitches and wrapped the other end about the capstan drum. He ordered six hands to install the six wooden bars in the capstan. With them in place, "heave along," he ordered.

The hawser constricted on the capstan drum, squeaking and popping as it bound on the whelps. The hitches that bound hawser to chain rolled tight, tortured about the hand-sized links. The hawser stretched, became thinner. Six crew leaned into their bars. The hawser shimmied on the drum. The force became too great. The capstan crew could move no further.

"Heave along on the windlass," the Captain ordered.

With six people on the capstan and twelve on the wind-lass, the chain did not budge.

"Avast heaving." The Captain told Nobby to shut down the engine. We drifted away in the light wind. He ordered the crew on the capstan bars to push in the other direction, using the capstan's lower gear. He ordered Brian to have the crew try again.

"Heave along on the capstan. Heave along on the windlass," Brian ordered. The windlass bars clanked in their sockets as we called out a rhythm and heaved. Nothing.

"Double bank the capstan," he ordered, and a second person jumped into place behind each of the six capstan bars.

"Stand by to heave along. Heave along!" he said.

We strained on the windlass. Sweat stained our clothes. Our skin seemed to grow more tanned by the minute and veins on biceps pulsed, turgid with blood.

"Port lift. Port down."

Hawser bit into chain and capstan drum. We worked in time. The anchor gave an inch. We strained. It crept towards us link by link.

Four feet later, the knots securing hawser to chain had reached the end of their throw.

"Avast heaving," said the mate. He retied the hawser.

Eighteen sailors strained. Sweat dripped across sunglass lenses. Hair stuck to foreheads. Rust smeared hands. We grew grumpy.

With only ninety feet of chain remaining below water, we could get a hold of it, and the anchor rose four inches with every stroke. The Captain ordered that the engine be started. Brian ordered me to the wheel.

I walked quickly aft. My arms were sore and shaky, but I knew I would not need strength to steer the ship into the cut. The Captain spoke to me quickly of the current. I assured him I understood how sensitive the steering would be, steaming against it.

I wondered how fast it was moving and calculated that it was very near its maximum speed. Yet to wait for the current to subside would mean losing the last daylight, and with it our visibility of the cut's reef walls. *Can the ship go fast enough? Can we back out? It's shoot the cut or put to sea.*

Without delay, the Captain put the engine in gear and ordered me to shape up on the cut. I could easily see where the Captain wanted me to head the ship. A tense mound of rushing water frothing at its edges defined the cut. I made for the middle.

The engine was above an idle. The mate stood on the fo'c'sle head looking towards the rushing water. The decks were still. I realized that no one could help now.

The ship slowed as it entered the faster current. I heard the water rush loud around the hull plate. The ship slowed and held station. The Captain signalled Nobby to increase the throttle. The ship advanced.

Standing alongside the wheel, I sighted down the deck planks and aimed for a distant point on the island's far side. I shifted the wheel inches at a time, aware of the shore's closeness on each side of the bow, correcting before she could peel off towards the bank. I kept an eye on the Captain for orders as he moved quickly from rail to rail, always trying for a better view of the channel walls in the failing sunlight.

Water surged within the cut. I thought of the *Roxburgh*, her breeched hull high and dry three miles away. I cleared my mind. The steering grew ever more sensitive. The Captain increased the throttle. He gave tidy indications with his fingers when he wanted me to inch farther from one of the coral walls.

I could now see them through the boiling water, their surface crenulated like a great petrified brain. The water grew faster. I entered a state of calm—only the helm, the cut, the Captain's gestures. He ordered more throttle. We barely eked ahead. I knew the slightest error now would catch the ship, send her against the wall. I moved her a touch towards the centre as I felt her wander; the Captain's fingers confirmed it. Halogen light lit the dock. We were getting closer. Crew stood by the hawsers prepared to throw heaving lines ashore. The current grew. The Captain opened the throttle wide. Grey diesel smoke blasted from the funnel. That old slow-turner clattered like machine-gun fire. We inched ahead alongside the dock. The Captain ordered the throttle back a touch. We held station with the shore.

The Captain looked back at me. With the tips of his fingers rubbing together as if he gestured money, he directed me to move slowly towards the dock, and almost imperceptibly I turned the wheel. I moved it back to centre as the current caught the ship and crabbed her towards the dock. The Captain's tongue searched the sides of his mouth. Crew shifted fenders over the side. Bow, stern and spring, the lines went to the dock.

For two hours we worked to secure a fendering system that would manage the current, chafe and range of tidal height. It was well past suppertime when we finished. I walked forward as we were finishing and the Captain's voice rang out from above on the bridge: "Good job, Rigel." The compliment shot through me like a drug.

With the ship secured, we gathered at the aloha deck for a late supper. It was nearly 2100 hours and we were tired. On the dock, a group of Takaroan men gathered to drink and look at the ship. We heard them laugh at a pack of small, feral dogs that spent their lives chasing each other to mount a yelping victim.

In the morning, our watch painted the offshore side of the ship from the skiff. There we learned that the island's children were nearly as frenzied as its dogs, running and jumping into the current, being carried along to climb out farther down the dock. Every so often a child dared climb aboard ship and dive off the bow or headrig splotched with paint.

Crew filtered in that evening with stories of the *Roxburgh* and the town's ice-cream stand. I was eager to get off the ship and explore, so my dock watch went by slowly.

The next morning, I awoke early and trundled to the main salon, hardly aware of its gym locker smell. My friend Don hadn't shown up until late at night and I wondered what adventures he'd had.

"Good morning."

He rolled over, looking sated and smelling sour. He grinned as he reached into the trough alongside his mattress and handed me a matchbox with a hibiscus flower printed on the top. The edges of the box were worn and its cardboard was moist like it had spent a long time in his sweaty pocket. A carefully tied string bound the matchbox tightly shut. "Open it," he said.

I pulled aside the string and pushed open the box. It was chock full of black pearls—round, tear-shaped, smooth, ribbed, purple-black, blue and steely.

"Holy shit. Where did you get these?"

"Lucky Luc gave them to me. He had a bowlful on his table and told me to take some. Every time I took some, he told me to take some more."

"But where were you?"

"On some distant *motu*, I don't know where. I met a young guy with a Vespa. Tim. A skinny kid. Long hair. Self-esteem issues. He took me on his Vespa drunk out of his mind racing across the Tarmac."

"The Tarmac?"

"There's an airstrip. Pan-Pacific flights stop here. He took me to his uncle's house. I drank Cutty Sark from a jelly nut and we smoked weed and someone offered me his granddaughter."

"Oh my god. Did you accept?"

"No. But they gave me the pearls and then we came back here. One of my friend Tim's cousins kicked his ass on the dock and he was so angry. That's why I think he has issues."

Don had done it: he'd found adventure with the locals. I wanted to go immediately. Don climbed down from his bunk and we walked into town and had ice cream for breakfast. We joined Tom and Andrew and ran into Don's Vespa friend, Tim.

We finally prevailed on Tim to take us to the *Roxburgh*. Growing up across the road from the great ship, he had apparently never come to appreciate its novelty. We pushed through low pandanus fronds and there, resting on big white coral stones, the *Roxburgh* towered above us. I was struck that after ninety-two years on the beach she gave the impression that she could be dragged off and sailed away.

The side facing us looked sturdy enough for sea duty. An enormous bower anchor dangled from her fo'c'sle head rail. Her rivets looked solid and the hull plating had suffered only an even dusting of rust. Only the bow and stern had been rent through.

I walked closer, and as I approached, she seemed to grow up out of the stony beach. Amidships, a hole was rent in her bilge where her back had been broken on the reef. We entered there and walked aft through the lower hold, which was as big as a cathedral. Shafts of sunlight darted through the deck to illuminate the remains of cement ballast poured between her frames, still in near-perfect condition. The coolness and the thundering surf that echoed within gave the sense that we were in a seashell.

As is often the case, many factors led to her destruction. Obviously, she'd been caught in a hurricane on the lee shore of the Pacific's most notorious stretch of reefs; but it was the lack of cargo in her hold that had made her float so high and thus unmanageable that day in 1906, as she skidded over growing seas, her rudder and keel unable to gain the traction that could allow her to be turned away from danger. A sailing ship needed cargo in every sense, and she was bound from Caldera, on the west coast of South America, to Australia with just a small amount of sand ballast. In Australia she would have been loaded with grain, one of the last cargos available to these ships.

Everything about that shipwreck breathed authenticity. It felt weird walking her decks, having arrived on a ship converted to imitate her. Nearly all of us were at least two generations removed from the last man to work in a vessel like this that was engaged in commerce. Adventure travel is a sort of commerce, but seeing this ship that sailed because she *had to* made me wonder why we imitated her, when clearly we didn't have to.

I had just finished reading Stephen Hawking's *A Brief History of Time.* He'd offered a proof that the timeline of the universe (big bang to dispersion or collapse) and the timeline of our own lives actually go in the same direction. The direction, he asserted, doesn't really matter, but that both have the same direction does. What it means is that time (memory, aging, causes and effects) is characterized by a loss of order—the loss of an original state or structure.

I felt that the *Picton Castle* was a mini-universe—a small-scale entropy machine—where the original order was a way of life as distant as the rusted shell of the *County of Roxburgh* that lay beneath our feet.

Why do we try to freeze time in 1906? Aren't those memories and practices also subject to the same decay of time? Or are love and the unchanging sea enough to keep them complete?

Soon we left the *Roxburgh* to surf and sip rum on the beach with some islanders. At the end of the day I headed back to the ship, wondering what I'd do with the next day on the island. But when I arrived, the Captain was pacing the deck.

He passed orders. He looked over the sides. He examined the lines and ordered bo'sun Josh to hoist the boat we had resting on the dock. He was waiting for word from a supply vessel that needed our berth that night. "Is everyone here?" he demanded.

"No," I replied.

"Round everybody up. I need everyone back on the ship, now."

"Round everybody up," I repeated, then turned and ran through the streets. I'd seen that the current was running back out to sea. I prepared myself for the ordeal of steering the ship down current. When a ship moves downstream slower than the current, her rudder has the opposite effect.

I found only one pack of sailors out for some late night ice cream. We hurried aboard. The engine was running and the docklines were singled up. Brian took a head count. He ordered general quarters and hustled to his position on the bow, searchlight in hand. It was dark.

I ran to the wheel. The Captain briefed me quickly on steering downstream and I told him I understood.

He ordered that the bowline be cast off and the bow spring. The outrushing current caught hold of the bow and peeled the ship off the dock. Her stern was pinned by a spring line leading forward from the quarter. Soon she was perpendicular to the dock and swinging wide across the channel into a spot widened by dynamite.

The Captain powered the stern away from the pier into the current. With a few helm orders we were washed quickly away from the channel walls and into open ocean.

CHAPTER 22

Stolen Knives

Apataki, Tuamotu Archipelago, to Bora-Bora, Society Islands
25 April to 23 May

FOR TWO NIGHTS AND A DAY, WE SAILED TO AN UNINHABITED
atoll called Apataki. We steamed between white sand *motus*,
or small islands, with palm trees bursting from them and
opened the throttle to beat the fast current that boiled and
twisted around reef heads and shallows.

The Captain guided us through, keeping an eye on the
sunlit reef rippling green and blue through the water. Then
we dropped the hook, furled all sail and spent an hour
more squaring and levelling the yards to a state of perfection, as if we were on display in a crowded harbour.

That day, Brian turned thirty-two. For supper, Pasha
prepared roast beef and mashed potatoes, Brian's
favourite. After cake, I watched a number of crew stand up
to give him a gift. Nothing big, just special items from
their personal stashes: a wedge of Laughing Cow Cheese,
a bottle of soy sauce, gum, a Pop-Tart, peanuts, a can
of Coke.

"I can't imagine a better way to spend my birthday," he
said. "It's such a privilege to be in the lagoon of a deserted
atoll, halfway around the world, with all of you."

The next day, we were invited to snorkel. While most of the crew splashed around in the water, I began work on a knife for my father that I'd been designing since the Marquesas. I based the blade shape on Brian's knife—a traditional German sailor's knife of a style once issued by the *Sea Cloud*, a four-masted barque out of Hamburg. It was utilitarian and handsome, with a straight blade one inch wide that curved to a point like a spade. I intended the handle to be more ornate and form-fitting than Brian's, with a guard to prevent the hand from slipping into the blade. The lanyard hole would be a copper tube, flanged at its ends to act as a rivet. The handle I wanted to cross-hatch, like a pistol.

I heard the crew splashing around and raving about the sights. It made me wonder why I worked so doggedly on the knife. I thought back to the previous summer.

It was a hot day for Nova Scotia. The ship was half finished and we were circumnavigating Cape Breton to raise money for the rest of the conversion, working on the ship the whole time. We'd stepped all masts and crossed all yards but the royals. As we travelled, we bent on new sail and the Captain drilled us on setting and furling. Only one of us had worked on a sailing ship as technologically advanced as a late-nineteenth-century split topsail rig, and it was good to learn the details.

We were steaming on a windless passage between ports and had just furled the foresail after a drill. From the well deck, by the galley house, I saw something fall from the foreyard, way out over the water.

"Oh my god, Rigel," my father said, searching his waist and looking concerned, eyes wide through his glasses. "I think that was my knife. How did it come off?" he said in disbelief, knowing how greatly it was frowned upon to drop gear from the rig. I imagined that, in sliding along the yard, the tang of his belt buckle had been pried open and the belt was released. It spent a few minutes snagged on a piece of gear before it finally let go and fell to the sea.

It was not just the disappointment in his eyes but how he'd sharpened it to a razor's edge at every opportunity that made me see how he'd adored that knife. It was a gift from his mother, something she'd bought for him on her travels to Italy. It was a slender thing, hand-forged in Sweden, with a hard core that could take an edge and soft cheeks for flexibility.

I found a good blade for his replacement knife. I needed carbon steel, not stainless—something that would sharpen nicely and develop character over time. I'd had my eye on a galley knife for a while, the only one that wasn't stainless. It was a cheap Brazilian make, but the steel was good. One of our six previous cooks had broken the tip off and the edge was deeply nicked. I told Pasha I'd take the knife off his hands. And though I knew its poor condition didn't make it mine, I took it.

The nicks and the break helped justify the act, but there was something else. Many months after my father lost his knife and resigned from the ship, we were walking on the shore by our home in Rose Bay. "The ship stole my knife," he said. "Now that was a sign."

I furtively took the damaged blade to the engine room as the rest of the crew splashed around, smacking fins, clearing snorkels. I climbed down the steel diamond plate ladder on bare feet to the steel floorboards aft of the massive engine, alongside the propeller shaft where engineer Nobby had a bench.

With a marker I drew the shape I wanted the knife to be. In the *Ernestina*, Moreland had shown me the qualities it should possess. "A sailor's knife should be simple and sturdy. It should have a straight blade, able to go in a sheath—not a jackknife. That way you can get it with one hand. It should have a roundish point and a thick blade so you can use it to pry open paint cans."

Engineer Nobby had a bench, a vise and metalworking tools there that he let me use. I secured the knife in the vise, drilled out its rivets and smacked off the cheeks of its handle with a hammer. With a hacksaw, I cut out the knife's outline. Shifting the knife in its vise, I tried to prevent it from vibrating and chattering the saw's teeth off. Still, many broke and it became hard work. In the hot air, with the diesel engines radiating heat, I became covered in a layer of greasy sweat that soaked my hair and ran into my eyes and waistband.

With Nobby's coarse bastard file, I gave the blade a new taper. I shaped the belly of the blade using a technique he'd shown me to create perfectly fair curves. Then, covered in steel filings that sparkled in my sweat, I cleaned up the tools and took my new blade and scraps on deck.

I placed the knife in the fo'c'sle and drew some water from over the side to clean myself up. I felt good about my progress. But when the crew returned from snorkelling, I realized that I had missed out.

They raved of the colours—the purples and blues, the pinks and greens; of the complexities of coral orbs and fans and fingers; of a profusion of fishes; of the wavy purple lips of a thousand giant clams.

The passage to Tahiti was short and sleepy, with the ship on an easy broad reach. We'd set all sail before the cool, fair wind, and now hardly noticed when our curving bow scared up schools of flying fish that soared from our headrig.

Sunrise illuminated the tall green pyramid of Tahiti, draped in laces of golden street lights, a few miles away. We cleaned ourselves and we cleaned the ship. We pulled alongside and new crew were there waiting for us, people I didn't recognize, others I did. Mildred had overcome her first physiotherapist's predictions and strengthened her ankle enough to rejoin the ship. Drummer Todd had returned. Baker Beth, a cheerful friend of the ship, had come from Lunenburg to help in the galley. Loco Kim's wife, Jill, had arrived with a mailbag.

We eased alongside the pier, just off a street busy with cars, walkers, black-pearl jewellers, restaurants and tattoo shops. Yachts were anchored close to shore, their sterns tied to the piers, their chains leading ahead, so they looked like horses tied to a rail outside a tavern.

As we doubled the lines, Mildred summoned Pasha from the galley. She handed her bags to him and told him to take them below to her bunk. Then she quickly left the dock for her air-conditioned hotel room. The other new arrivals, less seasoned, more eager to fit in and be a help, met their shipmates and secured chafe gear to the docklines.

In the hot sun of noon we mustered around the cargo hatch. I took my usual position in the periphery next to Don and third mate Tom. Like me, they hoped for a letter from loves at home. Many names were called, and it was hard to bear the sight of crew holding an envelope with both hands, concentrating so hard they might be hoping to see through it.

Finally, Jill gave me a letter from my family that she'd carried all the way from Lunenburg. Later that night, when I had a moment alone, I opened three letters from my mother, my father and my sister.

I opened the one from my dad. All at once I yearned to connect with him, but was afraid of what that connection might yield.

Rigel, my son,

Two months have slipped by since I last sat down to write to you. Miles and gallons have passed under you as you continue on your adventure. Needless to say, we follow your voyage with

*avid interest and, in my case at least, a little jealousy. I am so
happy for you, though, that you are getting such a rich experience and trust that you are taking all that you can from it . . .*

*I believe that there is a balance in the universe, and that if
you have been given an opportunity to learn that is one in a
million, or ten million, then you will likewise have an opportunity to enrich the lives of that many. This should not be a burden, but an even greater gift. I don't know how all of this will
unfold, but I'm sure that it will and I know that you will always
be joyful and spread joy around you . . .*

*Send me good thoughts and joyful ones and live these days to
their fullest, 'cause you're living them for me, as well. I love you.*

The letter gave me mixed feelings. He'd had trouble
getting back on his feet when the ship left town, and that
hurt to hear. But I was glad to have his blessing to be on the
voyage.

The next day, I left Papeete to hitchhike around Tahiti by
myself. I would get away from the claustrophobia of the
ship and look for another spot to surf—hopefully a beach,
not a reef. It was easy to hitchhike in Tahiti; people were
trusting and generous.

A short ride brought me to a beach. There was no surf,
but at least I was away from the city. I sat in the sand and
tried to relax, but soon became restless. I walked on in lush
grass alongside the narrow blacktop. My hair brushed the
low branches of white-blossomed trees. Soon a sweat broke
on my forehead from the rising humidity. The sky grew dark
and I knew it would rain. I no longer looked for a ride but for
a shop, a bar, anything to get me out of the rain already
starting to fall.

There was a tree ahead of me, heavy with star fruit. I took
one down and sliced into it with the Swiss Army knife my
father had given me. It was bitter, but good.

Hidden beyond the branches of the star fruit tree was a sign, *Musée Paul Gauguin*. The museum was a modest bungalow. No guards. The sky opened just as I entered, and I made a silent wish that no one from the ship would be there. Outside, big drops of rain slapped the gravel drive in a constant hush.

I walked in the mind of the artist. I admired the sugary Polynesian women he chose as his subject, so warm and calm and irresistible that he'd left behind his wife and family for them.

The *Bounty* mutineers, some of whom stayed ashore for months, rarely returning to the ship, formed ties with lovers and families here. To an extent it was these ties, combined with the relative weight of this new experience over what they'd known in England, that compelled them to steal the *Bounty* and stay in Polynesia.

I examined an artifact displayed in the middle of the room: a wooden box, dark like walnut and oiled so it looked even darker. It was rectangular and carved out of a solid block. Gauguin had sawn off the top and gouged out the inside. It was not a simple holder of trinkets. The artist had carved a miniature of his own corpse inside, so that the box was no longer the cheerful thing it appeared on the outside, but his coffin. I wondered if it symbolized his resolve to stay in Polynesia.

The hush of the rain was soothing, and I walked to a quiet corner of the museum. I pulled a pad of unlined paper from my backpack. It was wrinkled from rain. I wrote Ariel a letter.

I'm in the corner of a room of the Paul Gauguin Museum in Tahiti. Today, I'm on a hitchhiking tour of the island, checking out the surf spots. It started to rain an hour ago and I ended up here. Pretty convenient, but I hope it stops soon so I can hitch home in comfort.

I'm five or six months into this voyage and I'm starting to get over the growing pains caused by taking on a new lifestyle. I still don't know how long I'm going to continue working on sailing ships. Sometimes I think I'd like to run my own.

I got some letters from my folks here. Reading them has made me miss them terribly. I guess I'm a little sad that I didn't get any letters from you. I know your letter could have been returned. There is a policy here to hold them only for a few weeks, and we are far later than that. But I also realize that you are busy crafting a changed life out of all the moves, travelling and new friends. So it makes sense to put some stuff behind you. Still, I want to maintain a connection, a different kind of friendship. Where we used to enjoy wasting time together, I now enjoy sitting down and writing you long circular letters. I miss you.

Love, Rigel

I wondered, after the heavy rain stopped, why, in Polynesia, I missed so much a girl whom I hadn't seen for nearly a year. The *Bounty* mutineers didn't look back. Gauguin didn't look back. Perhaps I was too wrapped up in the past, or in a hope for the future. Perhaps I was disappointed because the promise of Tahitian women, advertised on Hinano beer labels, didn't yield the expected.

Each night, you check out the bar scene. You buy a matchbox of weed and, stoned, walk to the bars. On the way you meet a couple of girls. Always they're more outgoing, more flattering, more hungry than any women you've ever met. Their legs are longer, slimmer. Their bellies harder. Their breasts perkier. Through your altered state you try to hold the thread of conversation. You grow suspicious that maybe you are, in fact, too lucky. You tune in to her voice, notice her strain to sound more feminine, notice her Adam's apple, the hard line and shadow of her jaw, and you make some phony excuse to leave. You (already wise) watch

the white foreign men move in as they grin with the knowledge, *I am going to get lucky tonight.*

Don, a student of anthropology, who'd had the honour of
fending off the advances of Miss Tahiti Transsexual 1997,
told me that Tahitians have always had a place of respect for
men who wish to be women. But where are the women who
wish to be with men?

From Tahiti, we steamed a few hours to neighbouring
Morea. Each stop, each day off, we collected memories of
Polynesia—of dances, tattoos, waterfalls, of kind people.
From Morea we sailed for Huahine.

With all sail set, we meandered at two and a half knots.
Drifting very slowly, there was plenty of time to think how
we were travelling around the world sometimes slower
than we could swim. Still, the ship was more full now, and
it was seeming less and less likely that the voyage would
implode for lack of crew.

But the ship's harmony was disturbed like the mud at
the bottom of the channel in the harbour of Huahine,
where we dropped the hook one evening in chilly rain and
climbed aloft to furl all sail. It wasn't long before a local
authority was shouting to the quarterdeck from his skiff,
telling us to move to a more suitable anchorage.

The mate called us down from the rig to weigh anchor.
We worked with arms goosebumped by cold rain, watching
the steeply, sloped landscape of Huahine bounce up and
down over the windlass bars.

That evening, at anchor farther from town, when darkness set, we had an after-supper rum punch. In the glow of
the anchor light, Jesse, Tom and I stood around the fife rail
of the foremast drinking from plastic cups. Jesse had
cleaned himself up after weighing anchor. His hair was
neatly parted and combed into a ponytail. He'd washed off
the smudges of tar and grease that darkened his face

each day as he wiped sweat from his eyes. He pulled his plastic cup of Goslings and water from his mouth and smiled mischievously. "Nice job making the royal footropes three feet too short."

I thought with injured pride of the royal footropes I'd made back in Lunenburg, and how we'd only realized the flaw when we crossed the yards halfway to Pitcairn Island. Though it had been over two months since the deed, I lashed back. "I just made them to spec. Maybe it was the guy who gave me the measurements," I said, insinuating the Captain. "Nice job making the fore t'gallant stay eight feet too short."

"That wasn't my fault!" he said, offended. "Maybe it was the guy who measured the t'gallant lifts too short." He smiled in complicity.

"Or the lower masts too long!"

"Or the mizzen-topmast too long!"

We were busting into devilish laughter at the instant the Captain walked towards us and entered the glow of the anchor light. I saw over Jesse's shoulder that he'd realized the subject of our laughter. His face lost its granite confidence. He looked deeply hurt, then turned away and walked to his cabin.

Jesse saw me stop laughing and leaned against the fife rail as if catching his breath. "Why didn't you tell me he was behind me?"

"I didn't know."

We stood around for a couple of minutes, finishing the rum the Captain had supplied, feeling like dogs who had bitten their master.

When it was time for the ship to leave Huahine, the next evening, the Captain ordered the mate to heave along on the windlass. We crew heaved away, and after the first shift, Brian sent me back to the wheel.

I checked the wheel for midships, then looked up at the rig against the tall green slope of Huahine. All square sails hung neatly in their bunts, cast free from their gaskets. The engine was off and the slow clank of the windlass was the only sound, echoing off the slopes.

"Sheet home the fore lower topsail," the Captain said calmly and slowly.

The crew obeyed quickly and the chain sheets rattled clearly above the sound of the windlass.

"Hard right." He turned towards me and spoke the order, then looked to the foredeck. "Set the outer jib and sheet to starboard. Back the fores'l."

The ship rotated, pointing her bow away from the shore towards the sea. The Captain ordered the rest of the sails set, and they glowed warmly in the fleeting tropical sunset. He told me to steer the vessel between the tiny wavelets that lapped at the entrance to the barrier reef. Despite the sun's low angle I saw the reef's colours, luminous beneath the water. That same low light deepened the reds and browns of the quarterdeck's pine planks. I felt a sense of goodwill run through the ship, and couldn't help but think that the Captain had attracted our frustration for a period and then diverted it to the sea like a lightning rod.

After a nighttime passage, we entered the cut through the ring of coral and *motus* that cradled the forested island of Bora-Bora. That island's two black towers of basalt jutted high above its forest.

The day after arrival, at anchor in the middle of a protected bay, we had a morning muster. Already crew looked longingly at the shore.

"Bora-Bora is circled by a protected lagoon. I'd like you to use the longboat to make an expedition around the island," the Captain said, while offering his description of the island, recalled from his visit twenty years before. He handed the floor to the mate.

"We're spending six days here. I've broken down the watch system so two groups can take the Monomoy long-boat on an expedition. However, the only way it will work is if the first group leaves today."

The crew eligible for the first circumnavigation shifted on their feet indecisively. I understood the fear that a group activity could destroy the autonomy that we coveted ashore, but the trip seemed attractive. It was a chance to have a mission, to make it what we wanted.

"I'm in," I said.

"Rigel's in," Brian said. "Anyone else?"

No one would jump forward and commit, acting as though, if they had another day to decide, they'd go, but now the notice was too short. I saw the adventure that had already taken shape in my imagination disintegrating, leaving me no options but to wander tourist shops in Bora-Bora and waste the days, drunk on overpriced Hinano beer.

Brian spoke up again. "It ain't gonna happen if you don't go."

"Yeah, let's go." It was Patrick, speaking through a toothy smile.

Once Patrick was in, everyone wanted to go. With his sense of humour and generosity, it was a guaranteed good time just to be near him. Friends Don and Marcello were next. Second engineer Claire and Jean quickly followed suit, and I found myself at the centre of the provisioning effort, compiling a list and coordinating the supplying of the boat, excited to lead the expedition. Everyone acted in a flurry of enthusiasm and I did my best to stay out of the way.

Soon, Brian approached me. He stood close and fixed me with that look he reserved for delivering disappointing news. "Rige, Dan wants me to go on the expedition."

"Sure."

"I think he just wants someone to be there to make command decisions if necessary. You know?"

"Of course." He knew I'd let myself think I'd lead the expedition.

"I just don't know if I want to go."

"No, it'll be good."

"It will be good, won't it?"

"We'll make it good."

"We'll make it good. It looks like you guys have this provisioning under control. I don't want to interfere. I'll get ready." Then he turned and strode to his cabin.

Shortly thereafter, Doctor Beth approached. She was excited about the trip as well, and told me she was going to bring the first aid.

But she wouldn't need it. We camped two nights under the stars. And while the eight of us sailed, sitting comfortably in the open boat, Don and Patrick played guitar. Brian stood on the stern sheets and steered with the long sculling oar most of the time. Claire, used to the solitude of her role on the ship, always found helpful tasks apart from the mob efforts of the rest of the crew. I made adjustments to the lug rig that made the Monomoy look even more like a whaling boat, and I talked to Marcello. Ever since he'd predicted to the minute the time our transom would cross the last of Panama's locks to the Pacific, I'd been interested in getting to know him.

"Can I see your knife, Marcello?" I asked, pointing to the black sheath that dangled from his plaited leather belt. Marcello pulled the knife from its sheath and frowned because faint lines of rust marred its surface. Its handle was ebony, with six small bronze rivets arranged in pairs. The blade glowed with the inner warmth of hand-forged steel. It was heavy and thick, but its daring curves and artful proportions made it a pleasure to hold. "Where did you get it?"

"Oh . . . Well, I was flipping through a hunting magazine. I don't hunt any more, but I used to. I came across this ad for handmade knives in Montana. I called the guy and he said, 'Sure I'll make you one, but I have a twenty-year waiting list.'"

"No."

"Yeah, really. So I called him a couple days later." Marcello held his hand to his ear like it was a telephone receiver. "'Hi, I'm calling from the Department of Lands and Forests in Quebec. We have a Russian ambassador coming for an important visit. I would like to present him one of your knives this summer.' And he said, 'Send me two hundred bucks.'"

"Two hundred bucks? You did that?"

He giggled. "Yeah. And a couple of months later, I'd forgotten I'd ordered it, a package arrived in the mail. Lookee here."

I pressed Marcello for more stories like this. He told me that in Morea, he, Patrick and Don spent a free night at Club Med because they'd borrowed the ship's video camera and pretended to be doing a publicity piece. With each story I gained a deeper appreciation for his cleverness.

Marcello was soft-spoken but a constant source of enthusiasm for the crew. Just about everyone on the ship wanted to spend time with him—especially now that it looked like he might have to leave the voyage, just when it was getting fun.

"My brother hasn't fully paid me for my pet hotel," he said. "That's why I might have to leave. I'll know for sure when I can get into town and make a call."

And when the expedition was through and he did get into town, the news was that he'd have to leave. The parties at the crew's adopted boarding house, Lait du Coco, centred on his departure. His popularity grew, and in the days that followed he found a lovely girlfriend ashore. Her Martinique father had given her the tight curls in her black hair, which she sometimes wore bouffant with a hibiscus bloom behind her ear. Her first name was Hinano, like the beer label. She explained to us that *Hinano* was actually the name of a native flower; and something girlish in her curious eyebrows, her small flat nose and the dark freckles over her high cheekbones hid the fact that she'd explained the difference a thousand times before.

When it was time to leave Bora-Bora, the noontime sun lit up the blues and greens of the lagoon. We stood by the windlass to weigh anchor. As we strained on the bars, this time laughing and eager, we heard the roar of a powerful speedboat approaching.

It was a many-coloured V-bottom thing—a work boat, driven by Hinano's father. Marcello stood beside him, his arm around Hinano, who wore a string bikini that revealed her delicate frame and a row of simple triangles tattooed down the curve of her spine.

They circled the ship as our anchor broke the water's surface. Marcello and Hinano tossed flower blossoms from their boat as they circled and circled, until the ship was surrounded by a halo of hibiscus petals. Then they turned and left as we pushed off to sea.

With my duties completed, I went to my bunk to write in my journal. I grabbed the book and looked for a pen. When I shifted my pillow to feel around, I found the cold handle and leather sheath of Marcello's knife.

CHAPTER 23

Adoption

Bora-Bora, Society Islands, to Rarotonga and Palmerston,
Cook Islands
May 23 to June 14

Sunday morning, sailing to Rarotonga, Tom and I stared east, waiting for the sun to rise. Already, bright Venus had risen in conjunction with Saturn. Jupiter had been up for hours. An outstretched hand held at arm's length marks half the territory owned by each member of the zodiac. Using my hands, I measured off the constellations until I deduced the sun would rise in Gemini. The eastern horizon was deep blue where sunlight seeped into the night. It felt good to be back at sea.

Standing on the quarterdeck, I had the impression that, instead of sailing west, the ship was actually fixed in space and it was the earth that turned under us, while we churned it up in a frothy wake, faintly orange now in the sun's spreading light. This route, lying between the most common jumping-off place in the Society Islands and the most common entry point in the Cooks, was heavily trafficked by circumnavigators. I almost expected to see their tracks.

Sky and water turned a paler blue. Saturn faded away, then Jupiter, then Venus. The air grew hot with the sunrise.

Tom pulled off his T-shirt to reveal his new tattoo, a pattern of bold, unconnected black shapes that covered his shoulder in an ellipse. A similar band ran beneath it. It was still scabbed and inky black, glossy with ointment.

"What's that a tattoo of?"

"Um, it's an amalgamation of three Polynesian sea gods in one entity. See, one looks out at you, one looks forward and one looks aft."

I looked closely and saw an abstract skull deeply embedded in the image.

"It's supposed to be a spell of protection," Tom said.

"I feel safer already."

Tom turned to look at the square sails that pulled on main and fore. He scanned the taut leeches that traced the sails' scalloping outline from lower to royal, then he frowned as he saw the manila braces, stretched and draping, tired from the night's work. "Better grab the watch and take up on the lee braces before you do the deck wash."

"Braces. Deck wash." I repeated his orders in shorthand and rounded up our hands.

After watch, I went to my bunk to dig out my old leather jacket with the *Picton Castle* logo on its back and carried it to a hideout under the fore fife rail, in the shade of the foresail and the coils that hung there. Carefully, I sewed up the seams that had dry-rotted in storage. I'd put aside Dad's knife until I could get more materials, hopefully at the next stop, in Rarotonga. Nearby, Becky worked on a ditty bag. And Kim worked hard on his dory.

From my private den under the fife rail, I watched Kim climb the small ladder to the galley-house roof, crowded with four and a half boats. The half-boat was what remained of Kim's old dory, which he'd hauled off the shore of Wreck Bay. Only its dented surfboard-shaped bottom and three lonely frames remained intact. The splintered planks and frames that he'd dragged back to the ship added to the collection of scrap wood that we stored up there.

On the roof, Kim stepped gingerly in bare feet over one boat and onto a pile of dry planks. He held his breath through the galley's coal smoke and ducked under a sail to the remains of his dory. With pliers he pulled nails from the salvaged frames, stem, bottom and transom. Then he returned to the deck to whittle toothpick-sized plugs with his pocket knife, its blade worn narrow from years of frequent sharpening.

"Hey Kim," I asked from under the fife rail, "how'd you get into dories?"

"I tried to start a dory shop while I was scalloping," said Kim, "but I went out of business. I'd never built a dory before and was making it up as I went along. Then I bought the Dory Shop. You should've seen it."

I thought of his shop. Two boxy wooden buildings overhanging Lunenburg harbour on pilings with a wharf in between. Shingles on walls and roof. Buff-painted dories spilling out the door.

Kim looked down to whittle at his plug and continued. "The pilings were rotted off. The sills were rotted off. Things were crumbling into the water."

"Who showed you how to make the boats?"

Kim put down the rough little plug and started whittling another. "Well, it was difficult. 'Cause it was like trying to re-create a boat from archaeology. You know, there were patterns and markings on the walls by the machines, but it was like trying to decipher ancient runes. There were a lot of blanks. This old-timer, Freeman, who'd worked at the Dory Shop for thirty-five years, was the only guy who knew anything about making dories. I offered him fifteen dollars an hour, which was a princely sum, to just sit there and tell me what to do. But he wouldn't do it. Still, Freeman came by every once in a while and stuck his head in the door and told me what was goin' on with whatever it was I was trying to figure out. And after a while I got it all."

"He made you work for it," I observed, thinking how similar this teaching experience was to the ones I'd had in ships. No one ever showed me anything unless I'd taken the initiative to do it wrong first.

"Freeman's still with us. He's doin' good, too. So I know that building dories isn't bad for you."

Later, Kim went back to the galley-house roof to glue those plugs into the vacant nail holes. There was very little left to build on, and he'd had to scrounge for materials. Kim had formed quick bonds with the Pitcairners, and while we were still teasing him about his dory surfing, he trudged with five islanders into the woods, where he sawed frames from the sharply bent branches of a bourau tree.

Eight hours passed quickly while we mended. At 1600 hours, I was on watch again. Kim continued to work on his dory.

Ever since the beginning of May, when I'd realized that only one year remained before our return to Lunenburg, I'd been thinking of what to do next. I could see myself in the distant future, the skipper of a steel topsail schooner. Maybe a hundred feet long. A ship that could be sailed with a smaller crew. To prepare I'd work on the *Tole Mour*, a ship that took adjudicated youth on long Pacific passages. *I could put my heart into that*, I thought as I ran up the ladder to the quarterdeck.

My mood improving, I found myself with a growing involvement in the ship's classes. The next day, after the daily ship cleaning and rig tarring and rust chipping and repainting, I helped bo'sun Josh lead a training session for the newcomers on eight essential knots. Each of his eight lessons carried a piece of wisdom unique to the optimum function of each knot. "Though it's not as pretty, when you tie a figure-eight knot, leave a foot of line between the knot and the bitter end. That way, if your knot stops a line from being pulled through a block, you have something to grab a hold of."

For an hour after lunch break each day, I partook in Brian's ever-popular celestial navigation class. I listened to him stress the need for pinpoint accuracy—to stand directly over the chart, to use a sharp, sharp pencil, to understand how an error of a fat pencil's width can throw a site off by miles. Celestial navigation gave me contact with what I liked most about physics: the classical age, arithmetic descriptions, planetary motion and the elegant geometry of optics. It was a thrill to compute even the simplest of celestial operations: finding latitude by measuring the sun's angle when it was at its greatest height above the horizon, local apparent noon. Add that measurement to the sun's known angle from the equator, subtract the result from ninety degrees and presto—our approximate latitude.

When it was local apparent noon, I reached into the sextant box the way Brian had taught on his first day of class—with the left hand, fingers outstretched to grasp the frame, avoiding the delicate components. After pulling it from the box, I transferred its handle to my right hand. Then I flipped the shades over the mirrors, allowing enough light that the sun looked like a shiny nickel on dark velvet. Brian had said, "If you get salt water on your shade, wipe it with a damp cloth to dissolve the abrasive crystals. If you get fingerprints on it, shoot yourself."

"You've never had a teacher like me," he'd warned us.

Dan lectured on mooring a ship to a dock and sailing her off again. Discussing our dockline nomenclature—*headline, bow breast, bow spring, forward leading midships spring,* etc.—he said, "We use what I think of as the simplest version. Actually, there's one that's a little simpler, but it's too simple. They just number the lines from bow to stern: one, two, three, four, five, six, seven, eight. We can do that, but we're not gonna do it. It's just not part of our heritage to do that, any more than we're gonna call the port side the left side. The day we start calling the port side the left side is the day we start using numbers."

His discussion on sailing off a dock began with the example of the *Picton Castle* leaving Lunenburg under the power of her headsail. "You know, you read a lot about backing topsails, but that's done less than you think. You'll usually find that there's enough windage up there anyway to achieve the same effect. We use the squares to back and control less than the fiction books often indicate."

Using a whiteboard and marker, he brought an imaginary ship away from a pier and alongside again in a range of conditions. The next day, he brought the *Picton Castle* alongside a concrete pier in Avatiu, Rarotonga.

After a night of drinking and dancing in Avatiu's clubs, I stopped with some shipmates at a playground. I grabbed the rails of a merry-go-round, walked it like a capstan, then ran and jumped aboard. The spinning landscape of darkness and street lights became fluid, and I jumped off to lay in the grass. The stars swept across my eyes and I breathed deeply, fighting the spins. I propped a foot flat on the grass to stop the turning in my head and stomach.

I heard the meow of a kitten. The most pathetic sound I'd ever heard—frightened and alone. I stood and walked towards the mewing. From under a bush, two luminous green eyes looked up at me, bulging from a white diamond marking that made the head appear smaller by comparison. Egyptian markings ran from its eyes, and I felt them latch on to me.

We walked back to the ship and boarded by the aloha deck. At first I was too wrapped up in the joy of fatherhood to notice Nobby's disdain, and saw only Claire's amusement.

Said Nobby, "Jesus Christ, Rigel, you can't have that here. Give it to me."

I passed him my kitten, whom I'd named Maggie, and he picked her up by the scruff of the neck, dispassionately, as if she were a fish fillet. "That's a healthy kitten. Her mother's probably looking for her."

Nobby's opinion held weight. He managed all animal husbandry aboard. The ship's oldest cat, Mr. Fick, was also a Brit. And because Mr. Fick suffered from feline leukemia, he was beset by respiratory problems and persistent bladder infections. Nobby cared for him with the same pragmatic tenderness he gave the ship's four aging engines.

I walked back to the bush where I found her, placed her beneath an overhanging branch and walked away.

The kitten, tail pointing straight up in the air, wound between my legs and tacked in front of my sandalled feet. I kicked her and walked on. She wound around again, her paws a blur as she kept up. I tried to leave her in the park and run off. She cried and chased me.

I gave up and lay down under the bush, hoping her mother would come and take her. Soon, in the cool air, on the soft grass, with the last bubbles of drunkenness leaving my head, I fell asleep.

After a few hours with the kitten curled up like a snail asleep on my head, it rained. Her mother was not coming. I decided to give her to the shelter run by the vets who'd been treating Mr. Fick's leukemia.

Jesse was on watch when I returned. He quietly observed as I fed her a heap of dry cat food nearly as big as she was. Maggie quickly consumed it, gurgling and purring as she ate.

In the morning, before muster, Pasha's sun-browned hand pushed aside my curtain to reveal a complement of radiant shipmates. The kitten vomited a worm of half-digested kibbles onto my chest, which I quickly gathered and threw out my porthole. Then she reached her head down and attempted to suckle my teat.

Later, in the scullery, the Captain walked in behind me, grumpy. "Were you drunk?"

"Yes."

"What were you thinking, bringing a kitten on board?"

"I'm going to take her to the animal shelter when it opens on Monday." We'd arrived, as we often did, on a long weekend.

"Good." The Captain pumped a jet of coffee into his cup and left.

I wasn't the only one who doted on Maggie the Cat. It seemed that her every move endeared her more to the rest of the crew. It was her indomitable will to survive—the way she motored through the water like an Evinrude when Josh shoved her over the side to teach her the danger of the rail; the way she attacked brooms, pounced on feet, attacked Mr. Fick, the large sea cat dying of leukemia.

Mr. Fick remained unflappable. Even though his illness made it hard for him to breathe, he had patience for the kitten. With each advance of the growling Maggie, the old black cat flipped her on her back with his paw, claws retracted, pinned her there and walked away. She attacked again, and he patiently flipped her every time.

Captain Dan, who seemed to be softening his position towards the new kitten, spun her around in his arms and accused her of having a "toxic level of cuteness."

Later, we opened the ship for a typical tall ship day of tours. It was meant as goodwill towards our new port of registry and a field day for the schoolchildren. Visitors shuffled on and off the gangway, where I stood watch. The local veterinarian had come aboard and was down below treating Mr. Fick, whose condition had seemed to worsen greatly. Since the day before, he had not been able to get up off the floor. I knew she and Nobby were debating whether or not to euthanize him.

The vet returned to the deck carrying a cage for the kitten. I was about to stick her in when a family walked past and the children asked to hold her. One of them pinched her tight, making her squawk, and the other grabbed at her tail.

"Where did you git ah?" asked the father in a thick New Zealand accent.

I told him that I found her abandoned and that she was going to the shelter.

"Oy. Ahl adopt ah. We noid a mousah. We'll keep ah lean and mean."

The vet placed Maggie in the cage and gave me a quick look. She walked to her car.

At the end of the day, I lay on the cargo hatch. Halogen street lights reflected off the glossy tar that coated the lower shrouds. I felt a little satisfaction that we were finally catching up with the ship's maintenance.

Josh walked quietly down the gangway and lay on the hatch beside me. "Man, will you look at the tar on those shrouds. Look at it gleam."

"We're down to the short strokes now."

"Fuck off."

We laughed. At the very best, we hoped that the ship would be in peak condition by the time we returned to Lunenburg.

"What have you been up to?" I asked.

"Helping Kim. He'll have two rows of planks on by the time we leave."

"Holy shit. Where are you guys working?"

"There's a local artist who built these open-air market stalls with roofs. A hurricane destroyed one of them and Canada came through with the relief money. He flies a Canadian flag over the building now. I think that's why he took Kim in."

When it came time to leave Rarotonga, Kim returned to the ship with his shell of a dory in the back of a truck. The scrap wood moulds that he'd bent the planks around stuck over the gunwales, and the Pitcairn Island frames that he'd chainsawed to thickness—wearing only shorts and flip-flops, squinting bushy eyebrows against flying wood chips—sat in the boat, ready to be installed. We loaded his project aboard the ship.

Shortly after, the vet arrived with a cage. Handing Maggie to me, she explained that, the night before, she had run into the Captain at a restaurant and talked him into allowing the cat aboard.

When I thanked Dan, he replied sadly, "Well, one's dying. We might as well get another."

It was time to leave. Locals had filled our fruit and vegetable lockers to the brim with oranges and coconuts and melons. It seemed the whole island had come to the dock to wave farewell to our vessel, which had swapped its U.S. Virgin Islands registry for one in the Cooks. We flew the Cook Islands ensign. She was their ship now too.

The wind that blew over the island was light when it reached us, tied to the dock in Avatiu's harbour. We set most of our sail, cast off our lines, forward then aft, and sailed into the Pacific.

The seas rolled steeper than we'd ever seen in that ocean. Hiding out with Maggie the Cat in the bat cave, empty since the Galapagos, I could feel the ship pitch hard with the steep swells. I was sketching the topsail schooner that had been on my mind. She would be white, with a clipper bow and steep counter, able to handle a following sea like the *Picton Castle*. Even down in the bat cave I could feel how well she moved with the seas. I could feel how her twenty sails pulled in the stiff wind and dampened our roll. It was winter—peak trade wind season in this part of the Pacific—and the weather would have been rough for a yacht.

I came up to the aloha deck for lunch and looked over the stern. The transom below and the quarterdeck above framed the sea and sky. The horizon angled one way and then the other. It disappeared when a deep blue swell, ridged with black crescents and whitecaps, reached up over the transom and we descended to the trough, which enclosed us like a mother's arms.

I imagined my ship travelling to distant ports for valuable cargo, filling tanks with wine that I would bottle and distribute, its prices bolstered by the notoriety of our voyages.

The *Picton Castle* was sailing from Rarotonga on her way to Palmerston Atoll, which lay directly on the route to Western Samoa. Palmerston Atoll, with a land area of one square mile, was settled by one man and his three wives in 1863. The man was an English cooper and ship's carpenter named William Marsters. His wives were from Penrhyn, an island in the Northern Cooks. The four moved there with the intent of brokering coconut and sea cucumber from the island for a trader who helped Marsters set up there. The trader never returned, and the Marsterses never left. With William Marsters as that island's strict autocrat, the family established a tribe that grew to one hundred, shrunk to thirty, and today hovered at forty souls, still living with remarkable self-reliance.

We approached within miles of the atoll and clewed up gans'ls and royals to shed some speed. We could see the atoll's seven-mile-wide footprint, a ring of submerged coral that interrupted the constant march of swells and whitecaps, casting a wind shadow that reflected the light blue sky.

We clewed up all sail. The Captain fired up the engine and followed locals in aluminum skiffs into the lee of the island. We edged up close to the exposed reef, into the shallows, just past the ledge. When the locals said it was all right to anchor, the Captain ordered, "Let go!" The anchor found the reef and clung to it like a cat's claw while we drifted back with the wind.

"Up and furl!"

I swung around a turnbuckle on the fore shrouds and pushed for the royals. The new crewmen had become fast and nimble in the rig, and it was growing hard to be one of the first two there. Swinging from the shrouds to the footropes, we grabbed folds of canvas and pulled it under our torsos, feeling the scratch of canvas on our bare stomachs and the strong trade wind press hanging folds of sail against our legs.

Our criss-crossed masts and yards cast a long stark shadow on the water. The atoll stretched out ahead. The reef was jade and jagged, curving in a circle to the distant other side. Six small islands punctuated the ring of coral like jewels. Those islands were fringed with white sand and choked with palms and glossy tangles of leaves.

On deck, the locals were wandering about, wearing T-shirts and shorts. The women wore their black hair long while the men cut theirs neat and short, though some of the young men had mullets. There was a group of three men forward by the fo'c'sle, so when I hopped off the shrouds, I introduced myself.

"Hi, I'm Edward," one man said, and his right eye twitched as he spoke.

I smiled and shook his hand, looking him in the eyes. He had a handsome face and seemed a touch self-conscious about the betrayal of his eyelid.

"Cory and Terangi, my nephews." Edward gestured to the two young men. Cory, the older, was tall and well proportioned, and had the affected lack of interest of an adolescent. Terangi, his younger brother, was awestruck as he gazed at our lofty rig.

"Do you want to come with us?" Edward asked.

I hesitated for a second, thinking that things were happening rather fast, then answered, "Yes, thank you very much. Let me grab my stuff."

When I came back on deck, Edward, Cory and Terangi were climbing over the rail into their aluminum boat. I joined them and was told we were waiting for a couple more. The four of us stared uncomfortably at the ship above. I was relieved to see Josh and Karen finally step over the t'gallant rail.

Cory started his loud outboard and headed for the shallow green reef. The light aluminum craft hopped up on a plane and skipped fast across the chop, blowing our hair back, vibrating our cheeks.

Snapping the tiller from side to side, Cory knew instinctively the deeper parts of the reef. Coral heads whipped past just feet from the vessel's thin skin. He howled. He sped us past markers made of tree branches. Past a WWII pilot boat that lay breached and rusted on the reef.

Cory gingerly edged his skiff up to the sand of Home Island. Daily wear threatened his family's only boat more than his reckless speed crossing the reef. We hopped out into the water and watched while he anchored away from the shore.

We followed the three Marsters along a path that led into the island. It was lined with tall palms and bushy trees bursting with leaves like a rubber plant's. The ground went from sand to small rocks of broken coral, and it was sharp on my bare feet. The Marsters paid it no attention.

Soon we broke into an opening of cool white sand. Around the edges stood three houses, two of them concrete and one wood. Fat chickens pecked meat from broken coconuts in a coop. A family sat on the porch of one of the houses looking at us curiously, flashing up their eyebrows as a gesture of greeting. They told us to sit, and we met Edward's middle brother, Simon, a wiry, bearded, energetic man with a pronounced stutter. And we met his oldest brother, Goodly, who was portly, with a reassuring smile and measured voice that carried a strong trace of William Marsters's Gloucestershire burr. Edward introduced his fiancée, Shirley, who stood against the wall of the house. Having arrived recently from Rarotonga, she seemed nearly as uncertain in her location as we did. A young child clung to her knees.

After offering a round of cold coconut water from young coconuts that the family kept in the fridge, Edward suggested we go to the volleyball court, where crew and islanders were getting together for a game. Josh, Karen, Terangi, Edward and I walked down a wide path through an orchard of tall palms, past the island's thundering electric generator that ran twelve hours a day, to the treeless town centre with its eight houses. As we arrived at the sandy volleyball court, it occurred to me that my hosts were outsiders to the community.

Edward wanted to wait on the periphery by a short palm. After a rousing game, he beckoned us to go back to the compound. I hesitated to return, figuring the rest of the crew ashore were spending the evening with thirty islanders, likely drinking, singing and playing guitar.

On the way back, Edward explained to me that William Marsters had divided the main island up into three equal plots, with a compound for each of his wives and her children. That division still existed today, with a level of family squabbling you'd expect from a group living so close. My concern about missing the crew's fun lifted when we arrived at Simon's house to the smell of food.

In the spare concrete dining room, Shirley served us taro and deep-fried parrotfish around a wooden table. So fresh and tender, the fish melted away from its crispy batter. Whenever I finished a piece, Simon encouraged me to eat another so vehemently that I felt it would be rude to refuse. Only on the verge of physical pain did I prevail on him to stop feeding me.

"You know, if you're fishing on the reef and would like some help, I'd love to come along," I ventured.

Simon acknowledged my offer with a cautious look.

With all the plates empty, I excused myself and tried to help Shirley wash the dishes. She smiled and said no, thank you. But when I insisted, she seemed to grow uncomfortable. Simon, at the head of the table, cleared his throat to tell me I was upsetting the family order. I sat down.

After the table had been cleared and dishes washed, we went out to the porch. Edward, Simon and Goodly cradled two ukuleles and a guitar.

As they played and sang soulful, warbling harmonies, I admired Simon's ukulele. Clearly homemade, its back was half a coconut shell and its neck the same mahogany-like wood that Edward's house was built of. The face was made of thin plywood decorated with Magic Marker, and its strings were fishing twine. Its bright lacquer flashed in the porch light as he played.

At midnight, the town generator was shut down and it was time for bed. I walked across the compound to Edward's house. The full moon seemed especially bright, shining straight overhead, the same colour as the cool sand beneath my feet.

The next morning, Simon took us around the island. He showed us the pit where he burned coral to prepare the concrete he'd used to make his house. We walked through his garden of taros, with their diaper-shaped leaves, and other vegetables that helped sustain his family. We climbed the island's highest point, a twenty-foot mound of sand called The Mountain.

Simon invited us inside the old home of William Marsters. When we entered its one room, I saw oiled wood and great knees and rivets. I felt like I was walking upside down in an old wooden ship. Simon explained that the house had been built from wrecks that had washed up on shore.

Simon led us towards the turquoise lagoon and opened the door of a shed, revealing two wooden boats. He proudly showed us their construction details. The hulls were round-bottomed and lapstrake. A mast and boom lay across the thwarts with their tired old sail. I tried to imagine how much more difficult it was for them to sail over the reef and back, against a foul wind, when the tides were disagreeable or when it was storming. I thought of how much outboard engines had simplified their lives. I thought of fishing.

After a lunch back at the house, Simon and Terangi prepared for their work on the reef. I offered to help Terangi as he gathered his net, and noticed that he'd put his mullet back in a ponytail, modelling Josh. Smiling, Terangi handed me an old pair of white boots, one with a gaping hole in the side. I did not complain, seeing that his boots were worse than mine.

Simon, Edward and Terangi loaded me, Karen, Josh and Don in their skiff and headed across the lagoon to Cook's Island. As we pulled away, I could see the great Pacific swells roll in. They reached the sheer volcanic sides of the reef and jacked up steep and tall and top-heavy. I heard their crash over the outboard's roar.

We pulled the boat up on the island's shore and walked to the reef. I could see its shallow line stretch to Home

Island, a mile away. We were talking to the affable Edward, standing on concrete-hard coral below the high-tide line, when he reached down for one of the plentiful, plum-sized snails that clung to the coral. He pounded it hard on the reef until its dark shell cracked. Then he picked off the white corkscrew meat and chewed the flesh off the hard operculum that had once covered the snail's opening. I grabbed one myself and slammed it on the reef. I chewed on the tough, salty meat, trying to ignore the feeling that I was munching my own tongue.

When I looked up, I saw Simon and Terangi charging down the reef with their net, already hundreds of yards away. It was now or never. I ran.

I plunged into the water, and quickly it was past my waist. As water surged out of the lagoon, the surface stretched clear and I saw an unfamiliar footing: the reef's white bones, sporadic heads of living coral, red, blue and green. As I ran through deeper water, canyons of black appeared. I jumped, hoping momentum would carry me over. As I negotiated the difficult terrain, Terangi and Simon were pulling ever farther ahead. A wave crashed in and the water rose around me. I ran on, knowing I'd lose them if I stopped. Now Simon and Terangi ran nearer the reef's edge, so I moved farther from the lagoon. Clear water and canyons. Deep water and gauze. I pushed on. I stepped on a coral head. My bare foot slipped from the hole in my boot. Wincing, I felt it slice on the reef. I pulled it back in. Simon and Terangi were stopping periodically to fish and I was gaining. They moved nearer the lagoon. I moved nearer the edge.

A breaker, larger than the others, crashed near me, and the water rose around my torso, my armpits. The water lifted me off the coral floor. I scrabbled for footing and realized as I drifted that the water would pull me from the reef, over the volcano and into the mouth of the very next breaker.

I took a breath and dove, opening my eyes. On the uneven coral floor I found handholds. The water rushed out. Like the anemones and fans that clung to the coral, my body streamed towards the Pacific. Sharp coral cut the calluses of my hands.

When the current slowed and water drained, I stood and flipped my hair back from my eyes. Simon was intent on his net. Terangi looked my way. He gestured me in from the reef's edge with great sweeps of his skinny arm. I expected to see reproval or concern in his face, but there was none, just friendly guidance. I felt for him an instant bond of respect.

Terangi and Simon had just caught a couple of beaked parrotfish, with brilliant green scales big as feathers. Simon deftly snapped their necks and threaded a length of twine in their mouths and out their gills. He handed me his precious catch to carry. Terangi told me to follow.

Soon, a school of parrotfish carelessly exposed their triangular green dorsal fins in the water rushing fast from the lagoon. Terangi handed Simon the small hand net with its weights dangling in the water. Simon inspected it and passed an end to his son. "Go!" he said.

Terangi sprang to the other end of the canyon, pulling the net out with him. Then his foot caught on the uneven floor and he splashed clumsily into the water, scaring the fish.

"Ach, stupid boy," said Simon sharply. Terangi stood up, embarrassed.

We walked again and I looked at my fish to make sure I would not lose any from the twine.

It was not long before we found another school holding station in the current. The two hunters set up for attack. Terangi sprang and closed the net around four big parrotfish.

One by one, smiling broadly, Simon broke their necks and threaded them on the twine for me to carry.

We netted several more fish before I heard the skiff idle in behind us, carrying the balance of our party. With the boat next to us, Simon, proud of his catch, quickly slit the bellies and let the entrails be carried out to sea.

Back at the compound after our duty on the ship, I gave Simon a bottle of rum for a birthday gift. He in turn unscrewed the top and shared it with everyone. Inevitably, the instruments came out, and I attempted to play along on Simon's coconut ukulele. Just before the lights went off with the island's generator, he said, his stutter softened by alcohol, "You may have it."

My respect for the Marsters's resourcefulness grew with each day. Finally, on the last day of our visit, the whole island hosted a barbecue on the beach. The Captain allowed all but a skeleton crew to come ashore for the entire feast. There, the crew shared stories. Brian had gone spear fishing with his host family to provide us with many of the small fish. Never were there fewer than two sharks lingering around, he said, attracted by the fish blood. Patrick had made friends with one of his hosts, a man his age who'd gone to school in Rarotonga and, like many of the island men, had brought back a pretty wife. Patrick told us how his friend had manhandled one of the black-tipped reef sharks out in the lagoon. I told him of the tunas we'd caught with Goodly one day, longlining off the reef—how we'd learned to slit their carotid artery, bleeding the fish rather than clubbing them. Some of their rich meat was prepared as sashimi and *poisson crue* at the banquet. Doctor Beth and brain surgeon Dave had removed Edward's wife's bad tooth. Kim traded goods for three tamanu trees, each over three feet wide and sixty feet tall. He felled one and quartered it lengthwise on the spot in his flip-flops. The ship now owned two trees on Palmerston.

I ate until full, then passed the rugby ball with guys from the ship and island. I started to throw long spirals, and it made me feel like I was back home, at a barbecue, in the fall.

CHAPTER 24

Life Woven of Seabeads

Palmerston, Cook Islands, to Samoa
June 14 to 25

MIDDAY, WHEN SAILS WERE SET AND WE WERE HEADED west away from Palmerston, I saw second engineer Claire digging around in her bunk cluttered with carvings and geology texts she'd kept after graduating from Bryn Mawr a couple of years before. I knew the island had had a deep effect on her. It seemed that everywhere we went, she formed bonds with young people, particularly young women. I'd seen her talk with the Captain about providing assistance and education to the young people on the island, so I asked her, "What did you think of Palmerston?"

"I thought it was beautiful. A beautiful prison." She shocked me, told me the difficulties, the lack of options, the naïveté of the island's teenage girls.

I thought of my new friend, Terangi, who had burst into inconsolable tears when we weighed anchor. *Why did he cry? Because his new friends were leaving? Friends like Josh, who he emulated with his ponytail, his tucked-in shirt, his rolling walk?* His friends had disappeared; friends who'd appreciated his tenderness, which seemed almost a liability

277

on that austere island. Maybe he'd cried because he wanted to come along but couldn't. They said that Terangi had once made a trip to Rarotonga for school. He was there a month before he had to return to Palmerston because of homesickness. Maybe it was a prison, but it was a prison Terangi didn't want to leave.

I walked out of the fo'c'sle to the deck. Our heading was nearly downwind. The yards were braced square and did nothing to dampen our roll, knifing through the air as the ship swung side to side. The new cook's Jimmy Buffett tape was on automatic reverse for the tenth day in a row and I thought I might throw it overboard. When the port side rolled high, I walked past the galley, and it smelled strongly of the nutmeg that she'd poured in her weekly Alfredo sauce. I grabbed one of the short, ripe bananas from a bunch that hung from a boat skid and continued aft, timing my movement with the ship's roll.

In the scullery, I took down a cup from its hook and placed it under the coffee Thermos spout. A gurgling spray of cold coffee misted out. Empty. I left the scullery and walked forward, covering my ears past Jimmy Buffett purgatory, to my bunk, full of half-finished projects, half-finished letters and dirty laundry.

A dark feeling of claustrophobia pulled a haze over my eyes and rang in my ears. I lay on my back and imagined tree houses. A towering trunk of mahogany. Spiralling stairs, supported on branches grafted in place—all different species of tree, spraying out vibrant leaves of a thousand hues.

The next morning on watch, before sunrise, I heard Tom whisper from the charthouse, "Hey, it says in the night orders to wake Jean at 0600."

"Orange juice," I replied. "You gotta love her."

Just before wake-ups, I told Lori to wake Jean with the rest of the daymen.

"Sure. I don't have to do deck wash, do I?"

"No. Just report to the wheel when you've woken the daymen."

Lori smiled. I couldn't help but admire how she'd adapted to ship life. She avoided everything unpleasant to her by setting up a system of mutually beneficial compromises. Rather than do deck wash, she'd exchange her duty with someone else for some task less savoury to them, like wiping fingerprints, grease and rust stains from the superstructure and bulwarks every morning. Rather than haul lines, she always chose to slack the opposing end, saving her nails, which were long, shapely and painted as red as the capstan.

Just after sunrise, when yellow light traced the sea, we ran out the hundred feet of fire hose and scrubbed the fo'c'sle head. Side to side against the grain we scrubbed. We scrubbed our way aft—moving buckets, descending ladders, muscling the fire hose with its texture like sharkskin, scrubbing under the cat litter, rinsing away scattered sand.

Through a porthole I saw Jean with her long white braid trailing over her shoulder as she crushed orange halves in the press that she'd begged the Captain to buy in Rarotonga.

That afternoon, as I walked down the deck towards the fo'c'sle, Vicki stepped from fore shrouds to rail. A can of tar hung from a rope about her neck and shoulder. Tar streaked her nut-brown skin, gleaming in the ripples of her lean abdominal muscles, earned from months of twelve-hour days working in the rig. Holding her tar can with one hand, she hopped quietly to the deck and smiled at me, positively glowing from enjoyment of a day's work.

At dock in Western Samoa, a group of eight striking men and women—black-haired, with grass lava-lavas about their waists, arms banded in patterned tattoos—danced vigorously in unison to a loud drumbeat. The men stomped. The women wove their arms through the air. With lines across, our entire crew stood atop the quarter-deck and watched.

When the dance was through, one of the men came aboard to introduce us to his country. He told us he could arrange dance lessons for us, and when one of our crew asked him about his tattoo, he pointed to the patterned band encircling his bicep and said we should all get one. "Tattooing originated in Samoa."

They said the same thing in the Marquesas.

Pantomiming the motion of hammer hitting nail, he said, "We do it in the traditional way, and we always give tattoos to *palengis.*" When he said "*palengis,*" he smiled dis-armingly and extended his arms towards us.

"The tattoo clause is in effect," announced the Captain.

Ashore the next morning, Don and I walked down the quiet streets, wet with a morning rain. There seemed not much to do. We had learned by now to avoid the nearby bars. They attracted the greatest number of crew and, with them, a drunken apathy and many complaints about life aboard ship. There were restaurants, stores, bars, a movie theatre. Time was wasting.

"I'm going to get a tattoo," I said out of the blue, and was immediately filled with excitement over the idea.

"Where?"

"I don't know. Let's ask at the tourist bureau." We'd walked past this octagonal building some time before. Ordinarily, I would have scoffed at the idea, preferring not to consider myself a tourist, but Don and I entered the car-peted, octagonal room and faced a tall, well-dressed man standing behind a counter. The air-conditioned room felt dry and uncomfortable. My skin goosebumped and itched.

"Where can I get a traditional Western Samoan tattoo?"

"That's Samoan, not *Western* Samoan," he instructed.

I was reminded of Samoa's long resistance to colonial powers. I imagined that he didn't want his country defined in terms of its relation to the rest of Samoa, *American* Samoa.

"And if it's a tattoo that you want, you've come to the right place. The daughter of Samoa's foremost tattooer, Petelo Suluape, is sitting right behind you."

I turned around to see an attractive young woman with black hair brushed over her shoulders, hunched down in her chair, cowering from the unexpected attention.

I walked over and introduced myself. She spoke in an accent that was more North American than Samoan. "Meet me at the bus stop at one o'clock. That's when I'm going home to my father's house on the other side of the island."

I agreed and walked outside, stunned that it had been so easy.

The morning passed slowly, and as it did, I imagined that Suluape's daughter would not make our meeting, as so often happens with casual promises. But when we arrived, she was there waiting on a wooden bench at the bus stop.

She smiled briefly and said hello as we sat, but then quickly looked ahead to where the bus would arrive.

"Glad to see you," I said.

"Thank you."

"Where did you learn to speak English without a Samoan accent?" I asked.

"In San Francisco. I used to live there with friends. My father goes there to do tattoos."

"Are we going to your father's tattoo shop or his house?"

"To his house. He doesn't have a shop."

"Do you have a tattoo?"

"Yes." She allowed herself a smile, and with a hint of pride she rolled up her sleeve, revealing a narrow band about her bicep. The pattern was not as dense as those I'd seen on the men in the guidebooks. "It's a pattern reserved for women."

The bus arrived. Don and I followed Suluape's daughter aboard and sat together on one of the bench seats.

We rode for nearly an hour down a winding, two-lane coastal road with modern one-storey houses on one side and the ocean on the other. We entered a sparsely populated stretch where thick trees and vegetation seemed to reach out over the road. The bus stopped. Suluape's daughter stood and motioned for us to follow. "Here we are."

We followed her across the street to the head of a narrow dirt road puddled with mud and rainwater. We walked past many dwellings, called *fales.* Though some of their roofs were made of corrugated steel and others of weathered sugar cane thatch, all were of the same shape—long, with a ridge down the middle and slopes on all four sides. In those fales, devoid of furniture, lives took place in the complete open. In one, women and children played cards. "They're playing memory," Suluape's daughter said. "That's my aunt's house."

In fact, everyone on the entire road was a member of her extended family; there were perhaps ten fales in all. I walked ahead while Don trailed behind with our new friend. A former anthropology student, he unravelled the social structure of her village, island and country. An extended family that lives in a group is called an *aiga.* Each aiga elects a *matai,* who is highly respected, holds title to all property in the aiga and represents it to the greater village. Her father, Suluape, was the matai of her aiga. All the matais in a village form a group called a *fono.* The highest chief among the matai sits at the head of the fono. The members of the fono elect a *pulenu'u* to represent the village to the national government.

At the top of the long dirt road, we arrived at the last fale. Suluape's daughter gave us a quick introduction to her mother, telling her we were there for a tattoo, then took off her shoes and walked across the fale, apparently finished with us. Her mother, a large woman in a bright red cotton dress that flowed partway over the lava-lava about her waist, did not seem to relish our company, but she invited us into the fale, telling us in uncertain English that Suluape would be home soon from the school where he taught. I took careful note of the tattoos on her hands and arms; they were a simple matter of X's and dots. We removed our shoes and walked across the floor without talking, according to custom. We sat cross-legged where the children played and watched Clark Gable dance across the screen of a black-and-white TV. Suluape's wife did not want to talk, but eyed us suspiciously.

After half an hour, a silver Toyota truck, dirty and dented from hard use, sped up the drive, around the fale, and parked under an adjoining shelter. Suluape stepped out, a beefy man wearing jeans, a plaid short-sleeve shirt and a thick moustache. Like most Samoan men, he confronted us with a warrior's expression, hard and aggressive, challenging our intrusion, but then softened his features almost like an infant at the first show of our smiles.

We stood and introduced ourselves, told him I was interested in a tattoo. He smiled broadly and invited us to sit. "Where do you want it?"

"I was thinking of an arm band."

"OK." Suluape smiled again.

"I was wondering if I could look at a few examples of your work and choose a pattern."

"No," he said apologetically, and smiled as if to ensure no offence was taken.

I grew a little uneasy about the tattoo, not wanting to give over my skin as a canvas to a man I didn't know. My eyes began to wander over the varieties of tattoos covering his arms. I pointed to a tattoo of a bunch of bananas set on a red flag with a black horizontal stripe and three white X's.

"I got that in Amsterdam."

"A tattoo convention?"

"Yes."

I pointed to a so-called tribal tattoo, of a style popular in North America.

"Those are my initials." He traced out a P and an S that had been combined into one symbol. *P*etelo *S*uluape.

"And who's that?" I joked, pointing to an image of his face at a younger age.

"That is my portrait," he replied.

I pointed to a green, winged dragon. "Where did you get that?"

"Amsterdam. It covers another tattoo." He held his forearm closer to me and I could see the faint outline of a large butterfly, expertly covered by the serpentine body of the dragon.

Suluape would be stalled no longer. "Do you want a tattoo or don't you?"

"Yes."

"Good. Where?"

I had thought to get a tattoo on my left arm, opposite the Marquesan sun, but reconsidered. "My left arm. No, my right."

"Well . . . decide."

"My right."

"How big?"

I held two fingers to my bicep.

"Done."

Suluape stood and beckoned two of his young sons. Then he walked behind a blind and emerged wearing only a lava-lava knotted about his waist. Countless more tattoos were visible on his torso, but most impressive was his Samoan tattoo, parts of it visible just below his knees and more above his waist to the small of his back. There were many levels of pattern—long, repeating triangles made of many cuts—and finally the serrated pattern of the cuts themselves.

A calm descended on Suluape as he went to the shelter where he'd parked his truck. He returned with a steel bowl of implements and a bowl of pasty ink. He sat cross-legged in front of me, his two young sons beside him. He allowed himself a smile and said, "Ready?"

I unbuttoned my shirt and lay down on the floor mat, resting my head on a firm pillow. Suluape pulled a long-handled tool from his bowl. The serrated cutter, an inch wide, was lashed to the end of the stick like an adze head. His sons stretched the skin of my arm. Suluape placed the cutter in his bowl of black ink-paste, then placed it over my skin. He set a dense wooden rod over the handle of his cutter, breathed deeply and, with great control, tapped his handle with the stick. I felt cold ink touch skin. He hit harder. *Pain.* Skin separated. He shifted his cutter and whacked again. I controlled my breath and grew numb as minutes passed.

Suluape withdrew the large chisel. He told me to lie on my back to present the pale underside of my arm. As I turned over, I saw his work: six parallel lines of shiny ink interspersed with droplets of blood that seeped through my broken skin. He began again. Efficiently, accurately, he moved through his set of chisels, establishing a pattern, laying the foundation for the next, smaller set of lines. Three-quarters of an hour passed before Suluape's sons released my arm. Suluape wiped the tattoo, leaned back and smiled like a doctor who'd just delivered a baby. "It's finished."

I raised my head from the pillow and looked at the tattoo—a sharply defined pattern of hollow rectangles and zigzags set into my reddened skin. Suluape had added a fringe of evenly spaced, solid blocks, like the bricks around a castle turret.

"I love it. Thank you."

I sat up, amazed that it had not taken longer. Suluape smiled, apparently tired from his concentrated effort of spontaneous creation. I took the chance to ask him more questions before I would be expected to leave. "What is that chisel made of?"

"Boar's tusk."

"And that ink?"

"Candlenut soot and water. A boy's grandmother is meant to gather it for him from the date of his birth."

"Does this pattern have a significance?"

"It is called *life woven of seabeads.*"

"'Life woven of seabeads'?"

"Yes. *Seabeads.* You know, seashells."

"I love it. How much do I owe you, Suluape?"

Suluape smiled modestly, seemingly a little uncomfortable ascribing a monetary value to his work. "Thirty-five dollars."

He was so generous, giving a tattoo to a *palengi* like me. Thirty-five dollars seemed like a small amount for his work. I pulled a twenty from my pocket. Don lent me fifteen.

I stood to leave, but Suluape stopped me. He took a strip of cloth and soaked it in alcohol, then tied it around my arm. It bit into my cuts, but was cool and soothing. The cloth turned black with ink. When I uncurled my fingers and straightened my arm, I thought my skin might sever at the tattoo and, like a motorcycle gauntlet, slide off onto the floor.

CHAPTER 25

The Wind and How It Cleanses

Kapa and Nieafu, Kingdom of Tonga, to Fiji
June 28 to August 6

THE *PICTON CASTLE* SWUNG ON HER ANCHOR IN AN uncertain morning wind. Rain clouds were heavy in the sky. Off the stern was a stout cliff of Kapa Island. It had a pebbly shore below and a thick forest above.

"Boat call!" mate Brian shouted into each compartment.

Most of us already sat on the thwarts of the skiff that was tied alongside. A pickaxe and two shovels were at our feet. Engineer Nobby held the small octagonal coffin that Tom and I had built on watch a few nights before. Inside the coffin was Ficky, who'd ended his long battle with feline leukemia as we steamed up the seven-mile channel towards the island of Vava'u, our entry point into the Kingdom of Tonga, three hundred miles from Samoa.

While we'd floated past myriad green-topped islands, Mr. Fick lay below on the softwood floor of the bat cave, letting out short, raspy breaths. Nobby, his caretaker of four years, knelt over him until the end, saying finally, "He's gone."

Second engineer Claire put her hand on his shoulder to comfort him.

We'd been warned that the Tongan authorities would incinerate all our fresh fruit and produce as soon as we tied up alongside. With that kind of strictness, we figured they would not look kindly on our dead cat. But there was no time for a proper burial at sea. So, wrapped in a heavy-duty plastic bag, Mr. Fick was discreetly placed in a freezer.

Days later, once I had seen flying foxes darken the Tongan sky in great flocks, and the bustling market, and the fat sows that walk through the fields trailing long strings of curly-tailed piglets, I spent a day in the forepeak, fashioning handles for my father's knife. I worked with the branches of Palmerston ironwood that Kim had brought to the ship. Its grain was curly and yellow-red, peppered with pinhead knots. I wanted the handles to be fair and flat and matching, but the wood was so hard and the grain so uneven that my plane chattered across its surface. Or its grain caught on the blade, which pulled it from the old metalworker's vise or shattered it like stone.

Thankfully, I heard a shuffle from the ladder behind and turned to see third mate Tom's hairy feet enter the compartment, followed by his big calves. Tom's blue eyes were bright with some piece of mischief. "Hey, guess what."

"What?"

"Bill accidentally found Mr. Fick."

I imagined Bill, in the depths of the hold, balancing barefoot on our dwindling supply of bagged coal, peering into the freezer with a flashlight, the yellow eyes of Mr. Fick reflecting back from his frozen black coat.

"Anyway, I think we should make a coffin."

"What?"

"Yeah. An animal coffin. They're octagonal. We could make it out of scrap."

"Sure." I was ready to attempt something that could be carried to the end with certainty.

Within hours, we were driving small nails around the cedar lid, Mr. Fick curled up respectably beneath. Only later did we learn that the Captain had planned to sew him up in canvas and bury him at sea. We hadn't thought to ask.

Ficky had joined the ship in Ipswich, England, eight years before. At the time, the Captain and his first crew were working to ready the ship for her transatlantic crossing. He was proud of that cat. He seemed to admire Mr. Fick's cool, detached attitude. He called him a hard-case sea cat. Our coffin had changed the Captain's plans about a burial at sea, so he brought the ship near the pebbly shore of Tanna, where we could place his cat underground.

Ashore, eight of us jumped into ankle-deep water and searched for a suitable route to the plateau. We walked together into the forest, until ship and shore were out of view. The thick canopy overhead dimmed what light seeped from the overcast sky. The grass and moss, though thick and succulent, was pale green for lack of light.

We wandered towards a small clearing and agreed to dig there. Nobby asked me for the shovel I carried, and with his heavy engineer's boot he drove it through the grass. Quickly he dug a precise square. I was reminded that he'd grown up around farms—that he'd studied to be a soil scientist, and that his previous experience with engines had been on big farm machinery and cars. Everyone talked except Nobby, who dug in silence.

Soon the angle of his shovel made it difficult for Nobby to scoop out earth. He and Claire got down on their knees and reached into the hole with their hands, pulling out the soil.

"I guess we should put him in now, don't you think?" Claire said.

Nobby lowered the coffin into the grave. Light gleamed off the brass placard on which he'd tooled *FICKY* the night before on his engine-room bench. Then he stood and asked permission to read some words. We were silent as he read a eulogy from the Captain. He folded the page, smudging it with black earth, and placed it back in his pocket. Nobby pulled out another page and read "At Dover Cliffs."

We helped Nobby throw dirt into the grave. When it was full and he began to tamp down the mound with the back of his shovel, Karen said she wanted to plant a tree on top. We emphatically agreed, and broke up to search for a sprouting coconut. It wasn't long before Claire returned to the clearing with a grey and mottled coconut husk that had split with a healthy new plant, emerging like a blade from a half-open jackknife.

Karen placed the palm seedling on the mound and pushed dirt up around it. "This is how I'd like to be buried, in a simple wooden coffin, with a tree planted over my grave."

After our watch stood down that night on the way to Fiji, mate Brian walked into the fo'c'sle. All present flashed him that look reserved for officers who dared enter the fo'c'sle. He sat on a sea chest, crossing his hands before him.

"So. I want you all to know, we're looking at a shipyard period in Fiji. There's not going to be much time off. It'll run like a normal eight-to-five workday, and every other night you'll stand watch on deck for two hours." He waited for the groans to die away. "Look, we haven't had a shipyard period in a long time. We're halfway round. It's been very hard to make capital improvements to the ship. It's time. She needs it. You've had more time off here than on any ship under the sun. Besides, it might be a chance to do some interesting jobs and take something from start to finish. OK?" He finished and walked out with a disdainful expression.

I followed.

"She had daggers in her eyes for me," he said, referring to one of his most solid crew members.

"She'll be all right. Listen, I'm behind you." To do one job with permanence would make the shipyard period worth it to me. I needed to do something that required judicious skill and planning; something that would allow me to see a bit of myself in the ship, and a bit of the ship in me.

Just after sunrise the next morning, as I went to the engine room to shut off the navigation lights as I had every morning for the last six months during watch, I heard a scrabbling on the aloha deck, accompanied by Maggie's low growl. It was the same growl she'd make when someone passed too close to her food dish. I padded aft on the cool deck to see her drag a hapless flying fish behind the neat new oil barrels tied to our bulwarks with new cedar tables atop. Maggie's bright green eyes reflected the growing morning light as I pulled the fish, still flapping, from her mouth and snapped its neck. It was good luck to land a flying fish. It meant I could bait one of our hooks and throw it over the side on our trawl. It was a trick I'd learned from Brian, who had learned it on Palmerston.

The fish had already started to lose its freshness, growing slippery and smelling like rich soil and earthworms. Its dime-sized eyes were dull as I ran Marcello's knife around their sockets and pried them loose like cupcakes from a tin. Using a long needle, I threaded a steel leader through the fish from vent to mouth, concealing the shank of the hook. I lashed the empty eye sockets to the leader with a copper wire. As I attached it to the trawl line and tossed it over, I hoped we wouldn't have to wait long until we had something good to eat.

Soon after breakfast, we got a bite. I arrived to see Patrick hauling on the trawl, leaning into it with his broad bare back. Brian pulled on a pair of work gloves to haul on the wire-thin monofilament that led to the hook. Then the line went slack and the resolve in Patrick's shoulders melted. "Shit," he said, and speedily hauled in the line the rest of the way.

There dangled a flying-fish head. The sturdy stainless steel hook was gone. Only the loop it had been attached to remained.

"Did you seize the two parts of the hook together?" Brian asked.

"No, I didn't know about that."

"You're supposed to do that."

Back on the Atlantic, when the tackle box sat unused with its gear rusting, I'd put myself in charge of the fishing and liked to think I did it well. I was disappointed as I walked down to the freezers and returned with a backup flying fish frozen stiff on its steel leader. After baiting the line, I set up to replace the hook that had been lost.

I crimped eyelets in a length of heavy leader, passing it first through a double hook. Then, not because it was the appropriate seizing but because I thought it would look good, I pried apart the two halves of the hook using a sharp and rusty old knife. I slipped. I sliced into the crease opposite the last knuckle of my index finger. Skin separated. The tendon beneath spread its webbed surface. Cream-colored bone appeared. Blood welled up and pulsed down to my palm.

"Um . . . Tom, can you give me a hand," I said, trying not to draw attention.

"Sure. Whoa! Just hold on a second." Tom walked behind me to the nearby first aid chest in the outside head. He hurriedly snapped on some rubber gloves, tore open a gauze pad and applied pressure. "Someone get Beth."

Doctor Beth took me to the Captain's office, which doubled as the emergency room. She used a tourniquet to control the fast bleeding, then very methodically opened a sterile laceration kit and stitched me up with surgeon's knots. I tried to keep my mind off the embarrassment of having misused a knife.

The Captain and mate peered into the office, saying

nothing. Doubtless it had crossed their minds, the thought of dealing with a more serious injury like a severed finger.

In appreciation for the tropics' ability to incubate infection and for the gritty shipyard period to come in Fiji, Beth bandaged and taped my injured finger until it was as stiff and white as a parsnip. Whenever I used it, blood pressure would push at the wound painfully and I was forced to hold my finger in the air as if I were always raising an objection.

Three days after leaving Kapa, we entered Walu Bay, Fiji, and picked up our pilot. From behind the wheel where I stood as second helmsman to Becky, I could see the pilot's amazement at the number of women on the bridge in the typically male-dominated seafaring industry. Second mate Karen walked from radio to chart to bridge, second engineer Claire handled the engine controls, and ex–second helmsman Lori, who'd been promoted to the Captain's secretary, stood radio watch.

The city of Suva, we knew, was another mail port. After supper, we gathered on the cargo hatch bathed in the commercial dock's yellow halogen light. A new crew member had brought an army duffle bag full of mail from the ship's office in New Hampshire. We looked at that bag, expectant, like kids at summer camp.

I sat apart from my friends. Demoralized from my wound, the thought of a letter grew more important. By the time mail call came around, I sat on the hatch not talking to anyone. The night air, though hot, was also damp and made me shiver. I wanted just one letter.

Lori went to the front to collect mail an infuriating number of times. Beth called my name twice, the second time handing me a small package wrapped in brown paper and addressed in Ariel's childlike printing.

I stole off with it to my bunk, like Maggie with her flying fish. I released the tape on the wrapping and slid the box

out. Black and decorated with silver swirls, it looked like it
might contain the infinity of space. Pressed under the lid
were layers of letters that had accumulated unsent since
we'd left Lunenburg. She'd folded them to fit the box exactly. One letter was written on four thick pages, each a different colour, in different inks—black on navy, blue on yellow,
silver on Mylar. There was a Fisher Space Pen, and a poem
by bill bissett clipped from a Canadian magazine. I read it
hoping that it said what was on her mind.

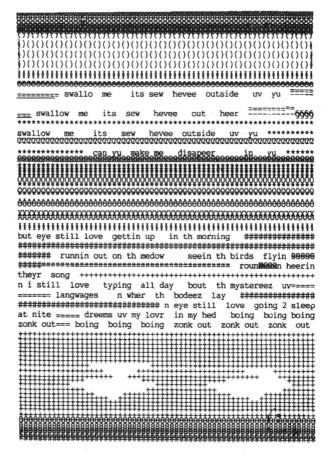

I decided that the next day I'd put together a package for her, made up of shells I'd collected, packed in fragrant shavings of sandalwood, and in one deeply ridged clamshell whose lips locked together I'd place the black pearl I'd been given by a surfer in Takaroa.

I pinned her poem to the overhead of my bunk, next to the *mola* of a parrot among hibiscus blossoms. A breeze came in through my porthole, fluttering the poem and cooling the sweat on my forehead and upper lip. I leaned up on one elbow and let the breeze hit me square on the face. I looked out at the docks and their stacks of containers. I gazed at the tall buildings of Suva and the forested hills beyond. I felt my bedsheet twisted around my leg. I felt my squeaky foam mattress. I thought of the bunk beneath it and of the steel hull and frames beneath that. And I thought of the ocean, of the earth's crust that it floats upon, the mantel supporting that, a spherical core of molten rock within, a mantel, a crust, a highway, and Ariel, one hand on the wheel, driving to her office in a red pickup truck.

The next day, we set anchor in the harbour and went to work. The schedule Brian had posted gave each of the professional crew a break of three consecutive days over the planned two-week work period. It was the first time since the Galapagos that a sharp division had been drawn between professional and amateur crew, who worked one day and took five off.

That division made some, who'd otherwise become involved in ship's work, take the effort less seriously. Some, who'd resented ship's work from the beginning, felt vindicated. And for some the time off came with a high cost: loss of sweat equity in a ship they were growing to love.

On the first day of work, Karen and I were set to measuring the length of cranelines to be strung between the lower shrouds. Sailors would stand on these while they furled the 'tweens'ls. While we measured and marked, using the horizon as a level, I looked forward to splicing the wires, thereby taking a rigging job from beginning to end. I wasn't far into the second splice, working awkwardly around my lacerated finger, when I overheard the mate and Captain mention my name in conversation from the bench where they sat on the bridge. Minutes later I gave over the measurements to Jesse and he silently went to work.

Brian then told me he wanted me to "mastermind" a project for him. It was the first time I'd ever heard him sugar-coat a job, and the transparency of it gave me a sense of both his deep humanity and how much I was going to dislike my new task. I was to fill checks in the ten yards with high-quality caulk from a tube, forcing it in with a putty knife, to keep rainwater from settling inside and promoting rot. It wasn't a terrible job; it was just that I'd been warned against putting hard caulk in checks when I lived in Nova Scotia. Some shipbuilders told me that it wedges the checks longer and wider, weakening the wood and eliminating any benefits of water protection. Brian brought my concerns to the Captain, but he had already weighed that potential damage against the problem of rainwater that currently settled in the unfilled checks, and decided to go ahead.

I decided that my job was to work humbly for the ship before myself, even if that only meant stepping in line.

I wrote a letter to a friend that night:

> And as amazing and expanding as this voyage has been, it has also been incredibly hard, especially in a professional sense. But because this profession is such a personal one and a dear one, my various disappointments affect me profoundly. Our

shipyard period is hard because it means a lot of shit work done artlessly. I feel that my hard-won skills and knowledge are underestimated and lie stagnant.

This idea of being a professional full-time traditional seaman has always been hard for me to reconcile. Perhaps it is that what we do sometimes seems like a watered-down contrivance, based on a vague idea of historical seamanship that now exists without context. There is still, of course, the context of the sea, but the impetus of commercial trade is gone in the world of traditional sail, and in the world of modern sail the love and art of traditional seamanship died with the invention of the engine and the GPS.

To my knowledge, there are no more active master riggers. Those still alive have already forgotten more than we'll know. I think that what I'm realizing is that this career is wonderful for the apprentice, good for the journeyman, but in my mind there will never be another master. Without the real context of time, traditional seamanship becomes hopelessly pedantic after a while. It reminds me of the study of Latin somehow.

But what is genuinely left is so good, good because it is experiential: understanding rope, responsibility, trust, rigging, thinking, leading, following and navigation mean a lot and if I have a role to play in this career it will be to pass along what I've learned. I don't want to live like the captains I've met. I dunno, that may sound sad, but I hope you realize, I'm doing what I set out to do. I'm exploring this career and I'm finding answers.

In Fiji, we did countless dirty jobs. As we covered and repaired blemishes on the ship, we transferred its entropy to ourselves. We were covered in layers of paint and rust and bruises from chipping hammers and caulking hammers and scrapes from wire brushes and grinders. Underneath us, the tide washed in and out of Walu Bay, carrying with it the sewage of Suva. Mildred, with her microbiologist's sensitivity, realized the health risk and requested that the deck washes stop. And soon the ship was a dustbin of grime and rust flakes.

Hired Fijians worked aboard, too, ripping up decking around the superstructure and torching and welding many improvements to our equipment.

We vacated the hold and shifted coal and loaded many tons more. We sent down the lower topsails and their yards with the ease of true journeyman sailors. Soon it seemed the entire ship was torn apart as we repaired and refurbished. We loaded food and painted and varnished. At the end of our two-week maintenance period, two more weeks were added so we could continue the important work being done.

Bare steel got five coats of primer and paint. Metalwork arrived from ashore—reinforcement for the steering gear, a new emergency tiller, lengthened funnels to catch air for the main salon and new cranes to support the lower topsail yards, replacing the only piece of rigging yet to fail.

On nights off, we took advantage of Suva's three-dollar movies at the cinema. We drank at bars that blasted dance music and sold cheap Fiji bitter, which was light enough to be refreshing in the humid air though bitter enough to satisfy my taste. We would wait on the dock for the last skiff at eleven, talking loudly with friends and wavering drunk by the water's edge.

On the last night in Fiji, we ran on fatigue, drinking and partying, not returning to the ship because she had been tied to the pier to bunker fuel that night. After all my friends left me at the bar for a night's sleep, I stayed out, caught in a whirlwind haze of booze and sweat, charged by a nervous insomnia, perhaps a side effect of our malaria drug. I wanted to soak up all the filth of that city—to drink all its liquor, inhale all its cigarette smoke, marijuana and clouds of dirty exhaust, screw all its women and wander its twisted streets until I found my way back to ship, which hid behind a mountain of shipping containers. At 0400, I stepped over the rail, nodded to the deck watch and crashed for three hours until it was time to leave.

In the morning, feeling weak, I turned to with the rest of the crew, helping ready the ship for departure. I felt more antsy to get back to sea with every minute, to fall back into the steady rhythm of watches, to let the purity of shipboard life wash away the grit of city and shipyard.

Mid-morning, the Captain commanded, "Brace up foreyards two points, port tack!"

We hauled together on the braces swinging those yards across the sky as crew continued to throw supplies aboard.

"Set the fore lower topsail!"

The chain sheets rattled around their sheaves as the sail stretched to catch the stiff trade wind.

"Set outer jib!"

Hand over hand, we hauled in rhythm until enough sail was set to pry the ship loose from her dock. Forward lines were cast off first, and she pointed towards the harbour mouth while drawing away from the pier. We braced the yards until the sails filled. We cast off after lines and the Captain ordered that more canvas be set to balance out the weather helm: main lower topsail, upper topsail, staysails, inner jib, the foresail that swept from starboard bow to port midships. The ship heeled in response to the stiff breeze that blew across the ship and slapped her with chop. You could feel her building speed.

The Captain took the helm and steered her through the cut while we washed down her decks. Bo'sun Josh had us scrub and hose the decks three times with soap to remove all the filth that had built up over four weeks without a deck wash.

And when it was done and we had shaped up on the islands of Vanuatu, five hundred miles away, I saw Josh on the fo'c'sle head. His big arms gently held the boltrope of the foresail in one hand. He wore a benevolent half-smile and seemed not to be aware of himself. These were working hours and he was usually chasing a never-ending maintenance list, but instead he drew the foot of the foresail towards the newly lengthened cowl vent, looked up the curving sail to the yard and back down. He was trying to divert wind off the sail and into the funnel to provide fresh air for the compartment below.

That night, we sailed on a broad reach, with the spanker sheeted out far and all sail reaching high and white and leaning over with the wind. On the quarterdeck, Kim assembled a kite that he'd brought all the way from Lunenburg and flew it on a long string aft of the spanker. We stood around him, taken by the simple spectacle, entranced as it turned in the air and dove for the ocean and rig.

CHAPTER 26

Magic

Port-Vila and Ambrym, Vanuatu
August 12 to 19

Six days out of Fiji, I lay on the fo'c'sle floor staring at the overhead. The floor was seventy years old—original equipment—three inches thick, with the soft part of its grain worn away, leaving elliptical ridges that pressed into the skin of my back, which shifted to port then starboard with the roll of the ship. The floor was cool, and it felt good on my back. I counted out the months we'd been to sea. *Almost nine.* I counted out the months until we'd return. *Just over nine.* I didn't usually indulge this kind of thinking, but when I did, I'd always lie on the floor to do it.

Jesse entered the fo'c'sle and lay on the two sea chests in front of his bunk, arms overhead, legs set apart to brace himself against the rolls—one under his bunk, one in the walkway. It had become his post-prandial ritual.

"Mefloquine Monday, Jesse. Don't forget." Jesse and I were still on the original dosage cycle, taking one pill to prevent malaria each Monday.

Jesse reached to the head of his bunk for the white carton of pills and pulled out a blister pack. The information sheet fell onto his chest. He pressed the pill through its foil wrapping, popped it in his mouth and washed it down with a gulp of water from a plastic bottle. He picked up the info sheet and opened its three folds.

"'Caution should be exercised with regard to driving, piloting airplanes and operating machines, as dizziness, a disturbed sense of balance or neuropsychiatric reactions have been reported during the use of mefloquine.'"

"Neuropsychiatric?"

"That's what it says. I guess that's what Betty had when she thought her light bulb was too loud."

"Don't forget that her cigarette was too long to light."

"Oh, man. Andrew says he has positive side effects."

"What do you mean?"

"It makes him happy."

"What else is there?"

"Um . . . here it is. 'Adverse effects: The most frequently reported adverse events are nausea, vomiting, dizziness or vertigo, loss of balance, somnolence, sleep disorders (insomnia, abnormal dreams), loose stools or diarrhea, and abdominal pain.'"

"I can relate to the abnormal dreams. Anything else?"

"Here we go. 'Less frequently reported adverse events: *central and peripheral nervous system:* sensory and motor neuropathies (including paresthesia), convulsions or seizures, visual disturbances, tinnitus and vestibular disorders, emotional problems (anxiety, restlessness, depressive moods, psychotic or paranoid reactions), forgetfulness, confusion, hallucinations."

"What is the percentage occurrence?'"

"It doesn't say."

"But the size of our crew certainly makes an event among us more likely."

"Why are we laughing?"

Soon, Jesse looked at his watch and sat up reflexively. "Oh. One o'clock. Gotta go to work."

Jesse had been a dayman for seven months already, working twelve hours a day on rigging projects. The routine of work and breaks had become so ingrained that he and Josh both admitted the lunch bell made them salivate.

I remained on the floor for another minute and then went to the deck to work on my knife handles. Jesse had seen my frustration upon chipping another piece off that unforgiving Palmerston ironwood, ruining my fourth attempt at a handle and two days of work. As a solution, he suggested I try using wood from a broken heaver that Brian had once used to wind tight wire seizings around the lower shrouds. Kim told me the wood was called martesano.

I had attached a portable woodworker's vise to one of the big forward deck cleats so I could work in the open. With a handsaw I had already cut two rectangular blanks that would make up the cheeks of the handle. This wood, like the Palmerston ironwood, was dense enough to sink. But unlike the wild and knotty ironwood, the martesano grain was tightly organized in tiny wavelets. It would at least be something I could plane without chipping.

Today's task would be to plane a sixteenth-inch rebate into each cheek, so when they were pressed against the blade, they'd reveal its spine on one side and enclose it on the other, where the fingers curl around. For this I would use Kim's rabbet plane, which had a blade that reached fully to one side, able to shave wood away along the full width of the plane's sole.

When I came to the deck carrying Kim's plane, Josh was sitting on the pinrail, his feet dangling above the bits where I'd attached my vise, the only place I could attach it and avoid getting splashed. It wasn't normal for him to sit there, or anywhere, during work. We all knew him for his almost impossible dynamism, working like a cyclone twelve hours a day six days a week, sometimes Sundays. Today his eyes were set on the base of the foremast and the long hairs of his black beard stood up around his jaw muscles. In spite of the smooth seas and fresh wind on our beam, he looked almost to be holding back tears of rage.

"You OK?"

He held his eyes on the foremast, then turned to look at me. "Yup."

"What's wrong?"

"Nothing."

"You sure?"

"I don't think I'm going to take mefloquine any more. It makes me angry—an asshole. I'm tired of being angry."

"Aren't you worried about malaria?"

"It's gotta be better than this." Josh slid down from the pinrail and ambled aft, his long ponytail swinging between broad shoulder blades.

I kneeled down and clamped one of the cheeks of my handle. Today was the end of a long-anticipated stage. I allowed the plane blade to protrude beneath the sole as little as possible; not just for accuracy, but because if the blade caught, even slightly, it would pull the thin handle from the tentative grip of the flimsy portable vise and threaten my fifth attempt.

An hour later, the handle was done and ready to be riveted to the blade. I looked forward to shaping it to fit my father's hand. At that moment, Nobby stopped by for a visit. Irresistibly drawn to any project, the engineer loved to shower the craftsman with bits of helpful advice garnered from his lifetime of tinkering.

He held one of the handles, looking it over. I felt he was examining it for flaws in my workmanship and it put me on edge. Then he offered advice on how I might improve the handle. I demanded it back. He looked at me, affronted by my lack of appreciation, and said, "OK, here ya go," and tossed it to me.

The handle spun through the air.

I reached. I didn't reach far enough. It hit one of the horns of the bits and bounced on the deck. It hit the edge of the Panama chock and dropped into the ocean frothing by at six knots. It sank to the bottom.

"Oh, dear. I am truly sorry, Rige."

"It's all right, man," I said as I picked up my tools and searched for that last piece of broken heaver buried in the forepeak, wondering why this project had become such a challenge, why I was stymied at every turn.

That night, I awoke from my sleep. I looked at my watch and realized that two hours would be too long a wait to use the head. I grabbed the sarong hanging over my curtain wire, wrapped it around my waist and walked aft.

Peeking in the mess, I saw a group of women, off watch, gathered on the benches, writing letters or reading, all of them wide awake.

Mefloquine, they all agreed, had caused the interruption in their sleep patterns, especially when the blood level was high, shortly after a dose. When they did sleep, their nights were bothered by violent dreams: a vegetarian beats a fuzzy white rabbit to a bloody pulp, a woman is frozen in her bunk while a man she hates looms beside her, not speaking, not moving.

I understood that ship life is characterized by high highs and low lows, but this was different. I saw it in the way we influenced each other's moods. I saw it in the way sarcasm deepened, the way we avoided each other's eyes, and how I doubted that anyone would ever again say something sincere.

The next afternoon, the Captain called a muster and we gathered about the stained cover of the cargo hatch, its synthetic fibre worn glossy by sleeping bodies and the scuff of bare feet. He kneeled down and laid a chart before him that showed his intended destinations: Port-Vila, where we'd clear in, Ambrym with the volcanoes, Pentecost with the vine jumpers and Santo with the wreck dives.

He pointed to an island on the chart. "That's Tanna." Then he pointed over the port beam, which rolled lazily up and down, to the real Tanna Island through a thin haze of humidity and dust. Our eyes were drawn to the smooth, dusty slopes of a volcano that belched a plume of dark smoke, drifting downwind with us. The Captain let the formality slide from his voice and sounded comforting. "Look. I just want to ask all of you to take it easy on each other."

I looked around at my shipmates surrounding the hatch, a ragtag group of homeless people wearing expensive sunglasses. Behind us the volcano left its smoky trail. Water lapped on the hull plates as we rolled.

The next day, we arrived at Port-Vila on the island of Efate. Customs arrived and those allowed ashore crowded the first boats. We climbed the ladder of the high concrete seawall and drifted through the open market, running fingers through baskets of smooth, cool shells.

While many of the guys wandered into the clean, modern, faintly European town to find a bar stool, Don and I headed off to try some kava, island beer that the islanders call *aelan bia* in Bislama, their pidgin language.

"It's supposed to be quite potent in Vanuatu," Don said as we leaned into the hill and walked to a long white building sided on two walls with lattice.

"Seems to get stronger as we head west."

We stopped talking as we entered the shelter. Afternoon light filtered in through the lattice and was diffused by the gravel floor. Men sat on benches fixed along the walls. They sat apart from one another, and their distance was enhanced by their silence and the meditative expressions on their ebony faces. They registered a second's discomfort as Don and I entered their space, which, while public, was rarely visited by outsiders.

We sat down on the benches. I leaned forward, elbows on knees, feeling awkward, intrusive, knowing it would be easier to walk down the hill into town and drink real beer among friends. I stood and walked to a short table where the bowl of kava sat. A man stood behind it looking at me expectantly. "Two, please."

He picked up a half-coconut shell and ladled in a dishwater-like liquid from the plastic punch bowl. He handed me the coconuts of kava and I watched him replenish the bowl, first dumping a satchel of powder, ground fine as flour, then adding water to suspend the grinds. It was the most commercial kava I'd seen. In Samoa, I had drunk kava freshly pounded from the dried root. In both Samoa and Fiji, it was served in wooden bowls.

I sat beside Don and passed him his libation. Observing etiquette, we put the shells to our mouths and drank what we could in one gulp, leaving some to pour on the earth. The liquid was warm, and I felt the fine powder work its way around my gums and under my tongue. It tasted like earth. I leaned back and relaxed, waiting for the kava to take effect, feeling my lips slowly go numb like I'd been given Novocaine by a dentist.

When Don returned with another shell full, I drank it and began to feel more comfortable in the unfamiliar surroundings, content to sit back in silence with the locals. A man with a bushy beard, thick hair and a pleasant expression entered the kava bar. Unlike the more reserved patrons, he made eye contact and flashed us a toothy smile. He sat next to Don and struck up a conversation that went on for over an hour, unflagged by the sedating kava. When the last light of day seeped through the lattice, he invited us on a kava crawl.

Our new friend guided us down the street to the next bar. We didn't stay long at these places. Just long enough for another shell of kava.

"There are over a hundred kava bars in Vila." His voice penetrated my awareness as it sank deeper into the mud and the dark of night. The more I drank, the more detached I became from my numb body.

"Let's go to the next one," said our guide.

I turned to follow. Spinning, I felt the dark buildings around me split in two, then catch up with each other. I followed our new friend, relying on Don to keep up my end of the conversation.

The last place was little more than a rusted steel roof with a few red light bulbs hanging from the rafters by their wires. There were more locals than ever and the feeling at the place was quite lively. I refused this round, trying to sober up a little. But it was too late. I now caught only snippets of events: shortcuts through yards, labyrinthine paths, clutches of conversation.

"Where will you sail next?" our friend asked.

"Ambrym Island."

"They practise magic there."

"Come on."

"Natives of Vanuatu are said to get magical power from the active volcanoes on their island. The power is proportional to the number of volcanoes. Ambrym has two."

He waved goodbye. Don and I walked down the hill to the seawall at the bottom of the basin, guided by gravity. A little brown bat alighted on Don's shoulder as we met up with Brian and Beth at the seawall, where they waited for the boat.

"How much did you imbibe?" Doctor Beth asked, ever clinical.

I answered her more graphically than I would have liked, disappearing behind a solitary bush. Earth to earth. *I'm going to find some magic in Ambrym.*

After a short passage, the *Picton Castle* anchored in a shallow bay of black sand. Large sailing yachts were anchored nearby, yet when a few wary locals paddled towards us in their outriggers, keeping a safe distance from the ship, I had the feeling that visitors here were uncommon.

I crawled into my rack early that night, planning to leave the ship before breakfast on my magic hunt. I looked out my porthole and was overcome by the island's sense of portent. Stars shimmered in the moonless sky more brightly than usual. A plume of sulphur, smoke and steam hung over the volcano and glowed orange from the lava bubbling beneath. I dreamed of the sorcerers ashore.

In the early morning, as crew pulled pillows over their ears to block out the first cock crows, Karen drove Marcello, Patrick and me ashore. Brian had sent me to meet the returning Marcello at the airport in Vila so I could help him find the ship. Brian understood the bond we shared because of the knife, and I felt lucky that Marcello had been able to return. If there was anyone who would be enthusiastic for a magic hunt, it was Marcello. I went to the airport alone and was surprised to meet ten of my shipmates screaming with adoration as his plane touched down, as if he were the Beatles.

Stepping over the bank of black sand, we walked under the cover of bushes, short palms and papaya trees. We entered a small village of neat thatch houses with chickens in the yards and the wholesome smell of cooking fires and vegetation left to compost. Standing at the edge of the village was a *tam-tam*, a sculpture carved from a log with a stylized human head and a long slit in the belly that was hollowed out as a sound chamber. The tam-tam was used as a drum to summon villagers together.

We three walked away from the coastal village into the forest.

"Marcello?" I asked.

"Yeah?"

"What was it like to go home?"

He took a deep breath. I could tell he'd been asked before.

"Everything was the same when I got back, except for me."

"What do you mean?"

He looked down at his big bare feet, one ankle encircled by a Marquesan tattoo, a *tiki* in the centre, alert and alien. "Like shoes. I never wore shoes. I was barefoot everywhere. On the street. In people's homes."

We walked under the shade of a thickening canopy.

The undergrowth became less dense and the black earth was hard packed. Villagers followed us in excitement at a distance, running at our flanks. The group grew larger as they followed. All wore shorts and T-shirts. Some wore flip-flops. Children poked their heads from thatch huts.

We met the chief in the village centre. He'd just pushed his way through some brush on an important errand. Though he was shorter than most of the villagers, his station was evident by the preoccupied look on his grey-bearded face, his pot-belly and his attire. He wore nothing but a thatch belt that supported a delicate woven basket as a sheath for his penis.

We presented his village with some T-shirts and fish hooks we had brought. He told one of the villagers to give us something in return. A man dutifully handed me a white woodcarving of a popular Vanuatan icon. It was an abstract human form with large disc-shaped eyes, a protruding lower lip, a penis emerging between bent knees, and hands crossed over a pregnant stomach.

We walked away from the village, back to the coastal path. We continued farther from the ship. "And the tattoo, Marcello?" I asked. "What did everyone think of your new tattoo?"

"I tried to tell them about it, you know? About what tattoos are like in the Marquesas—how bold they are and how we looked over the island for two days to find the right artist—about Raphael and his backyard, about the cats. But no one understood."

We walked through an orchard of coconut palms stretching in all directions like a sea of green, each tree choked with a necklace of coconuts. We passed the steel A-frame roof of a copra shed. Under it, the thick meat of coconut flesh was dried and then packed into burlap sacks for export. We passed a desperate and skinny old man, perhaps forgotten by his family. He had no teeth, and he shuffled himself through the black dust using only his arms and his one leg. He followed us with his one good eye; his other was opaque white.

"The showers, guys," Marcello said. "I was in the shower all the time. I think I showered four times a day. You can't imagine the luxury." He paused as if to let us imagine a hot shower. "And the women. The women in Montreal, in the summertime, are totally unreal."

We soon heard the approaching footsteps of a couple of young women. They giggled as they walked close together, carrying bamboo flutes, probably excited to do some trading at Loco Kim's Travelling Cargo Store. I gathered that he had set up on the sand to trade tools and clothing for bamboo two-toned flutes and carvings.

We turned off the coastal path to walk deeper into the forest. It was dry and dusty, shrouded by a high canopy.

Standing off the path were the tallest tam-tams we'd ever seen. Unlike the ones in the village by the ship, these had two heads, stacked like on a totem pole—one the face of a dog, the other a rooster. I picked up a stick to tap a tam-tam. It had a deep resonance.

Standing among these silent faces, running my hand across their carved surfaces, I wondered if this was the magic of Ambrym, the man-made spirits in the forests.

CHAPTER 27

Music

Ambrym, Vanuatu, to Malaita and Honiara, Solomon Islands
August 21 to September 8

THE NEXT WEEKS OF SAILING AND VISITING IN VANUATU
and the Solomons were fast and beautiful. The weather was
known to be squally, even in peak trade wind season, but it
was clear and strong, day after day.

The crew's growing strength was reflected in the steady
improvements on the ship—the retreating pockets of rust
and chafe and dry-rotted fibre, better food, cleaner heads
and more efficient stowage. You could see it in the way crew
avoided the toe-stubbing obstructions on the deck and
held their balance as the ship rolled and heeled, or as they
hung in a bo'sun's chair, replacing a block at the end of a
flexing yard that seemed to breathe the endless trade wind
high above a whitecapped sea.

I started work on another knife handle for my father.
When Nobby had accidentally thrown my fifth attempt
overboard, I began to feel paranoid. *Am I being tested?*
I laboriously shaped a new handle from the last remaining
fragment of Brian's broken martesano heaver. There
was barely enough wood, but I was able to complete it.
Feeling like I'd just slain a dragon, I placed the last

component in my project bag with the other parts of the knife.

It was around the new moon and the nights were dark. A halo embraced Jupiter. The Milky Way and the Magellanic clouds, normally dim, were bright and crisp. Surrounding islands broke up the swells and the deck was stable, so that beyond the outline of the sails you could see Violent Scorpius, Proud Orion, Gentle Centaurus and the steady Southern Cross, always above our port beam.

The stiff wind leaned into all squares and the spanker, sheeted out far on a broad reach. Even the least experienced helmsman could keep our speed over seven knots, carrying us first to Pentecost, then to Espíritu Santo, and finally to the town of Uhu on Malaita in the Solomon Islands. There, I was awakened midday in the grips of a mefloquine sleep.

The equatorial sun burned down on the deck above, turning my bunk into an oven, where I tossed, tangled in sweaty sheets.

"Rigel, wake up. They want you on the helm."

I barely registered the voice through my thick slumber, then I peered through my porthole at the glassy, undulating water the colour of polished hematite. I slid from my bunk to my sea chest, stepped into my shorts and buckled my knife belt.

I walked down the hot deck to relieve the helm. We were holding station off an island so thick with life that trees on the fringes were pushed towards the water by the inland vegetation, which grew all the way up to a rounded peak. Hovering over that peak, as if created by the humid breaths of plant life, was a cathedral of afternoon cloud, mounded impossibly high.

The Captain ordered that the engine be engaged and headed us for the mouth of a narrow inland river. Realizing that the quarters would be growing close as we entered, I forced myself to attention, though my eyelids still felt heavy. The clouds contained the richest shades of orange and gold in the afternoon sun. The broad fronds of the palms were so green and glossy that it frightened me, because it seemed they were made of rubber and that the sky was painted.

I responded to the Captain's instructions, turning the wheel spoke by spoke. Soon a bearded man in a dugout canoe paddled towards us and held station off our stern, absently sculling his spade-shaped paddle with one hand. More followed him, silhouetted against the orange sparkles on the water cast by the setting sun. Still more came, seeming to grow confident and joyous with their numbers, collecting by our ship in their fine dugouts like willow leaves arrested by a branch on their way down a creek.

We idled down the river's gentle turns while Tom, harnessed to the turnbuckles at the base of the fore shrouds, swung his lead line and shouted out soundings. When we reached a great bend where the river widened and the water deepened, we dropped anchor.

That night, after the mate had gone ashore to secure permission for our visit from the village chiefs who lived along the banks, we sat on the cargo hatch playing guitars. Cooking fires burned around us on the shore. Each one represented a mysterious family that lived just over our bulwarks. We felt safe in our ship, comfortable in its familiarity, unassailable.

I heard the sound of a canoe on the starboard side. The officer on watch peered over and quickly fetched the Captain. As crew gathered to muster by the cargo hatch, the lithe Uhu locals climbed over the rail and slapped to the deck in flip-flops, compressed thin from constant use. Each local reached down, either to help another board or to pull up what looked like musical instruments. Some were great logs of bamboo. Others were rows of bamboo segments arranged like a xylophone, but vertical. Some were small pan flutes, lashed together with fibres from the jungle.

Twelve young musicians, motley as their bamboo instruments, crowded together by the mainmast. They looked out on their expectant audience with the nervous blankness of a junior church choir. I was impressed by their courage to come to our ship, the dark and unfamiliar, from the warmth of their cooking fires and the safety of their thatch huts.

The music took the rhythm of children skipping over sand. They hit the open ends of their bamboo xylophones with old flip-flops, producing a haunting, sweet sound. A bass line took shape beneath. Two children took turns lifting and dropping two huge hollow bamboo logs. Each log provided one deep tone. Root note, then fifth. Root. Fifth. Pan flutes flew above all—free, soaring over the landforms of bass. Music shivered from the children, and soon we were invited to dance. Before joining in, I sat back in the shadows and listened, knowing I was as happy as I'd ever been anywhere, watching blue flashes of lightning far away on the horizon.

In the morning, I rented a small green dugout for five dollars. Don, Andrew and Marcello did the same. We paddled together upstream, far away from the ship, to a village that stood on the banks.

A man in his late thirties with a beard and short Afro waved us over with his long machete. We dragged our borrowed canoes up on the pebbles, and before we had a chance to feel uncomfortable, he smiled and introduced himself as Moses. His teeth and gums were stained deep red from chewing betel nut, a mild stimulant thought to improve memory.

Open and welcoming, Moses led us around his village. We followed him to the firepit where they danced in ceremony, and to houses, some made of planks and some of thatch. All of them stood on stilts, a nod to their relationship with the sea. They depended upon it for food and transport but respected it because it could rise up and flood their homes without remorse.

Soon, Moses invited us to his house. Though he was modest about its construction, I was impressed that he'd put together such a sturdy building with the few rusty tools he had. He held our attention with some of his treasures: a solid gold British coin from 1897 in beautiful condition, given to him by his father; and a blob of white stuff, hard and shiny as a cue ball, crenulated like the surface of a brain, that he had found on the beach, whose identity he could only express as, perhaps, *whale sperm*?

There was nothing else. He suddenly grew aware that he had no more treasures to entertain us. Then he remembered the family sash. "My older brother John has it. He is the chief."

We walked down the path from Moses's house on the fringe of the village to John's in the centre. John stepped onto his small porch as we approached, and Moses asked about the sash in pidgin. His brother walked back into his house.

"I'm not allowed to touch this—only the chief is. Women aren't even allowed to look at it."

When his brother returned to the porch elevated above us on the sand, he held a small swath of burlap, rolled up and carefully cradled in his hand, like an injured bird.

Moses looked to the ground in reverence and I sensed my friends growing quiet and respectful, craning for a look.

John carefully unrolled the foot-long sash, from his palm up his forearm. He presented it to us—a carefully woven network of fibre strung with small, oblong, green

shells. He held the sash between his hands and let the tas-
sels at its base swing free. They tinkled dryly, hauntingly.
And I took a closer look.

"Are those teeth?"

"Yes." John pointed to his eye tooth. "From every chief
in my family."

The eye tooth of every first-born male in his family
line. I tried to count them as they swung. There must have
been at least thirty generations represented there—six
hundred years.

John pointed to a worn brown tooth at the end of the
sash. I saw that two scores were cut into the enamel. Others
had three scores, or one. John told us the scores represented achievements in each chief's life. He said he knew the
name of every man who'd once owned a tooth on that sash.
He held it to his head as he did in ceremony, then carefully
wrapped it in the burlap swatch and tucked it away.

Before we left his village, Moses gave us some betel nut
and sold me one of his attractive spade-shaped paddles.
Then we paddled down to the beach near the ship, where
Doctor Beth and brain surgeon Dave were conducting a
free medical clinic for the villagers.

On the beach, we chewed the betel nut. It tasted like the
skin of a green banana, but it soon made us feel giddy. In a
light-headed rush, I saw the beach tilt away from me. We
stood up and ran, bare feet kicking up sand and pebbles all
the way to the stony shore of the Pacific, where breakers
crashed and whitecaps broke.

Many of our crew left Uhu with bittersweet memories.
On the eve of departure, some locals, whom we'd let spend
time aboard while we had work detail, stole shoes and mugs
from the ship. It was embarrassing for the elders, but in a
way it was a genuine South Seas experience. Captain Cook,
sailing these waters two and a quarter centuries before, had

experienced the same treatment from these less property-minded people.

I wondered what they thought as we steamed away from the island of Malaita with three of their perfectly fair, symmetrical, thin-walled canoes—the best we'd ever seen—purchased for fifty dollars each and stowed in our hold.

CHAPTER 28

Big Fish, Small Fish

The Torres Strait and the way to Darwin, Australia
September 13 to October 9

Mouth of the Torres Strait
Dear Ariel,

In many of the Pacific Isles, the catcher of a tuna will eat the fish's heart while it's still beating. That is what I did tonight, at the very end of the Ocean.

The water has turned green and the waves are piling up higher and higher as the water depth drops, now 100 metres.

I feel so good! The following waves are like giant white horses and the ship loves to be pushed along like this. I went aloft to furl the gans'l and the seabirds actually collided with me. I think they smelled the tuna blood on my beard. Josh shared the tuna heart with me. So did Maggie. And the sashimi after. Like chocolate in the sun. Heaven. We ate until full. This voyage is going to be a burning hot memory.

Mornings after I wrote that letter, near the end of the reef-strewn Torres Strait, the fishing line again went taut.

"Rigel, I think we have a fish," Tom said as he stood watch by the wheel.

I walked to the transom to haul it in. I could feel it wasn't big. Josh, up early for work, helped me land it. We pulled the slender fish aboard and, while I held it, Josh pulled the hook from its spiny mouth. A barracuda. The mate, awake now, stuck his head out of the scullery.

"Should we keep it?" I asked.

"Seems like more trouble than it's worth to have a fish that won't feed the whole crew."

"It could have ciguatera," I observed, having heard that barracudas are susceptible to fish poisoning.

"Ah, throw it back," the mate said, returning into the scullery.

I held the cuda over the transom and released my upper hand. It jumped for the water.

"Rigel." I heard the Captain's voice above. "Come see me on the quarterdeck."

I breathed out, knowing what was coming, and walked to see the Captain on the bridge. He was still bleary-eyed from sleep.

"Why did you throw the fish back?"

"We were concerned about ciguatera—fish poisoning."

"I know what ciguatera is, Rigel. I've had fish poisoning before. Do you know how many times I've had fish poisoning, Rigel?"

"No."

"Twice. Do you know what kind of fish gave me poisoning?"

"Barracuda?" I ventured.

"No. Tuna. Tuna gave me fish poisoning, twice. Not barracuda. I used to eat barracuda all the time, caught on the reefs of Barbados. If you aren't going to eat the fish, don't catch the fish. Don't hurt the fish, Rigel. You can go now."

I walked to the helm, where Tom was standing by. "What happened?" he asked in a low voice.

"He was mad because I threw the fish back. He thinks we're hurting them unnecessarily. Funny thing was, the mate was right there, Captain just couldn't see him."

Tom looked angry, fisted his hands. "The mate wants us to throw them back, the Captain wants us to keep them. I know how we make them happy: from now on, we fish with no hooks."

"Wha . . . ?"

"Yeah. Take the hooks off. Throw the lines back in the water."

"Good idea." I did the job with a strong feeling that I was doing something right for a change. Letting the wet trawl run through my fingers in our wake reminded me of a few days earlier, when we'd hooked the tunas that I wrote about to Ariel.

I remembered I had been in the forepeak, riveting my seventh handle cheek to my father's knife. My friend Don had mistaken the previous cheek for scrap, and cut a piece out of it to replace the bridge of his guitar. It was the last remaining fragment of Brian's martesano heaver. Don felt so bad that he helped me find a suitable complement ashore, and in the forepeak I peened the rivets that would hold it in place. The close work and the pitching of the hot compartment made me feel seasick, so I climbed to the fo'c'sle head for fresh air and said hello to the lookout.

She stared intently over the water. For the first time since the Atlantic, the Captain had posted someone specifically to spot for hazards in daytime. The partially surveyed waters of the Torres Strait seethed with possibilities. It was riddled with currents and wrecks and reefs.

The lookout gripped the rail as the bow surged down and flying fish took flight from under the headrig, soaring crosswind over a sea that raged with whitecaps. In the near distance an enormous cargo ship was overtaking us. An enormous cargo ship steamed behind us. An enormous cargo ship steamed ahead.

The mates and helmsmen had been tense as well, manoeuvring or holding steady among all this shipping. The Captain had adjusted the sail pattern to reduce weather helm, making it as easy as possible for the helmsman to keep a steady course. On the mainmast, three squares were set, from lower topsail to t'gallant, pulled tight as drumheads by the following wind. On the foremast, five sails were set, from fo'c'sle head to royal yard.

As we raced downwind with a strong following sea, the myriad Pacific islands behind and only continents to hop now, it seemed that the voyage would move ever faster. I scrambled down the ladder to the forepeak and worked to rivet my handle until watch.

It wasn't long after we reported for duty that we hooked the tunas, ate their hearts and had sashimi on the cargo hatch, wringing four tubes of wasabi sauce to the neck as the ship surged down the strait, between reefs, among shipping, over shifting sandy bottom, under growing wind, surrounded by laughing crew.

The Captain appeared on the bridge, hands on the rail, overlooking the feast. "Take in the main gans'l!" he yelled with a sharp edge of urgency, as if things had suddenly got out of control.

Jesse and our new shipmate Paul jumped immediately for the shrouds. My watch was on duty, but our best guy was on the fo'c'sle head looking at me searchingly, not knowing if he should leave his post. I motioned for him to come and sent Lori to take his place.

"Rigel! What the fuck are you doing!"

My stomach dropped when I heard the Captain yell, and I felt hot needles of adrenalin shoot down my arms. "Making sure lookout was covered."

"WHEN I SAY YOU GO YOU GODDAMN GO!"

I'd turned for the shrouds before he'd finished and pumped my legs up the ratlines. The racing adrenalin forced precision in my movements and I ran up, hearing the Captain's voice fade as I went. "If he ever . . ."

I felt the biting wind. I saw the banks of the straits not far away, and I heard the crack and snap of the flogging gans'l. It reared up over the top of the yard, where Jesse held on, crouching low for balance. Second carpenter Paul crouched beside him.

I stepped onto the footrope and threw an arm over the flogging sail. Together we grabbed a fold as the ship rocked beneath. Terns circled above. Terns circled below. We grabbed sail, jammed it under gut. A tern's wing hit my arm. The birds cawed in excitement. The sail under control, I looked at the nostrils in their beaks and wondered if they smelled the tuna blood.

We pulled together now and rolled the sail on top of the yard. We passed gaskets and descended while the ship roared down the frothing strait.

The Captain summoned me to the bridge as I climbed down the shrouds.

I swung around inboard, lowered myself to the deck and walked towards him. He placed his elbows on the bridge rail and stared ahead, expecting me to do the same. Instead I focused my eyes on his temple.

"When I tell you to go aloft, you'd better go."

"I wouldn't disobey you."

He turned to look at me. "Oh, don't even talk to me about that. That's a subject for another time."

"I was looking for relief for the lookout before going aloft."

"Rigel, the Captain was on the bridge. I've got it. I can look out. I always see everything before anyone else anyway."

His tone was kind, not the dressing down I'd expected. Still, I felt guarded and angry.

"Rigel, please don't fuck up any more. You're the best sailor on this goddamn ship. When you go the royal, I almost think you're going to forget to stop and try for the skysail even though we don't have any."

He disarmed me with his compliment. I'd liked my anger, liked that I'd stood up, ready to take his punishment on the chin. Now I felt ashamed. I choked down an urge to cry. Then scepticism slid in. I didn't believe him, or felt I couldn't afford the price of his approval. I pushed the event from my mind.

After watch, I went to my bunk. Dark seas churned loud outside my porthole and I couldn't sleep. I felt too alive.

Within days, the intensity of this passage clung to me like a hangover. I was looking forward to Australia. On the eve of arrival, I talked to Don about it.

"Yeah," he said. "I've been doing some thinking—about an agreement, a mutual understanding. Tell me what you think."

I listened closely. It sounded already like a familiar fantasy.

"I know I'll be in a bar somewhere, and sooner or later a little flirtation will start up."

"Yeah. Of course."

"I'll start into a conversation, let it get rolling, then just tell her that if she wants me for a week, I'm hers. I'll just let it be known that I want her, and I'll make sure there's an understanding that I'll only be in port for a short while, but that while I'm in, I'm available. If she doesn't go for it, I'll just have to excuse myself and keep going, because I'm on a mission."

"Yup."

"I'm sure someone will appreciate the honesty. I'm just tired of waiting around for something to happen."

"Good man." The story did sound familiar. I understood it as a desire for a dense and fresh relationship, a new start and an escape from the world of our ship.

"What are you doing, Rige?"

"Well, you know I just finished reading this book *Tracks.*"

"*Tracks?*"

"This woman, Robyn Davidson, wrote about her solo trek from Alice Springs across the desert to the west coast, packing her gear on camels that she'd trained herself."

"What?"

"Yeah. So I want to go to the desert. Maybe to Ayers Rock if I can make it. Don't tell anyone."

I was impressed by Davidson. I envied how she'd set out on her own without a prescribed path and let the desert change her, teach her. I wondered if this voyage could do the same for me.

I'd finally finished my father's knife and sewn a sheath from one of Nobby's old engineer boots, with holes in the soles so big he could have pulled them on over his head. I felt things were set right now. I had my dad's blessing and he had his knife. It had cut me free from my history.

In Darwin, I awoke before sunrise, climbed down from my bunk and slipped on my sandals. I looked at the bit of twine holding together one of the dryrotted straps and regretted that I hadn't found my boots. I tried again to remember the last time I'd seen them . . . *Panama?*

I shouldered the backpack I'd readied the night before and quietly reached behind Tom's sea chest for his WWII army boots—the ones he'd taken from Kim's supply before Kim had sold the last of them in Tonga, green mould and all. The boots, I thought, would give me terrible blisters, but I had no confidence in my sandals in the rocky desert, and I wasn't going to spend my money on new ones. No money for clothes at all.

The tide was low, and from the quarterdeck I had to climb twenty feet to the dock, which was nearly level with the lower yards. In the dark, leaving alone and without warning, I felt like a fugitive. Four days of freedom. The longest time away from the ship since I'd met Ariel in Quebec over a year before. After the two-week passage, I sought silence and solitude and oblivion.

Oblivion must have been my goal when I walked down that dock and reached inside an old tire for a stash of pot I'd bought and hidden the night before. I never brought the stuff aboard ship, refusing to let my pleasures put her at risk.

I left Darwin on a bus just after sunrise, bound for Katherine, three hundred miles south. There, I'd read, was a 7.5-mile-long gorge that had excellent hiking. I couldn't waste two of my valuable days in a bus on the way to Ayers Rock and back. I also figured that other crew would be heading to Ayers, or to the more popular Kakadu and Litchfield parks.

From my window seat, I could see the landscape open up for miles—scrubby trees, wildflowers and clumps of grass growing out of red sand. Road trains roared by with their sullen payloads of cattle. And soon we entered the city of Katherine, where I provisioned and hitched a ride for the last thirty miles to Nitmiluk National Park, cleaved in two by the gorge.

There was a visitors' centre where I had to sign in and receive my map of the trail. It was late afternoon and they were reluctant to allow me past, worried I might not make my campsite before nightfall. I begged and they relented. I was annoyed that even on my escape I had to placate some authority. I wanted to be like Davidson, who'd torn off every mask society had placed over her eyes—ignored every metric of success or failure, pass or fail—until there was just survival and her own authenticity.

However, I shimmied my pack high on my shoulders and followed the park service's blue triangular signs as I walked alone along a four-by-four track. I made good time but soon cursed my army boots. It was foolishness to think my feet could handle someone else's boots when they were barely used to the touch of sandals. I hid them behind a recognizable rock near the track, making a mental note to carry them back out. Then I put on my sandals and tied the rotten strap in place. I smoked a joint and was off to the desert.

I woke early the next morning and quickly struck my camp, which lay about a mile from the river. I had an all-day hike ahead to the farthest gorge accessible by foot trail. It was the height of the dry, when no rain falls and temperatures reach 120 degrees Fahrenheit in the afternoon. I'd have to get going early and cover as many miles as possible before the sun reached its zenith, nearly overhead. And I'd have to take it easy on my water. I had only a gallon and a quarter, and the pot was making my mouth dry.

The trail was easy to follow, defined by the deep ruts of truck tracks. But as I continued to walk, they grew shallow and the trail dwindled to a barely visible walking path that intruded less and less on the ironwood and plum trees. Coarse grasses sprung up, as did rocks and termite hills that stood like columns. I gazed at faces in the craggy rock standing high around me. An ape's face. A crocodile snout. A rainbow in a bead of sweat rolling down my sunglasses.

I relied more and more on the blue signs as I hiked, yet they seemed to grow less and less frequent. The trail went on plunging into a wilderness of towering rocks. Textured faces that looked like apes and crocodiles. *Have I gone in a circle?*

With increasing desperation, I searched for one of those blue triangles. The sun was directly overhead and provided no indication of direction. Then I wondered if maybe I'd wanted to leave the path. I decided not to worry and stopped for a lunch of crackers and canned mackerel in the meagre shade of a leafless tree. Its black trunk and white branches cast a shadow that mingled with cracks in the dried mud. Everything seemed burnt, tortured and dusty, yet with a peculiar vibrant personality. Maybe it was the air, which was sweet and slightly minty.

I thought of a friendly American guy I'd talked to back in Darwin. He'd introduced me to a friend: "This is Rigel. He fancies himself a sailor." It stung that he saw my chosen profession as some kind of delusion. *I am a sailor. I'm a traditional sailor. How the hell do you think I got here?* In spite of lingering questions about this career and its place in the world, I'd made it a firm aspect of my identity. Authenticity, to me, always came down to a decision: *I am a sailor.*

I opened my pack to stash the lunch garbage and refill the small water bottle I carried in my hand with water from the larger bottle in my pack. I was thirsty, and there were many hard miles before I'd have the chance to replenish my supply at the gorge. I pulled out the reserve bottle and was shocked at how light it felt. It was almost empty. I couldn't believe how careless I'd been: the bottle had a mismatched lid and I'd stored it on its side.

Reality hit home. Alone in an Australian desert. The dry season. No one knows where I am. Water gone. Sun overhead. No blue triangles. Lost. I felt it in my gut.

OK. Think! I scrambled to the top of a high ridge and saw a hostile landscape of tall rocks, sharp angles and scrubby trees, with Katherine Gorge winding its way through.

I knew the campsite was on the gorge. I would find it by hiking along the wall. First I'd have to get there. Boulders and bushes blocked my path. Mouth dry, I grew tired carrying my pack up short pitches and down, though walking through some scrub I scared a wallaby and was delighted to see him bounce across my path. Once, I stopped to release a brief orange stream of urine and noticed a proud sulphur-crested cockatoo roosting in a nearby tree. The pitches grew steeper and taller, which told me I was getting closer to the gorge. I was forced to scale the rock and haul my pack up behind me on a rope I'd brought.

An hour later, I made it to the gorge wall, steep and carved deep by the river below that'd run for 23 million years. Climbing, sliding, walking in my broken sandal, I connected with the track that led to a small beach where I would camp. Mouth dry, head pounding, legs weak, I shed my pack and all my clothes, then walked into the cool river. I tucked my two empty water bottles under my legs and floated. With only my nose above water, I relaxed, drank, watched a shadow creep up the southern gorge wall, extinguishing a fire of reds and oranges alive in that rock.

I bobbed in the murky water, completely silent, realizing I hadn't spoken a word for two days. I imagined the river must somehow run to the ocean and the *Picton Castle*. So far the voyage had been much of what I'd hoped for: long, involving passages and meaningful travel. Even the Captain's harsh treatment—part of me wanted that too, so I could rise above it with some steel in my soul.

After another day and night of freedom in the desert, I returned to the ship. It was high tide that night, and I was immediately impressed that the crew on duty had painted the hull. I stepped over the quarterdeck rail, its fresh coat of varnish glowing in low light from a kerosene lamp set for sailors boarding. The brass glowed and so did the newly oiled deck. She'd been rinsed with fresh city water, which washed away the salt and renewed her gloss. Still, it was the smell that struck me most. Familiar, yet I had never noticed it before. It was not diesel or tar or paint or coal or food, just the smell of home.

In the fo'c'sle, I said hi to Maggie, quarantined in her cage for our stay in Australia. She'd been out only once, to be spayed by a local vet. Weary on-duty crew told me how she'd wailed and clawed, terrified to leave her universe of the ship. It had been a hard week for them. On top of two-hour night watches, they had spent ten-hour days removing tons of goods from the hold—tree trunks, tam-tams, dugout canoes, trade goods—all to be stowed by our watch along with five months' worth of food and coal. I felt ready again to face it head-on.

CHAPTER 29

Bali

Timor Sea and Bali
October 9 to November 21

AN UNUSUAL FLYING FISH JUMPED ABOARD FROM THE
Timor Sea. Sailmaker Marge found it and held its rounded double wings apart so we could see the brilliant
shocks of yellow, blue and violet, rather than the typical
dull bat-like wings we were used to. I remembered when
Brian put the idea of flying fish in my head back in
Lunenburg and I wrote Ariel telling her they had wings
like a butterfly's. Seeing a creature from my imagination
held before me, I felt we had indeed travelled a long way.
Later, a manta ray, big as a baby grand piano, jumped
clean out of the water and flapped its wings once before
belly-flopping down.

These waters were active with sea life. And the sea life
beckoned the fishermen in their eighty-foot white trawlers
with big square transoms, tall superstructures and sweeping sheers like swayback horses.

We'd been warned of pirate vessels on these waters,
sometimes disguised as fishing boats. It was the increased
risk of piracy on the more northern South China Sea that
had prompted the Captain to scratch Thailand from our list

of destinations. Time was growing short, as well. We were
already behind schedule.

The afterguard had taken precautions to defend us from
possible attack. High-intensity halogen lights were rigged
facing out from the quarterdeck. If the officer on deck sensed
danger, the lights would be flipped on, blinding the assailants
while illuminating them. Brian assigned himself and three
crewmen to the ship's guns. All four were familiar with
firearms and could be counted on if it came down to the wire.

There was a backup strategy: surrender to the pirates,
give up the ship's coffer and hide everyone in the forepeak.

"I don't think they'll really want the ship," said the Captain
in a muster, looking up momentarily at the arcane rig.

This provoked laughter from the crew as we imagined
modern-day pirates struggling with the intricacies of
square rig.

"She doesn't have an owner's manual."

"We'll have to hide Jean's pin diagram," Jesse said.

Everyone laughed, including Jean, who still studied to
keep a working knowledge of the ship's one-hundred-
and-fifty belaying pins and cleats.

One night on Brian's eight-to-twelve watch, a pack of
fishing vessels closed tight about the ship. He ordered that
the halogens be lit and broke out the guns. The vessels
pulled away. Aside from that, the only real emergency on
that passage was thwarted by Bill, who, after a year as third
engineer, prevented the destruction of our propeller shaft
when he heard its main bearing go awry. He shut down the
engine and saved the vessel a costly haulout. The ship
slowed to a stop on the glassy sea that shone like a mirror in
the reddish afternoon sun.

While Nobby, Claire and Bill worked to repair the broken bearing, the Captain declared a swim call. I dove into
the swells and thought of the surf adventure Tom and I had

been eagerly awaiting. We couldn't wait to get to Bali and the famous beach break in the city of Kuta.

Days later, we entered the winding channel that led to Bali's Benoa Harbour, dropping the hook three times before settling on a location so tight with every imaginable vessel that we had little room to swing on our anchor. All around us were barges, yachts, oil tankers and colourful wooden sampans powered by outboards. But the most common vessels were the white fishing boats with high, flaring bows streaked orange by rusting fasteners. One had passed us as we entered. When it turned towards the dock to unload its catch of bluefin, it began a slow roll that I was certain would end in capsize. But the crank vessel stood herself up again and the fishermen inside lived to unload their cargo of frozen tuna.

Anchored nearby was a derelict wooden cargo schooner. I'd heard that Indonesia was one of the last places on earth where sail was still used to transport cargo, but not in this harbour; only in Celukanbawang on the north coast, far away from the tourist spots.

In the city, we walked over sandy cobblestone and looked for a cheap hotel. It was noon and the three-storey buildings provided no shade from the intense sun. The morning rain had burned off the street to hang in a thick vapour. Every shop burst with artistic wares—beautiful clothes, extravagant masks, antiques made to order and clay pots big enough to climb inside.

Soon we made our way to the beach and stood on the rise to study the waves. Directly ahead were a series of perfectly formed curls, five feet high, unbroken and stacked in even ranks. We watched them run towards the beach and wash over legions of surfers crowding the water.

Those surfers, and their hangers-on, came to Kuta like a great wave themselves. The Balinese, so welcoming and industrious, had opened their city to the visitors—to their needs and their pleasures. It seemed we'd arrived in Kuta after that wave had become too big for their culture to absorb. The wave had already broken, and when it pulled back to sea, it left at the high-water mark a detritus of hawkers, pushers, hookers, bungee jump towers, hamburgers and henna tattoos.

While the best surfers in Bali braved the coral or volcanic rock in search of bigger waves away from Kuta's crowds, I saw enough decent surfers here to be frustrated by my early attempts at paddling beyond the surf, as I tumbled through the waves, gasping for air and blocking rides. After a day of that, I got my rhythm and ducked the waves well enough. Floating beyond the break, we sat back on our boards, cooled by the waves and the spray ripping off their backs.

At night, there was little for us to do but follow the dance music that pulsed through the air over the wooden gates of the Sari Club. It seemed the only place to be in Kuta at night, and Tom and I were drawn through those gates by the scent of sandalwood incense, pheromones and sweat. You could see it evaporate off their bodies, the Scandinavians, the Australians, the North Americans, the Dutch, the Balinese—all there bouncing, grinding, drunk, loving life.

The men sniffed around, charging the sandy concrete floor in packs, yelling, grinning, shirtless, biceps swollen from paddling in the surf, glossy with henna tattoos, hefting extra-large bottles of Bintang beer. The women crowded the dance floors—loose hair, bikini tops, surf shorts, sarongs—bound together by exertion and sweat and pleasure and freedom. I bought myself a Bintang and tried to get into the mood of the place, but the Barbie song played one too many times and I felt out of place. Being shirtless too made me uncomfortable. I wasn't having the luck of my fellow travellers, and seeing everyone so wrapped up in each other, feeling the sexual energy that hung overhead like a cloud of static electricity, I became lonely and bothered and ready to leave.

The next day, after an early morning surf, I left Kuta for the small city of Ubud. It seemed the inverse of Kuta. Though tourism was still its lifeblood, Balinese culture dominated in Ubud, or at least was more visible. Visitors could walk through temples, witness ancient dances and attend extravagant cremations often followed by ritual cockfights. The dissonant, clanging sounds of gamelan music—xylophones, gongs and drums—played on street corners. Ubud was imbued with the splendour of Balinese art and expression.

In Ubud, I ran into chief engineer Nobby and we went to a *kecak* dance. On the ground, in the centre of a circle of spectators, sat one hundred bronze-chested men clothed in black-and-white checkered sarongs—a pattern representing the constant interplay of good and evil in the Balinese world view. The men waved their arms in the air and syncopated their voices. *Chak-a-chak-a-chak-a-chak-a.* Their voices seemed to echo off one another, shimmering as they undulated in a complex rhythm. Soon a woman clothed in gold brocade and crowned in a frangipani-flower headdress moved elegantly onto the stage, making the most profound expressions with just her eyes.

When the show was over, we noticed a pretty, long-haired young woman across the floor looking at us through the smoke of a costume that had been lit aflame. We introduced ourselves. Her name was Brigitte. She was a young, hippie dance student from California, come to Bali to appreciate their rich tradition of dance. We introduced ourselves and then, over a snack of firm, cold calamari, talked about spending the next day together.

After sleeping in our separate boarding-house rooms, the

three of us walked through forest temple ruins. I tried to befriend a monkey sitting on an old foundation. I let him climb on me and pick through my long hair. He repaid the favour by rifling through my backpack and biting the back of my head. Fearing I would soon die from the monkey bite, I asked Brigitte to bicycle with me around the island to the sailing-ship port of Celukanbawang after my four-day stint on the ship.

I did not look forward to the interim on the ship. Others had taken a break from the vessel at this point in the voyage, and though I didn't admit it, I understood their desire to do so. It wasn't the work; it was a feeling that the ship's gravity was taking hold—hauling me back.

On the bus back to the ship that night, I was overcome by feelings of self-loathing. All of my life's compromises, my confusion, my desire to stay away, swirled in my head. Caustic bubbles rose from deep in my gut, twisted around my insides and lodged against my heart. I wondered if mefloquine heightened the pain, and I buried my face in the Naugahyde seat ahead of me, bit the cold plastic and spun into a pit of anxiety. I squeezed my eyes, heard a ringing in my ears and felt the searing point of a cold sore push out on my lower lip, drilling its root deep down to my jaw. I was a worm turning in a thimbleful of dirt.

Back on the ship, the anxiety passed. The four days went by steadily thanks to hard work, long boat runs and eventful night watches. My days were spent managing a crew of four Balinese men who'd been hired to chip rust. All of us lay on our backs and pounded rust scales off the bottom of the cap rails, ridding the ship of one of its final few pockets of decay. The workers were paid five dollars a day, which was the going rate for Balinese labour. I was amazed that people could live on roughly two or three dollars less than what I was getting, on top of my food and bunk.

With four days of service done, I rushed back to Ubud with a light assortment of clothes, a first aid kit and my machete. I half expected my liaison not to show up, but when she did, I was eager to leave town before anyone from the ship saw us together and my six-day adventure became ship gossip and lost its value as an escape.

We did not get along as well as I had hoped. My cold sore had grown to disfigure my lower lip due to my regimen of intense sun and sleep deprivation. (I'd been awoken many times on the ship to help Tom fend off a fishing boat that swung into us as the wind shifted overnight.) The cold sore made Brigitte wary of me. I had developed a kind of protectiveness for her. This irritated her, and I was irritated by her irritation. We got what we needed from our tryst, but there was a feeling that we each would have chosen another companion if given the option. Any port in a storm.

I felt happiest losing myself looking down on the beaches of Amed. Brightly painted dugouts rigged with pontoons and colourful patchwork sails were pulled close together on the crescent shore. Beyond both headlands were other crescent shores, and beyond them, rows of boats stretching into the distance.

On the north coast, after a long afternoon bike ride, Brigitte stayed at our rented hut while I raced off on my bicycle. I pedalled as hard as I could to reach the town of Celukanbawang. Ten hard miles later, I breathed the intoxicating odour of fresh-sawn teak, cut and hauled from what remained of the Indonesian rain forests. I followed the odour to three white sailing ships tied to a dock. Though they were loaded past their gunwales with teak planks, it was evident that the ships were well crafted. Probably influenced by Portuguese explorers, the vessels were schooner-rigged, with gaffs on the fore and mains'ls, topmasts and three jibs. Their hulls were built with exaggerated bows and sterns that must have given them the reserve buoyancy they needed in heavy seas, loaded down with cargo.

The Indonesian Bugis people built these ships, called *pinisis.* For a thousand years they'd transported cargo to ports in Asia and Australia. It was said that the Bugis had a reputation as the most feared pirates in the Java Sea, inspiring the word "bogeyman." They crafted their ships entirely by hand, building them by eye and fastening their teak planks with wooden trunnels, or pegs. The sailing cargo trade has remained viable for them because of their ability to access the smaller islands of the Indonesian archipelago. Like us, they used engines to go to dock and pass through calms, but underway they hoisted all sail and would transport anything from lumber to crates of Coca-Cola.

At last, I'd seen a genuine sailing cargo operation. I wondered if their ships would one day disappear with the dwindling teak forests they depended on for cargo. And if their ships disappeared, would the Bugis, after a lull of forty years or so, realize the worth of that bygone life and scrape the barnacles off old sailors in order to dredge their secrets from them?

It was getting dark. I bought a soda to quench my thirst and rode back as fast as I could down a road lined with broad green leaves and palms.

When I returned to the ship, ready to press on across the Indian Ocean, the hatches were open and Balinese goods lay in piles about the deck. One of the skiffs was missing. The freshwater pump had a sign that read: *Conserve water. Drinking only*. The ship was not ready for departure. Bo'sun Josh brought me up to speed. Work that the Captain had contracted from local artisans was taking longer than planned. There was an undertone of concern in our conversation, because every day placed us deeper into cyclone season on the Indian Ocean.

As the days aboard went on in routine cycles of chipping, painting and stowing, the first of the contracted jobs arrived: our skiff with its interior painted Caribbean shades of blue, green, pink and yellow. Next came teak boxes to cover the steering gear and engine controls, carved with traditional Balinese motifs of the rice goddess and six-petal flowers.

Like Melville's *Pequod*, with sperm whale teeth along its rails for belaying pins so that her deck resembled the jaw of the beast she sought, the *Picton Castle* began to reflect her career of travel. She carried tokens from each port like trophies. In her mess room were Tongan and Samoan war clubs. Norwegian life jacket instructions were posted in the heads. A Lunenburg windlass stood on her bow. Galapagos cedar accented her aloha deck. And a Bermuda rum barrel was lashed to her bulwarks.

Each day, the Captain returned to the dock with Balinese furniture and carvings to stow for sale in Canada.

Our stay was delayed further. A golf-ball-sized abscess had formed on the side of the mate's jaw. Despite a course of antibiotics the thing had continued to swell to a painful extreme. Though he didn't show it, I wondered if this was his body rebelling against a growing road-weariness—a weariness of his long burden as the bridge between Captain and crew. He and Doctor Beth prepared for travel back to Darwin, where they had chosen a hospital. There, Brian would go under general anaesthesia and have the thing drained. Both they and the U.S. consulate felt he could not be safely operated on in Bali.

When Brian returned, we still needed two more days of preparation. Because it was unsafe to desalinate the contaminated harbour water, our water tanks had nearly run dry and we were now making runs to the yacht club to fill jugs for drinking and cooking. The water was too sewer-ridden for even a deck wash. Trapped in a harbour under tropical sun, the ship was parched, longing to cross the Indian Ocean.

CHAPTER 30

Family

Indian Ocean, Bali to Seychelles
November 21 to January 28

THE ROYALS WERE FURLED CLEAN AND TIGHT AGAINST
the stiff breeze. The wind was on the quarter and all sails
from the gans'ls down pulled full of wind. The ship moved
at seven knots and I was content on the quarterdeck, near
the helmsman, on a Sunday afternoon.

In choosing his route across the Indian Ocean, the
Captain had made judicious use of his weather maps and
took us past the fifteenth southern parallel, clear of the
tropical depressions and squalls that twisted about at that
time of year. On our path, fast-moving cotton-ball clouds
swabbed clean the daytime sky.

Then came the call, "Fish on!" Marcello and I pulled
together, watching water drops squeeze from the trawl,
expecting the fish to skip along behind like all the others. It
didn't. We pulled until our heavy trawl aimed straight
down. In the deep blue we could see a form of deeper blue,
slashing its tail, fighting for life.

Brian stood ready on the bench at the transom, toes
curled around the grating, sinewy muscles tensed as he
held his gaff like a harpoon. The hook was deep and the

341

trawl was strong. We hauled the fish to the surface, and the force of our pull made him roll onto his side so I could see one of his big round eyes. Brian struck out with his gaff, twisted it up inside the massive gill. He lifted and the tired gaff nearly splintered under the strain. The tuna fought, swinging its tail to get free. Tom reached for the narrow base of the tuna's tail. Together we hoisted the great fish aboard to the transom bench.

I was ready with Marcello's knife. I slid it into the gill and cut through the carotid artery. Josh jammed his well-worn knife into the fish's brain. Maggie the Cat twisted around my ankles.

We stood back and were now part of a large crowd that had gathered. The five-foot tuna kicked. Arrhythmic convulsions pulled his body onto the deck with a thud. Spasms grew faster, more desperate. Frothy blood issued from his wound. The fish turned over and streaked his blue scales with blood. He slapped the planks with his shivering tail and slid down the deck to the superstructure.

Onlooking crew laughed uncomfortably as if this was dark comedy. The laughing grew until, mercifully, the fish died.

The next day, the ship was abuzz with work. Five coats of paint sealed the steel we'd chipped beneath the rails in Bali. Now crew worked to encase the rows of seizings at the base of the shrouds in primer and white paint to stand out against the protective tarred marline. It was one of the few effects on a square-rigger done purely for looks, and it made me feel we were actually reaching the end of this long conversion project.

Mate Brian had shuffled the watches before we left Bali, and had taken over from Tom as the leader of my four-to-eight watch. While our watch carefully painted seizings, I told Brian about the progress of our work party. I could see through his zebra-patterned sunglasses that he looked me square in the eye.

"I've been thinking about that tuna," he said.

"Pretty big, huh." I thought of the time I'd helped Brian try to catch a tiger shark, anchored off Ambrym, where their tails were rumoured to stir the murky black water. He'd rigged an enormous hook baited with two pounds of salt beef, and prepared a lasso to hoist the shark upside down from the port yardarm, where it would gnash its teeth at the air.

"I feel kind of bad," he said. "It fought so hard."

The fish had sounded like a whale beneath our transom.

"Then we brought him to the deck, where its fins and gills were no use, and cut it with our knives."

I was taken aback by his sincerity. He demanded, like few people I'd met, his own deep introspection and growth.

"He might have been a king down there," he said. Suddenly he turned around to the general crowd on the quarterdeck and shouted, "BUMPING UGLIES! Someone write that down!"

To pass the time and bring the crew together on this long passage, he'd created a group project: list one hundred words for sex. I watched as crew gathered around him, joining in for another round of brainstorming, already at seventy-two. The forums were as popular as his celestial navigation classes, which had recently advanced from sun sights to star sights.

Every morning, Brian, Becky, Jean and I shot with our sextants the six brightest stars that were not blotted out by the rising sun. Later, on our off time, we would sometimes work out our position. But Brian would disappear into the charthouse to calculate it right away and plot his result on our chart.

As a nautical art, celestial navigation deserves to be preserved. That one thought allowed us to ignore the rewards of its practice. It helped us understand the motion of our planet through the solar system. We learned to identify stars when they were just beginning to appear at night, or perhaps peeking alone through a hole in a cloud-covered sky. The art completed us as traditional sailors. In a way, shooting the stars was a more lofty craft than crossing royal yards.

Brian's morning calculations left me in charge of the deck, an experience I seldom had under Tom. When Brian disappeared at sunrise, the warming air usually brought a wind shift, which necessitated a trim to the squares. This would be a small honour for me on most traditional ships. But in the *Picton Castle*, like the short-handed Cape Horners, only officers slacked the windward braces. Looking aloft, I held three braces like reins and eased them slowly, such that each higher brace was squarer to the ship, creating a spiral effect. This allowed the higher sails to make better use of the faster wind aloft. And if poor helmsmanship caused us to steer into the wind, the highest and smallest sail would be first to go aback.

Brian had refined this art to a high degree of precision. Trying to match him caused me to be miserly with the slack I gave the crew hauling on the other end. They shot me bewildered glances. But the learning and challenge were energizing, and even after thirty days at sea I wanted to keep sailing.

Off watch, I devoted a few hours a day to a project that would help organize the chronically disordered forepeak. I designed and helped Kim to build a set of swinging cabinets that would be installed on an unused wall.

The galley department too put in extra effort. With another cook let go in Darwin, baker Beth worked hard to put out delicious and plentiful meals. She was aided by a couple of spirited young Australian women. One of them, Annie, had joined us as a result of Don's foray into the

Darwin singles scene, and the other, Jade, had answered an ad in the paper.

With her long brown hair, high cheekbones and spaghetti-strap top as tight as the royals in a gale, Jade was one of the most fetching additions to our crew since Lee had strutted the decks naked in the Caribbean. Quickly, Jade paired up with Marcello, and they became a tight and isolated unit.

The rest of us grew more like family. With a warm Thanksgiving behind us and Christmas approaching, many crew became Secret Santas, sneaking around crafting gifts for each other.

The crew's high spirits were reflected in our caring for the ship. For that reason I should not have been surprised to see bo'sun Josh step onto the quarterdeck before sunrise on his day off, coffee in hand, knife belt strapped around his waist.

"Josh, I'm sorry. Did someone wake you by accident?" I asked. It had been some time since our watch had botched a wake-up.

"No, I had a vision."

Brian and I looked at him incredulously.

"Rigel and I are going to bend on the fore royal," Josh said.

I looked aloft. On the mainmast flew all the squares, but for the last couple of days the fore had been missing its crown, creating a gap like a missing tooth in an otherwise perfect smile. Brian broke the silence. "Sure. Go ahead."

Josh told me to rig the gantline that we would use to hoist the sail. I descended the ladder to the main salon and lifted the hatch where the rope was stored. Jumping down into the bilge, I found a long coil of soft manila that would reach from the deck to the top of the mast and back down to the deck.

With the rope slung over my shoulder, I climbed from the deck to the highest ratlines. Finally, I shinnied up the backstays to a block at the hounds of the royal mast, where the highest rigging converged. I had been from the very bottom of the ship to the very top in minutes. I paused to look at the cloudless twilight flooding the horizon in soft orange.

Josh was now waiting for me to toss him the line on the fo'c'sle head. I threw it gently forward and the coil of line unfurled through the network of rigging to the deck.

Climbing back down, I saw he had stretched out the foot of the sail and had begun to sew a leather patch to the boltrope, where continual flogging of the sail in light wind or rolling sea had caused it to wear away on the stay that ran beneath. Josh stitched quickly, though I could tell it was not fast enough for his liking. There was impatience in the way he pushed his needle through the layers of hide and canvas then extracted it with his pliers. I asked to help and soon we were both working fast to finish the job.

"Why are we working so fast?" I asked. "It's Sunday."

The bo'sun looked a little embarrassed. "The Captain wanted me to put this on loose, with big wide stitches. That's just not me, so I wanted to get it done and up there." He looked up the foremast.

I helped stitch faster, but the small, tight stitches were taking time. Stitch. Pull. Stitch. Pull. Soon the Captain stood behind us. We stitched, hoping we'd make it, but the Captain was observant as always.

"Josh, come talk to me."

I stitched. The sun rose higher and chased out the cool of morning. Bo'sun Josh returned.

"How was it?"

"Not bad," he said, though he looked a little red in the face. "Should have made it loose so it would dry faster after rain. That way the canvas won't mildew."

I wasn't sure if Josh accepted the argument or if he was

simply being a proper shipmate, not questioning the Captain's view. I admired Josh for wanting to assert his autonomy, even though it was technically the wrong thing to do. Like the Captain had said, a bo'sun has a mind of his own. In any case, we bent sail to its high yard, holding tight against the ship's rolls amplified so heavily aloft. We sheeted home the clews, hauled the halyard, and the *Picton Castle* pushed towards Africa with her full suit of sail.

That night, in the final hour of watch, I leaned with mate Brian against the charthouse, sheltered from the cool wind. He smoked a cigarette. We talked.

"Would you like to be a captain?" I asked.

"No, not me. It's too lonely at the top."

"Does it have to be?"

He crossed his arms over his black-and-white checked flannel shirt, quiet for a moment. "I've sailed under a lot of masters. Some are buddies with the crew and some are aloof. The aloof ones are better. You have to keep your distance to make the big calls."

"That's why Dan snubs the new crew when they say hi."

"Exactly."

We were quiet for a while. Brian threw his hand-rolled cigarette stub overboard and it was caught by the steady wind. "You have to be careful, though. If you're perceived as unfair or spiteful, you'll turn your crew against you. Drain enthusiasm. They won't care, won't turn to. That's dangerous."

"Right."

"I used to be like that, but I'm not any more," he said.

That night, in my bunk, a cool draught nipped at my shoulders. I pulled on a blanket for the first time since we'd left Pitcairn Island, and slept deeply. We continued west into flawless days and refreshing nights. Too soon, it was time to guide the ship northward to the Seychelles and then on to Zanzibar. As we approached the equator, nights grew hotter and the weather more fickle.

Just before sunrise off the east coast of Africa, our watch began the daily deck wash. I hosed down the fo'c'sle head as a band of crew scrubbed their brushes across the grain of the deck, a regimen necessary to preserve the wood and keep it swollen and tight. The water, drawn from several feet below surface, was cool on our bare feet.

On the main deck I noticed a couple of the daymen leaning against the rust-streaked bulwarks, staring at the eastern horizon, apparently unconcerned with the thought of getting wet from our hose. Patrick tucked his brush handle under his elbow and leaned in repose. I looked to the east.

High cirrus and low stratus draped the sun in robes of red and orange. The cotton balls that had chased us across the ocean were lined in gold. The sea was cold blue, and a shifting wind pattern whipped up choppy wavelets. The low red sunlight passed through the chop and turned its tips to flames. The sails turned red and then slowly paled to white.

With ten months solid on the four-to-eight watch, I hardly noticed the character of most sunrises. It's the danger of a rich lifestyle: you can get used to it. It was hard to believe that the beautiful scene was a bad weather portent, but by late afternoon we saw the horizon to windward smeared grey by a line squall.

"Just thought you should see this. Looks nasty," Brian told the Captain as they exited the charthouse to the deck. Even as they spoke, the squall neared. It appeared to close faster than any we'd seen since the North Atlantic. It frightened up tall chop beneath. I could see its form now— solid, slate grey, rolling like a tank tread towards our ship.

"READY ABOUT!" the Captain commanded as he hurried aft to take the wheel. He hoped to head the ship through the eye of the wind and onto the other tack before the squall could catch us halfway through, sails aback and spars vulnerable to breakage.

Brian stood at the bridge, quickly assigning positions to impose order on us crew. We'd only tacked the ship in controlled situations, many months before. It showed. Brian sent hands to the headsail sheets. He sent hands to the braces and the spanker. Anticipating that flogging sails and the roaring gale would drown out the Captain's orders given aft from the helm, he grabbed my shoulders and walked me briskly to the wheel. The Captain had it hard over now, and he yelled to the hands on the quarterdeck to set the spanker.

"Rigel can relieve you on the helm," Brian offered respectfully, urgently.

"I got it!" the Captain responded, so Brian hustled to the main deck to manage the crew.

Square sails on the fore and main luffed loudly and the yards bounced in their yokes. The air temperature dropped ten degrees with the approaching squall and I started to shiver, but more from adrenalin than cold.

We desperately needed the spanker set to turn the ship through the wind. Two seamen had almost cast free the long spiralling gasket that bound the sail to its mast. I joined Karen in casting off the many lines that held it in.

"Set the spanker! GET IT SET!" the Captain urged, gripping the wheel.

We fumbled with lines. I heard headsails flog on the foredeck with all the noise of a stampede, now cast free so as not to slow our turn.

The spanker was free. I helped Karen and her crew to sheet it home. The sail worked its way along the boom and gaff, flapping in the building wind. We turned faster now and the squares were aback. Crew were relaying communications between Captain and mate, and confusion grew. Crew braced the main yards. Brian heard a call to *let go and haul* as the squall's front—its towering smoke-coloured cloud, its panicked sea—was nearly upon us. The fast-growing wind pinned all squares aback, but the ship still had forward motion. The situation was fast growing perilous. The Captain had a chance to abort the tack, and he took it.

Brian noticed a change in plans and stopped the foreyards turning. At his post he could hear nothing but wind whistling in the rigging and the incessant flogging of headsails and spanker. He left the braces in mid-evolution to confirm that the Captain wanted the yards back around. The Captain did. So, Brian raced back to the main deck and yelled for his crew to haul so we could take the squall from aft, where supporting rigging was strongest.

"TAKE IN THE SPANKER!" the Captain shouted, a sharp edge in his voice as he pried on the wheel to shift the rudder. "Ease the SHEET," he commanded, knowing it would help the ship pay off and save precious seconds before the full squall could catch us aback. Someone eased the sheet without first considering the crew still hauling a line on the boom, and it dragged them across the mess-room hatch.

With yards around and spanker in, the line squall slammed the ship broadside. She heeled, accelerated, her scuppers awash, freeing ports awash. On the main deck, whitewater coursed around our calves as we hauled. The ship heeled more and soon the ocean looked ready to billow over the lee rail and onto the deck.

She was falling off now and Brian yelled for his shaken crew to sheet in the headsails GODDAMN IT!

Horizontal rain and all the squall's fury was upon us. It raced by the ship. It moaned in the rigging.

Brian climbed to the bridge to manage the Captain's commands issued from the helm. "Take in t'gallants!"

We were slow to slack halyards. We cast off sheets too soon. We shouted conflicting orders to each other as things unfolded into mayhem. Finally, with t'gallants bunted up and braces taut, we scurried aloft to furl while the ship raced downwind and the squall blew through us.

In the remaining hours of my watch, we tidied lines, reset sails and cleaned up from the abandoned day's work. At 2000 hours, I gathered our sombre watch.

"Everyone here, Rigel?" said the mate.

"Everyone's here."

"We're going to be in port tomorrow. Today was a wake-up call. We performed badly. Not just you. Everybody. Everybody from the mate on down. Prepare yourself for daily drills after this. See you at ten-of-four. Good night."

CHAPTER 31

Marcello, Jaded

La Digue, Seychelles, and Zanzibar, Tanzania
December 25 to January 29

THE DAY WE ANCHORED IN A SHALLOW, SANDY BAY ON the island of La Digue in the Seychelles, off-duty crew rowed ashore through the surf in our longboat. We spent some time playing in the waves, then Marcello and I hiked past the beach lined with giant cubes of sandstone, their surfaces eroded into rows of gentle wavelets that caught the shadows. We hiked the switchbacks of a dusty mountain trail that carved among the tall palms, evergreens and cinnamon trees. We were surprised and delighted to find a canteen at the end of the trail, playing Bob Marley on the boom box. So we drank beer and watched the glossy black backs of flying foxes as they circled beneath us.

Two days later, after my early morning anchor watch, I looked through the galley door and watched breakers swoosh onto the soft white sand.

Marcello frowned as he pulled breakfast, a plate of frittata, from the galley oven. "Jade's thinking of leaving and I don't blame her." He stuck a toothpick in the centre of the pie and, satisfied that it had been cooked to the perfect firmness, said, "They'd better wake up for this."

I knew the crew well enough to see that Marcello and Jade, now our head cook, had set themselves up for disappointment. The crew would stay in their racks until the last possible minute, sleeping off the exertion of the previous day's all-hands effort.

We'd worked hard that day, with reggae tunes jamming, from the time we turned to until the time we quit. We renewed the ship as quickly and happily as I had ever seen. In gear, five divers scraped three oceans' worth of grass and barnacles from the enormous surface of the ship's bottom. Six crew in boats, and two reaching down from the deck with rollers, had painted the hull. Three spot-painted the superstructure. Two set up the rig, tightening the turnbuckles at the ends of the shrouds. Many laughed as they worked. Bo'sun Josh moved quickly between groups, coordinating like a conductor, delighted to see a day's work unfold with some joy.

Christmas Day had felt good too. Baker Beth, before returning to school, had been the first cook to leave the crew with an entirely good impression. She had heaped the cargo hatch with a cornucopia of good food, a task I would have thought impossible thirty-four days away from dry land.

The Captain had again found every crew member a gift, from hand-forged Balinese krisses to cow bone needle cases.

I hadn't expected anything from anybody. When I received a gift from Josh, I was floored. I opened a brand new belt that he'd bought years before at the Sackville Harness Shop in my college town in New Brunswick. Back in Aruba, I'd thought that by now I'd feel close to home. I did, but it was because home had become the ship.

That's why it was hard for me to see my friend Marcello, once such a beloved part of our crew, slipping to the fringes. I had watched many grow tired of the "sweetheart deals" he'd arranged for himself on the ship. Word got around that he was one of the six paying crew to have received a discount rate for the voyage. It had been an incentive from the company for those willing to pay in full a year in advance. Marcello's hitch was that he'd paid in Canadian dollars, not U.S. funds.

"I didn't know it was supposed to be U.S. dollars," he had said on the phone.

"Oh dear," my father had replied.

"I sold everything. My pet hotel. My gun collection."

My father vouched for him to the Captain, and Marcello was allowed to join. The length of his stay on the ship would be ambiguous.

When the professional videographer hired by the ship in Aruba had quit in the Galapagos, Marcello, a trained photographer, agreed to take on the role. For his services Marcello secured from the Captain the professional crew salary of fifty dollars a week, yet he remained on the amateur crew shore-leave schedule. When there were interesting cinematic opportunities, such as the crew doing hard physical labour, Marcello brought out the video camera. While his video work was certainly a legitimate activity, he was paid to do it, irritating many other amateur crew who valued their contributions just as highly as Marcello's. Second mate Karen, in a grumpy mood, summed up their feelings on the way to Australia: "Where's that useless piece of shit Marcello?"

Feeling under fire and unappreciated, Marcello distanced himself from the rest of the crew. And after Australia, when beautiful Jade joined the ship, he retreated to her. We watched him read her fortune in her palms. We watched her young face light up in amazement at how his predictions resonated with who she thought she would be.

For her part, Jade told him about her youth on the pearl farm, her aboriginal ancestry. She'd tell him stories too, like the one about how the deserts flood, and wallabies float on the water using their lower legs as pontoons, their tails as rudders.

Weeks after Christmas, anchored in the ancient harbour of Stone Town, Zanzibar, it appeared Marcello had mellowed out his angst. I was on my liberty time, returning to the ship on a volunteer cargo mission, bringing some prospective tire buyers to see Kim's wares.

Marcello greeted the boat as we approached. He leaned his elbows on the cap rail, hunching his sculpted shoulders, looking totally content.

"I thought you were off today. What are you doing here?"

"Helping Jade. We're provisioning the ship tomorrow. Then we'll be looking for something to do."

"Cool. I'm going to sell some tires."

I didn't sell any tires. They were just too expensive for the Zanzibaris, and like we had feared in Panama, they would stay in our hold all the way around the earth.

Days later, after my diving excursion, I returned to the ship and sat on the cargo hatch with bo'sun Josh. It was night and we were discussing the work we'd do over the following five days to complete the building of a new t'gallant yard, which would replace the one we'd broken while setting sail for an impressive entry to Stone Town.

Third mate Karen sat down next to us. She put her hands on her knees and spoke excitedly. "I don't think I'm supposed to tell anyone this. But you can keep a secret, can't you?"

"Sure," we said, turning to look at each other.

"Well . . . Marcello and Jade are gone, and they took the provisions money. It's so juicy. Our first embezzlement. Apparently, Marcello called the office and said, 'We're in transit.'"

"What a jerk," Josh said. "How could he do something like that?"

I thought for a minute. "With a perfect piece of Marcello reasoning. Everyone who left the ship has requested a refund, right?"

"Yeah."

"Well, he just took his in advance."

The next morning, we had a muster. Captain Moreland announced that Marcello and Jade had absconded with four thousand dollars. He said that Jade had even complained that he hadn't given her enough money to provision so they'd have more to steal.

Usually, when a cook goes ashore to provision, a crew of the larger men from the ship would accompany her to discourage muggers. Marcello, with his tall, muscular stature and his black belt in tae kwon do, had convinced Brian to let him bodyguard alone.

"And that's what we get for trusting them," the Captain added.

A member of the crew asked if legal action was possible, perhaps at the Canadian border.

"Unfortunately, since this happened in Tanzania, there's nothing we can do. They appear to have known this and planned well in advance. For days they had been emptying out their cabin, leaving a few items so as not to arouse suspicion.

"Marcello's girlfriend has been informed. He'll have some explaining to do back in Montreal. Anyone who still thinks Marcello is a good shipmate should seriously re-evaluate that idea."

Some crew were vocal in their anger. Bill wanted to give him a mouthful of bloody Chiclets. Third mate Tom, with characteristic feelings of persecution, asked, "How could he do this to me?"

I still enjoyed carrying Marcello's knife, though it lost some of its lustre. All the more when I learned that he and Jade had had access to an emergency fund from the Canadian consulate but denied it because it was a loan, or that they'd stopped for a four-day safari on their way home.

Still, I wasn't going to let the drama of Marcello's departure overshadow that of Kim, forced to leave the voyage because his father was dying back in Canada.

"I can hardly stand to leave, Rige. I can't tell you how many times I've dreamed of being aboard the ship as we round Battery Point in Lunenburg harbour," Kim said.

I felt bad for him. He was one of the few people on the ship who never complained. Only the Secret Santas had irritated him, constantly requesting his tools and wood-working advice as we crossed the Indian Ocean while his own time aboard grew short. "They keep bugging me, Rige. It's enough to start old people fucking."

Kim had struggled in each remaining minute to cobble his dory back together. Using his chainsaw, he milled capping from perfectly curved branches of Palmerston wood that we called *dilo*. He cut seats out of avocado wood from the Galapagos. All the while going from galley-house roof to the subterranean recesses of the forepeak to collect his tools. In the last days of the passage Captain Dan gave Kim two days off so he could finish painting his dory and leave the ship with a clear conscience.

One final carpentry job would make it difficult for him to leave. Chief mate Brian and Kim worked together for the first five days of our stay to shape a replacement fore t'gallant yard from one of the two pieces of black spruce that the Captain had had the foresight to bring with us. When finally the spar was shaped, it was left for me to finish. I would fit and fasten the yoke, which would slide on the mast, and install the hardware used to attach the halyard, lifts, braces, sheets and the sail itself.

Kim also left me a jar of maple syrup.

"Here's a little jar of heaven. It's from the trees of Arthur Dauphine's land on Second Peninsula." I took a furtive drink of the syrup and stashed it in my bunk, thinking of Dauphine's land back home, where he had his famous block shop. Arthur had manufactured many of the blocks on the *Picton Castle*.

Later, pleased with the work we'd done to complete the outfitting of the t'gallant yard, Josh and I affixed two of Dauphine's blocks to its bunt and prepared to hoist it aloft. Hardly anyone was on the ship. What few there were, Josh asked to walk the capstan. The job of crossing the yard he left to me.

"You know I've never led a yard crossing."

"Well, it's about time," he said.

When the syncopated tinkling of the capstan pawls sounded, I started my climb aloft, coordinating the crew who remained on deck. Slowly, I followed the yard's ascent. As I climbed, I registered every turnbuckle and shackle with a renewed sense of pride. I saw every splice in every ratline, and felt the mild pull of tar still a little sticky between every turn of marline wrapped around every shroud. At the top of the t'gallant mast I shackled the starboard lift and brace to the yardarm. Hoisting the yard farther, I shackled in the port lift and brace. I levelled the yard.

Clapping shut the parrel that attached the yard's yoke to its mast, I looked out over Stone Town. Muslim minarets and Christian spires reached not quite as high as our yard. Every shutter of every whitewashed building was flung wide open to invite fresh air, however humid. The doors, thick and studded with silver, copper or iron, spoke of the city's age and layers of dominion. The smell of the shoreside bazaar with its charcoal-cooked seafood wafted past us— octopus, crab, prawn, lobster, curries, kebabs. I heard the rumble of small motorcycles speeding dangerously along cobblestone streets, barely wide enough for two bikes to pass abreast.

In the harbour, ancient dhows sailed gracefully. I thought of the dhow that had carried Kim away from the ship; of how he'd walked to the dhow harbour and must have inspected some of the 110 ancient sailing vessels registered there. The old, wooden, open-decked cargo vessels were tied up in rows and smelled of the fish oil used to preserve their teak planks. He stepped aboard one that would carry him to the mainland port of Dar es Salaam—the same port that Marcello and Jade snuck to in Zanzibar's high-speed ferry.

Kim must have helped the African sailors push the ship away from the docks and haul on their old rope halyards. Hand over hand they would have hoisted the three lashed-together logs, their yard, which supported a great triangular lateen sail. They'd have gybed easily out of the harbour, dipping that yard from one side to the other as they worked their way to windward.

When night fell, a kerosene lantern must have lit Kim's dhow. He must have lain back on a sack of cement or maybe a coil of coconut-fibre cable. I imagined he stared through that ancient rigging at the southern stars, sorry as hell to leave the ship, but glad to do it in style.

CHAPTER 32

Esprit de Corps

Zanzibar to Barbados
February 13 to May 26

"Rige. Wake up. It's twenty minutes to four. Time for watch. It's cool and clear."

The wind was strong on the beam and the ship heeled sharply to port. Taut square sails on fore and main carved up into the night. The *Picton Castle* dug her shoulder into the water and a hissing bow wave surged alongside. I turned to look at the sky over the low rail.

Where's the Southern Cross? It had always been there, over the port beam.

No, wait . . . We're going south. I looked over the bow and saw the bright little constellation lying on its side, wedged between the fo'c'sle head and the foot of the fores'l. I hurried to meet my watch on the quarterdeck, counting the months that the Southern Cross had been above our port rail: *more than thirteen.*

Congregated by the life raft outside the charthouse, my watchmates were equally amazed by the change in scenery. Patrick traced a bare arm from the Southern Cross along the Milky Way, which arced over the ten square sails set on fore and main.

It was Sunday, and in my free time I decided to start one more project before the end of the voyage. I'd finally make a box like the one I'd seen in the Paul Gauguin Museum. I planned to use a short log of tau wood that Pitcairn's Charles Christian had harvested on neighbouring Henderson Island and given to me. I remembered the other Pitcairners remarking on its value as we loaded it aboard ship from one of their longboats.

I pulled the tau wood stump from the hold, and with Kim's sharp ripsaw I began to saw it in half. An hour later I had one flat side exposed. The wood was darker than walnut, with swirls of milk and dark chocolate defining its grain.

Inspired by my celestial navigation classes, I chose a planetary theme for my box design. The basic shape was an ellipse, like an orbital path. I planned to make the sides come straight up like a hat box. I would make the lid into a domed ellipsoid. In its hard, smooth surface I'd inlay yellow wood—a fireball to represent the sun. Around the outside I would carve the signs of the zodiac and the planets. I would saw the lid free and hollow out the inside like a dugout canoe. I would leave a galaxy of stars in relief on the inner surface, and carve a model of my hand, full-size, exact to the fingerprints.

There should be just enough time before we return to Lunenburg. I planned it as a gift for Ariel.

That afternoon on the fo'c'sle head, in the warm breeze scooping down off the foresail, the Captain gave an informal lecture on the evolution of sail design. It had the feel of a 400-level college course, and almost every member of the crew listened with interest. The lecture began with the Arabic dhow, passing through the Chinese junk and ending, of course, at the square-rigger.

Our connection to Arab dhows and Chinese junks was relevant here. For hundreds of years the junks had voyaged from the China seas to Ceylon, India, Arabia and as far as here, the east coast of Africa, where old Chinese coins are sometimes dug up. In these ancient ports, handy junks, with their battened and balanced sails that pivoted near the middle, had manoeuvred among the simpler dhows, which also carried a balanced sail. Through the lecture I learned that our square sails, pivoting at the middle, were quite like those of junks and dhows.

Going south along the coast of Africa, those Arab and Chinese ships would have similarly caught the northeast monsoon that blows from India and Arabia, down the east coast, from January to June. The other half of the year it blows from the southwest.

Learning about those old sail designs taught me more about our own. Our yards, which separated the individual square sails, could be considered battens of one enormous super-sail, allowing it to be tuned with precise control. A super-sail is a dangerous thing in the sudden squalls and storms of the Cape of Good Hope. So, the next day on the cargo hatch, the Captain gave another lecture, this one on striking sail before a squall. He brought out his full model of the *Picton Castle* to illustrate his discussion.

Pointing to the miniature spanker, the mizzen topmast stays'l, the main royal and the gans'l, he explained the importance of first taking in the sails farthest aft. This reduces weather helm, which can drive the ship's head into the wind. If that were to happen, all square sails would be aback, and the stabilizing force of shrouds, backstays and braces would be useless. The sails would push back against the masts, relying on the few forward leading stays. Not only would we lose manoeuvrability, we could break yards or have a dismasting.

After his introduction, the Captain delegated the training to mate Brian and retired to the charthouse to carry on with his day's work. With the air of a football coach Brian broke the crew into small units and created a spirited sense of competition between them. Within two days all crew were striking and furling sail with alacrity, running up ratlines, acting on pared-down commands and growing confident.

On the third day of training, as we gathered for drills, a dark line squall tumbled towards us. The Captain ordered the spanker brailed and the royals stowed. With dispatch we broke into groups to attend to the three masts.

Running up the main shrouds, I saw from the corner of my eye the spanker brail into the mizzen-mast like a theatre curtain opening for a show. By the time we reached the royal yard, it had settled into its lifts as the sail's clews skittered up to its middle. My heart pounded from the effort and the raised voices below. We swung onto the yard, horizontal rain and hail pounding our bare backs. The ship surged. Canvas flogged. We grappled. Slammed it in. Formed a skin. Rolled it back. Secured it down. Stepped to the shrouds. Climbed down to the gans'l yard. Grappled sail. Slammed it in.

Down on deck with sail secured, the crew talked loudly, swapping war stories. We'd done well. Engineer Nobby was the only one to lose any canvas that day. Three of his shirts had blown from the laundry line.

A week into our passage to the Cape of Good Hope, we were still training each day—tacking, wearing ship, striking sail. On Saturday night, around supper, a customary calm settled on the ship in anticipation of the day off that would follow. Eighteen-year-old Annie, promoted to head cook when Marcello and Jade absconded, had risen to the challenge. She prepared ziti with meatballs, a green pepper salad and a passion-fruit cake for dessert.

As we neared the entrance of the Mozambique Channel, there were few swells and the current was slack. A moist, gentle breeze blew over the stern, and I sat on the fo'c'sle head with Crista, a new recruit from Boston who'd signed on in the Seychelles. A slender crescent moon was about to follow the sun over the western horizon. There, we knew, was Africa. In the deep twilight we could see the entire western horizon raked with blue flashes of lightning, yet over the ship the sky was perfectly clear.

I'd snorkelled with Crista on the small atoll of Aldabra, the southernmost of the Seychelles, inhabited by eight scientists and one hundred thousand giant tortoises. An experienced diver, Crista led me through shallows, chasing black-tipped reef sharks. And in the deep water I watched her hold her nose and go to the bottom, her long red hair flying behind her like a sea anemone and her translucent white fins looking lovely with her fair skin.

The island researchers had told the crew about a narrow winding channel that cut from the atoll's lagoon to the ocean. Just like in Takaroa, the water rushed in and out twice a day with fierce speed. If we caught the current when the ebb was at its fastest, it would make for an exciting and beautiful drift dive.

I piloted a skiff full of divers to the narrow reaches of the channel. I opened the throttle of the forty-horsepower engine to buck the boiling current that rushed from the lagoon. All along the channel walls were black coral, jagged as lightning forks, and columns, beautiful and imposing. At the end of deep water we hooked an anchor over a coral ledge and the divers left the skiff like paratroopers from a plane, disappearing fast behind.

The next day, it was my turn to try the dive. Having taken an open water course on the island of Gizo in the Solomons, I had some skills, but no equipment. Crista lent me hers and told me to be careful, with genuine concern in her eyes. I relished her concern. It felt good to be cared about. But I also felt a familiar resistance to shipboard romance rise up. Still, the voyage was stretching on; friends had paired up; and a traveller who was not yet road-weary would be a welcome companion.

Drifting underwater down the narrow channel, I felt I was flying. I hugged the contours, floating up over boulders and down into cavities, always looking forward in case the current would ram me into a column. As I went farther, the current slackened and I followed the spotted potato groupers, the dottybacks and the damselfish. Anemones waved in the surge and canary yellow fish darted in and out. Triggerfish, their scales in the pattern of South Africa's flag, swam by in schools. I flowed out to the end of the channel, where barracudas and nurse sharks hovered, mouths open for the feast.

Now, sitting on the fo'c'sle, eating ziti and watching the lightning, Crista told me the reason for her unusual concern that day. Not long before, her boyfriend had died in a diving accident. In a routine exercise his instructor had taken him fast to the surface. Something went wrong. His muscles tingled, then seized. Blood frothed from his mouth. He died in the boat from decompression sickness.

I told her about Ariel, how things had been at their best when we'd said goodbye, how much I still thought about her, how I would continue to.

Drills continued, and we crew continued to grow tighter and more competent. With the refinement of their skills, many of the amateur crew were on par with the professional hands. One morning, the fore royal snapped full of air and its starboard sheet of stretched manila parted with a bang. Seamen raced up the shrouds to secure it even as the orders were being given. Bo'sun Josh quickly eased it into its lifts and clewed up the sail.

The Mozambique Current carried us to the vast, muscular city of Durban. Using sails forward and aft, the Captain manoeuvred our ship to the dock like the agile three-masted Chinese junks, and nested her alongside with modern supertankers and freighters, their half-exposed bulbous bows nearly half as big as our ship. We had fit in better with the dhows of Zanzibar.

The Mozambique Current flowed into the Agulhas Current, which whipped us around the southeast coast of Africa. On that current, chased by a force five wind, we raced at twelve knots. The seas were grey and rolling. Strong wind and swells twisted the stern around. Sails on the main shadowed the wind for those on the fore, and the resulting weather helm made hard work for the helmsmen. The strong air had a cold nip. At a frigid seventy-two degrees Fahrenheit, it forced us to dig out mouldy boots, hats, jackets, scarves and blankets. Hot coffee tasted better. Sleep gave more rest. Work had more vigour.

The sea smelled rich and alive like the North Atlantic. Pilot whales joined us. So did sharks and sunfish. Albatrosses soared overhead and bobbed on the water. Penguins torpedoed by. Seals popped up their heads. Sails on the foremast spilled and filled.

In one day we logged 232 nautical miles racing with the current along the southern coast of Africa, until finally the wind went afoul. That night the entire sky was ripped by lightning and the ship tossed on confused swells, tipping over sea chests in the fo'c'sle. The wind went fair in the morning, and with the coast in view we scudded around Cape Agulhas, which divides the Indian Ocean from the South Atlantic.

We rounded the Cape of Good Hope and arrived at the harbour mouth of Cape Town. In the bone white light of the setting half moon we could see the great truncated outline of Table Mountain and a blanket of city lights that spread from its base to the sea.

A living gale whipped up from the shore and we spent the night hove to. In a chilly dawn I watched a cloud that had settled atop the level surface of Table Mountain. It rolled and spilled over the sides, disappearing before it fell to the city below. A native South African who'd joined in Durban told me that cloud was called the Table Cloth and the wind that blew it over the city was called the Medicine Wind.

"It blows the city's ills away."

Like that medicine wind, a college friend of Kristin, a young black South African man named Sandile, ran aware- ness tours through Cape Town's historic sites of oppres- sion. He always conveyed the spirit of optimism that saw South Africans through their hardest times.

A group of crew went on a tour to Robben Island, where Nelson Mandela and many others had been imprisoned for their resistance to apartheid, now run as a museum by for- mer inmates still dedicated to the cause of freedom. Sandile led crew to an African National Congress rally. He took us to the township of Guguletu, where we saw a rotting stream and a dusty highway separating destitute shanty- towns patrolled by army vehicles from the sleek modern city.

But for most of our time in Cape Town, the professional crew was required on the ship to facilitate an inspection if necessary. Though very few details filtered down to us proles, it seemed that an unverified claim about our status with respect to U.S. Coast Guard regulations had been posted on our website and caused a bit of trouble with them. They made their clout felt all the way across the Atlantic, threat- ening a costly haulout.

We were to remain on board most of the time to be ready to facilitate and keep the ship looking her most impressive. We killed time with painting, polishing, varnishing, cleaning, tightening furls, squaring yards and touching up the waterline. We made the ship more beautiful than she had ever been.

Though the air of secrecy that surrounded the unexpected maintenance period bothered me—and at times left me furious, hoping the authorities would fly us all home—it didn't seem to bother the engineers in the slightest. Nobby and Claire had unbolted the ports on the sides of our massive engine and spent many a day pulling out bearings, checking tolerances, assessing how extensively they would have to rebuild the engine upon its return to Lunenburg.

I saw them one day from the fiddley that spanned the top of the cavernous engine room. The two engineers lay with their backs on the diamond plate, reaching their arms into the crankcase, balancing a bearing on their fingertips, their faces very close. According to Bill, the two had been refusing his relief, preferring to work by themselves. Nobby combed his pompadour with more care. Claire seemed more silent, and a little amazed.

It was shocking that their friendship had so suddenly elevated to love. I thought to write Ariel a letter, but first I looked in my bunk for something she had written long before that I kept in a box with her letters. It was the first thing she'd ever written me, a poem, before we had parted ways in Lunenburg.

I found it folded into four and stained with tar at its edges. I had read it many times, though it had been difficult for me to understand. It ended:

If I am the final verse
— the last stanza
waiting on your tongue

and held,
fixed
pinned
by green-green eyes
— let go a little
and begin
your show
again.

I would.

A long time ago—it seemed like forever—I had driven Don to my old home in Rose Bay, near Lunenburg. We were there to meet Captain Moreland and see his slides of the *Romance*'s first circumnavigation. The day was clear and bright. The early afternoon sun glanced off the deep snow and dazzled through the windows of the dining room where we sat.

My father pulled down the orange paper shades and sat next to me. The slide projector made a white spot on the wall. I felt the warmth of its vent fan like a trade wind. Captain Dan clicked the carousel around. We all watched low, sandy islands with willy-nilly palms in the Caribbean; the machine that is the Panama Canal; the friendly faces of the Pitcairners; the horsemen of the Marquesas; the *County of Roxburgh*; and smiling, chocolate-skinned, bare-breasted women with flowers in their hair somewhere in the western South Pacific. We thought we could smell the coconut oil on their skin wafting through the room, carried on the projector's exhaust. We saw five hundred or so perfect sunsets. We saw whales and towering masts and a crew living utterly self-reliant. Barongs and gamelan bands shimmered on the screen. The tall swells of the Cape of Good Hope enveloped us. Then we pushed on to the South Atlantic with Captain Moreland.

"This is the best leg of the voyage," he said.

"Why?"

"Because the crew is into the voyage by now. They are sailors. Voyaging around the world is *what they do*. And with only one ocean to cross, they're almost home. The way you see things on a world voyage is very different from how you see them now. You will forget the novelty of your experience. This is what we will have to guard against.

"When I was chief mate of the *Romance*, we sailed to some isolated South Pacific island, it doesn't matter which one. Skipper ordered me to let go the anchor. The chain rattled down through the hawse pipe. It made a racket, and a crewman who'd been sleeping in the fo'c'sle came on deck. He looked around at the tiny white islands and the leaning palms and the crystal blue water. 'Oh, great,' he said. 'Another goddamn tropical paradise.'"

Many nights out of Cape Town, just after the skies cleared and we once again grew used to the sea's motion, I felt a sour cloud lift from the spirit aboard. Maybe the last of the mefloquine had left our blood, or maybe it was the improving weather and the return to tank tops. Maybe it was that we realized our voyage would soon end.

Patrick asked if he could break out the six djembe drums I'd bought in South Africa with what was left of the cargo money Kim had left in my care.

Patrick, an accomplished drummer, had been the pulse of just about every band at our university. Drummer Todd had been playing professionally since he was a teenager. A new crew member had experience in a fife and drum corps, and a technical ability that the two professionals admired. Drumbeats bounced between the three with the sureness of a spirited horse gaining its gallop. I joined in, tapping the rim of my drum on the offbeat. Cowboy Brad jumped in as well.

BOOM BOOM. Brian pounded a wide, resonating drum made of dark wood that he'd picked up in South Africa. He almost always bought the biggest of everything. He bowed his head and passed the drum to Patrick. BOOM BOOM. The rhythm took on a resonating backbeat.

The sun set and Todd returned to the deck with his twin kendang drums from Bali. There were now enough to go around. When it was dark, the rhythm pounded on. The ship rocked like a metronome, swinging its way homeward. Claire picked up the smallest drum and played high tones, slapping her hands like the wings of a dragonfly, syncopating, darting, rapping around everyone. The night was cool, but sweat sheened her smiling face. Third mate Tom looked to be in a trance as he dug up a rhythmic skill I'd never imagined he had.

We pounded on towards St. Helena.

That island, sturdy and forbidding as a fortress, rose on the horizon at sunset one Sunday. We eased into the shallow bay to anchor at our last truly remote stop in the world, where the residents open their homes and hearts to you.

Set in the centre of the South Atlantic, it was not hard to see why St. Helena was chosen as the last prison of Napoleon Bonaparte. A few lights burned in the small town. Deep ocean swells washed against the cliffs on the lee side of the island, and, strangely, the booming electric sound of a modern dance bar pulsed its way through the air to welcome us that Sunday night, although it was unclear how many of St. Helena's seven thousand citizens were inside.

The last day, we waited at anchor for the Captain and Doctor Beth to return to the ship after clearing us through customs. I sat on the fore upper topsail yardarm, replacing the sail's lashing. I took a moment to look around and noticed a grey object, as big as a bus, circling the ship.

"Hey! I think there's a whale down there!"

"That's a whale shark!" Josh said, leaping to the rail to confirm. He looked to the mate, who was quick to post a couple of lifeguards, then Josh ran below for a mask and snorkel. Splash after splash, crew dove into the water in fluorescent fins and shorts. Soon, nearly everyone circled the ship, following the peaceful fish like the remoras that clung to its tail.

I worked my way down from the rig and threw on a mask and snorkel. The shark was forty-five feet long, and seven feet wide at its enormous, blunt head. Rows of white spots covered its grey and ridged upper half. Its great mouth was shaped in a gentle, goofy smile. I watched as crew dove down to touch the shark. It returned the favour by ascending nearer the surface and swimming slowly around our ship, clearly enjoying the attention. Cowboy Brad grabbed the shark's dorsal fin to ride it like a bull, losing skin from his thighs to the shark's sandpaper hide.

When it was time to weigh anchor, we were sad to leave the gentle giant. I believe it was a little sad too, staying with the ship until we pressed on to Barbados.

I had been made the ship's carpenter for the South Atlantic crossing. Though this meant less free time for personal projects, I relished constructing things for the ship. I'd always wanted to measure myself by how I contributed to the ship, and now my skills as a builder had been recognized. Every day, I started work at 0630 hours at a small bench next to Jesse and his rigger's vise. While he spliced wire rope, I shaped two big cleats for the spanker boom. Because I could now make something tangible each day, I usually worked a little past quitting time, producing curly cedar shavings with my plane that annoyed the other daymen as they tried to clean up.

As I worked at fitting and fastening exotic wood, I could observe my former watch continue without me. They used skills and attitudes that I'd helped pass on. Maybe I had been contributing after all.

Doing good for the ship buoyed my spirits. But I finally wondered if I'd really come here to see what I could do for the ship, or if I was here because of what I'd hoped the ship could do for me. *Do I need the ship any more? Do I need another ship? That's the only question that matters now.*

We were starting to look ahead. The ship itself was nearing completion. Chain sheets went on the t'gallants, wire sheets on the royals. Things were running smoothly everywhere—except in the galley.

Annie, the youngest member of the crew, had continued to work in the capacity of head cook, even though a highly experienced ship's cook had joined us in South Africa. Leaving her in that position seemed a nod to Annie's hard work and perseverance after Jade had left her in the lurch.

New to leadership, Annie demanded respect rather than accept that she'd already earned it. As the days went by, she set down more and more rules for the crew to obey. Crew rebelled. Some of her help even behaved negligently, drinking on duty, ignoring instructions. Annie became more rigid. After day forty there was little new to talk about, so we filled the air with complaints about her bossiness. Annie became less open to suggestion, finally refusing to make any pizzas without anchovies. This caused outrage among the cheese pizza—loving crew. I was thankful when another distraction entered our world.

A school of bonitos picked up our trail. There were so many that it appeared we could throw a spear into their midst and pull one out skewered each time. This was not the case. After a week's worth of attempts, only Josh had been able to spear one. Still, many came aboard by hook and line, their scales gashed by our many attempts with the spear. And for one last time the diet of fish caused our sweat to take on a sharp tang, like the sweat of Pacific Islanders.

Past the equator, where the bonitos turned tail and left, we entered the doldrums. We alternately set all sail in puffs of wind and furled again while we steamed through the lulls. I had predicted this would go on for weeks when the Captain announced a firm arrival date for Nova Scotia, one month away.

It meant I would have to scrap my ambitious plans to ornament the elliptical box. That Sunday, I worked as fast as I could to gouge away the dark, hard wood inside and leave the outside plain and smooth. Don sat next to me in silence.

I felt something was wrong. "This has been quite a crossing," I said. "Can you believe we've been forty-five days at sea?"

"Well, yeah, actually I can. It hasn't been that good for me. Like, every time I walk into a compartment—the mess or the salon or even the aloha deck—everybody shuts up 'cause they don't want me to hear them rag on Annie. Sometimes they don't even shut up and they go right on ragging in front of me. She's my girlfriend. And then there was the line crossing, when she was tarred and coated in flour."

I felt bad. I'd been in on the fun too, ragging on her when there was little else to talk about.

"Has everyone forgotten that she saved the day when Jade and Marcello left? Doesn't that deserve some kind of respect?"

"She is kind of inflexible," I said, thinking of the anchovies.

"I know, man. It's just that I'm afraid she's becoming a whipping girl for a crew that's been at sea so long, they have nothing better to talk about. I just don't want to see her snap. Where is the leadership? Why are they letting this happen?"

I shrugged. I was supposedly part of that leadership, and I did nothing to discourage shipmates from bitching about our eleventh cook.

"I used to think that this was a place where people were judged on the merit of their work. That's bullshit. You know, she seems so poised."

"Yeah. She does."

"Well, every night she cries herself to sleep."

Don got his wish the next day at lunch break, when Captain Moreland called twenty of his long-time crew to the quarterdeck. He steered the ship, dressed in his black vest and flat-brimmed straw sailor's hat. It seemed he was using the wheel as a prop to hide a twinge of discomfort. He stared at the sails.

He said that Annie was on vacation for a couple of days to unwind. That the tension of having everyone rag on her for six weeks straight was a bit much. He explained that her job was the hardest "day to day" job on the ship, and said to remember that she was only eighteen. He couldn't have done the job when he was her age, he said, and asked us to consider if we could have either. He told us to have a little compassion. He told us that she'd agreed to make some plain cheese pizzas next time.

When he finished, I walked to the fo'c'sle. I was pleased that Captain Dan had spoken up for Annie, and it disturbed me that much of her distress was caused because we couldn't get out of our own skin. I looked out my porthole. I had recently read something on the nature of authority and wanted to see it again. I thought of the Captain and how he handled himself. I looked through my bunk for *Mount Analogue*, a novella the size of a pack of cards that I'd read in the Mozambique Channel. A passage had arrested me. I'd read it again and again, and I wanted now to copy it into my journal. I found the short volume and flipped through.

I have brought you this far, and I have been your leader. Right here I'll take off the cap of authority, which was a crown of thorns for the person I remember myself to be.

I scribbled down the passage and read it again. *Could it be? Nah.*

CHAPTER 33

The Port Is Near

Lunenburg and the Way There
June 2 to 23

WE SPENT TWO WEEKS IN THE CARIBBEAN. THE FIRST
we spent entertaining the ship's primary backer on a passage from Barbados to Antigua. The second week, Captain
Dan gave us a generous amount of time off and we used it
well: water-skiing off the island of Tortola, getting wasted
in Jost Van Dyke, saying goodbye.

The night we left the British Virgin Islands, I stood on
the fo'c'sle head and listened to the engine chugging with
an eagerness I hadn't heard since the voyage began. The
ship pitched slightly as she punched through oncoming
waves. I stood on the bow and closed my eyes, letting the
cool nighttime breeze wash across my face. I could almost
smell the fresh-cut grass and sweet wild roses of
Lunenburg in springtime. I looked over the bow towards
home and saw the North Star low on the horizon. I looked
aft to see the Southern Cross sparkling like a handful of
diamonds. I wished I could take them with me.

We steamed north to Bermuda.

Stepping on that island, onto the very same dock we'd
fled to with our steering gear jury-rigged one and a half

years before, I felt satisfied by our tidy accomplishment, like we'd been trailing a rope around the globe and just now tied it in a knot. Josh's sister, a Bermudan, ran across the dock, eyes soft with tears, cheeks flushed, her smile so sincere and bright that I thought she must be the most beautiful woman on earth. She put a hand on the back of Josh's head and squeezed her cheek against his beard.

Tropical storm Arlene forced us to stay in Bermuda longer than Captain Dan had planned. When we left, a chilly wind blew over the stern, filling all our sails, helping our tired engine drive the ship home. On the next-to-last day, Jesse clapped the final seizing on the rig, replacing two cable clamps that mate Brian had placed on the mainstay in Lunenburg three years before. The rig was complete.

That night, I lay on the cargo hatch next to Patrick, our backs sticking to the rough canvas cover as the ship rolled. We were giddy with the thought of homecoming. Patrick and I stared aloft between two walls of taut canvas. We were not looking at the stars but at the homeward-bound pennant that pointed the way from mainmast to Lunenburg. Ripples curled down its length and snapped into the air like a coach whip.

"That pennant . . . I haven't seen it before," Patrick said.

"It was made by a Lunenburg kite maker. She had me present it to the Captain before we left, and he tucked it away as soon as I gave it to him," I replied. "Did you see the dragon on it?"

We looked aloft, silent for a time, absorbing our last night underway in the *Picton Castle.*

On our final morning, a glowing coastal fog embraced the ship. The Captain ordered the engine all stop. Mate Brian launched the skiff so that Jesse and I could touch up the rust streaks and peeling white paint that had appeared since we'd left Bermuda. There was a slight breeze, and the ship rolled peacefully as Jesse manoeuvred the skiff around her hull, which had scars and blemishes more familiar to me now than those on my own skin.

"There's a spot," Jesse said, giving the throttle a twist, heading the boat towards a black patch where the white had peeled, revealing the ship's former colour.

"I got it." But it rolled underwater and couldn't be reached. We waited for the ship to rock back. When it did, I quickly wiped off the salt water with a rag and smeared on the white. With the roller's stroke I remembered the anger I'd felt the first time I was told to paint wet steel. And I remembered Fiji, when I decided I'd just do what I was asked as well as I could.

We circled the hull, covering the last of her blemishes, then Jesse headed us to the davits where the skiff would be hoisted. As he revved the engine, I assumed I'd be stationed in the skiff for our approach to Lunenburg, as I'd been for our most recent landings.

We hoisted the skiff. Captain Dan engaged the ship's engine, driving hard to make his appointment. The engine pounded faster than before, causing the ship to shiver. The fog retreated some with the strengthening sunshine, and the ship seemed to fly. We heard the whine of an outboard, then a large white skiff with a flaring bow burst into our fogbound arena. It was Kim, Skipper and the mate's dog, Deadeye.

Seeing a change in the wind, Captain Dan ordered, "Brace up three points, port tack!" The whole crew responded. It was now impossible to tell old crew from new by their performance on deck.

Captain Dan gave the order to set the spanker. The crew hustled aft to set the only sail still furled. It snapped in the breeze as it stretched from the mast to the ends of its boom and gaff. The same wind that rose to fill the spanker parted the remaining fog, revealing the protective bluffs of Rose Head and Ovens Point. Crested with evergreens and golden moss, those bluffs reached into the ocean like the paws of a resting lion, guarding Rose Bay, my childhood home.

"Rigel," said the mate, "get some good clothes on and relieve the helm."

I went quickly to the fo'c'sle, my heart racing, and pulled on the red smock I'd worn as skipper of the Lunenburg ketch *Eastern Star*. I walked aft to take the helm. The *Picton Castle* moved quickly now, under the power of her sails more than her engine. As we passed the string of white houses on Feltzen South, our escort grew. Loco, Skipper and Deadeye returned to the ship in their skiff. When they took position off the stern, I saw their passengers. Baker Beth was there. So were Bob and Lynn, two crew who had left the ship in the Galapagos. Patricia Lynch was aboard, wiping mascara from teary eyes.

Kim's skiff was joined by Lunenburg's whale-watching boat. The *Eastern Star* sailed out of the harbour and fell into position in the shadow of our spanker, shaded from the sun and wind. Soon, more vessels joined us: a wooden cutter, a small schooner, a fishing boat, an inflatable skiff. The flotilla grew. As we neared Lunenburg's breakwater, the Captain disengaged the engine. The wind picked up. Whitecaps appeared on the surface and the ship heeled in response.

I turned the wheel right a touch to balance out the weather helm. Captain Dan stood behind me, and with his voice full of kindness, said, "Do you remember what you said to me when you were twelve, Rigel, at the helm of the *Ernestina*, bound for Lunenburg?"

"Yes."

"You said, 'I can't believe I'm at the helm of a tall ship and I'm taking her home.'"

The Captain walked forward to the charthouse, leaving me with this happy memory of who we once were.

Our steel hull slipped past the breakwater, with its boxy lighthouse. Just ahead, the three-masted, full-rigged ship of war, HMS *Rose* waited in ambush. Holding position in front of Lunenburg's rusty deep-sea draggers, she looked like she'd just sailed out of Nelson's navy. Her hull was black and yellow, bulging and muscular. She fired cannons in a deafening salute. The grey smoke of burnt gunpowder shrouded her, and was soon swept away by the same wind that carried us deeper into the harbour. The green hill of Lunenburg's golf course fell behind, revealing our old dock.

Our once snow-dusted pier with its small crowd of well-wishers now bristled with family and friends. Deep into the harbour stretched a long row of red, blue and black fishing trawlers. One of them sounded a long foghorn blast. That foghorn was joined by another. A shrill air horn joined in, all resonating joyfully.

The Captain ordered some left rudder and we took a course parallel to the shore. He gave commands to take in sail and the crew responded brilliantly. Not a mistaken line or a confused face. From top to bottom, yards descended and rested in their lifts like doves alighting on branches. The square sails were bunted up and pulled close to their yards. On the deck, below this display of retreating canvas, crew handled the sails with callused hands—marionettes bowing at the end of a long show.

Captain Dan ordered me to turn the helm hard left. He ordered Claire, at the engine controls, "Ahead half." I heard the musical rush of water kicked up by the propeller rippling past the rudder. The ship responded, turning ninety degrees into the wind.

With the sails in, Captain Dan stood on the quarterdeck rail for a better view of the dock. Holding one of the main backstays for support, he turned the vessel for his final approach to the crowded dock. The ship turned until it appeared he had aimed her directly for our old finger pier. The ship slid ahead, too fast.

"Oh no," the second helmsman said. "There's gonna be a crunch."

"No, he's got it. It's just right."

The Captain gave the order, "*Astern slow*," and the stern crept to port, aligning the ship with the pier. Slowly she glided alongside, like a weary traveller sliding into her slippers.

"Lines over!" commanded the Captain.

Soon the ship was secure at her berth with the engine off. I left the helm and shuffled down the ladder to the main deck. I stood on the rail where I could reach my father, mother and sister, who were waiting to greet me. We held each other in a long embrace.

"What a thing you did, Rigel. What a thing you did," my father said over and over.

Epilogue

Our first night in Lunenburg turned into drunken revelry, ending when the bars closed and we stumbled back to the ship. Of the seventy-seven sailors to sign aboard, twenty-three of us had sailed around the world together over thirty-seven thousand miles to forty-seven ports in twenty-two countries. We'd gone through thirteen cooks and countless trials together. Yet things dissolved quickly the next day. Every minute, the ship felt more like a hollow shell. Partly it was the emptiness of the bunks—sheets stripped away, clothing and knick-knacks packed in bags and boxes, shipmates absent. But there was a deeper emptiness in the quick disappearance of our routines.

We held the last ship event, the *Picton Castle* Awards Ceremony. It was a chance to involve family and townspeople in our ship's society. I had seen the small awards committee twittering away on the last leg of the voyage, thinking up ways to recognize our quirks and contributions.

I walked with some crew to the ceremony on the waterfront in the middle of town. I pushed aside a rubber door flap and entered the long marquee tent. I took a seat with some friends behind a folding wooden table and faced the stage.

The Captain started the ceremony off with a short speech, clever and funny. He offered a broad thank you to everyone who'd helped get the ship away from her dock and around the world. Then the goofy awards began: *Most Curious Sailor, Cleans Up the Best, Cutest Couple.*

Drummer Todd thanked Kristin for being the *Best Listener.* "For being the person you're most likely to spill your guts to when everything has gotten really black. Someone you trust, that you're comfortable with . . . that you can talk to."

Crew Member Most Likely to Hurt Himself, Best Dinner Wake-ups.

Kristin approached the microphone to give the award for the *Most Inspirational Crew Member:* "She is the most independent and positive human being I know. She does nothing halfway. When she has galley duty, we get chilled, fresh-squeezed orange juice instead of tap water. She sections our grapefruit. She makes mocha coffee. And she was my absolute inspiration climbing Kilimanjaro. I was whining. I was hating it. I paid a thousand dollars to do this hellish task. She didn't know she was pushing me, but she was. She's gentle. She's my hero. She's Jean Burke!"

"Jean Burke! Jean Burke! Jean Burke!" the crowd shouted.

Mildred Broome was declared *Crew Member with the Cleanest Laundry.* Patricia Lynch received an honourable mention.

Crew Member with the Strangest Plans for the Future: I won for my tree house reveries.

Doctor Beth gave the *Above and Beyond the Call of Duty Award:* "This is for the crew member who gave of himself, freely, fully, on watch and especially off watch, the crew member who did so much for the good of the ship, for his shipmates. Never grumbled about it and just lent a helping hand so many times. He came here as an amateur crew and he's signing off as our third engineer and communications officer. Bill Wellington."

Most Functional Seasick Crew Member, Best South Pacific Dancing, Best Nails, Most Difficult Person to Wake for Watch, Best Belcher, Most Likely to Sail Forever, Most Likely to Retire from the Picton Castle *with a Pension Plan.*

Doctor Beth awarded the Captain's sister and brother-in-law for their hard work managing the ship's home office. Next she awarded bo'sun Josh for being the *Most Indispensable Crew Member*—for his enthusiastic leadership and constant hard work.

Brian spoke next: " . . . This individual came aboard the ship, needed to lose a couple of pounds, fresh out of university, just a dumb college kid. But he had all kinds of potential . . . He's become an awesome shipmate, always helpful, knowledgeable, he's become a teacher, he's become a leader, and he's really become a man. And it's my great, great, great pleasure to present the *Most All-around Improved Award* to Patrick."

Brian next awarded Loco Kim the title of *Most Safety-conscious* to a round of applause and laughter.

Bo'sun Josh took the microphone with nervous excitement. "This award recognizes so many different aspects of a person's personality and style and spirit. So we had to count the votes under strict election polling techniques. Everyone voted. Some of us voted twice. I did. I didn't win. I got two votes.

"You know, you may not bare your heart and soul to him, but if you're feeling down, it's the person most likely to give you a punch in the shoulder and get you laughing again. Or if it's two o'clock in the morning and it's blowing a gale and you have to go stow royals, this is the person you want *next* to you. Or if you're ashore and you have a couple of extra dollars to spend, this is the guy you want to spend it with. So without further ado, under the category of *Best Shipmate*, my very good friend . . . myself! No, Rigel Crockett."

I walked to Josh on the stage, my face flushed. Captain Dan and Josh gave me a hug. Josh asked for a speech. I couldn't think of anything, just, "I voted for Josh. Thank you."

The Captain took the stage and thanked the ship's chief financial backer for raising the funds to get the ship past Darwin, Australia. He thanked the company's vice-president, the creator of the ship's website, the company's attorney, all of whom worked gratis. He again thanked his sister and brother-in-law for managing the ship's office. Then the Captain thanked his crew. "There isn't a day that goes by that some of the crew didn't think, myself included, that we're carrying the ship around on our shoulders. But this award is for the people that *I* could not have done the voyage without. The people that carried me, and this vision, though it wasn't always beautifully spelled out, as a nice organized operation would be. There are three people in particular, in spite of everything, who have helped *me* pull this off. I would start with . . . Nobby."

Nobby smiled, parting the curls of his reddish beard. He walked with his usual huge strides as Captain Moreland pointed to a spot on the floor.

"Nobby's been with the ship since Manhattan. He thought it would be a very funny thing to be the chief engineer of a ship that's going nowhere." The audience laughed.

The Captain spoke again. "Brian Donnelly." The audience cheered while Brian took his place. "Brian is the chief mate, and a more qualified chief mate I can never ask for. There is no other mariner on the planet who could have successfully worked with me on this voyage. Brian has read my mind when I couldn't read it myself. And that's a task.

"And then Beth." The audience cheered for a long time. "Beth quit residency when the prospect of this voyage was 50 percent on, 50 percent off. She signed on as an AB and a doctor. She's become my administrator. She filled in every possible gap. Brian has been the chief mate of all maritime affairs; Beth has been the chief mate of everything else. And Nobby is the guru of the engine room. And I personally am absolutely in their debt. Not just for this voyage, but for the future. And I have something for them."

Captain Moreland reached below his table and presented Brian, Beth and Nobby with paintings that I'd seen him working on in the last weeks of the voyage. On a frame stretched with canvas, the *Picton Castle* ran downwind under a full press of sail, cutting a frothy bow wave, whitecaps all around.

"OK, guys, let's eat," the Captain said tiredly. The tent emptied.

Almost immediately after the awards ceremony, the mate's stomach began to hurt. It'd come on quickly. *Probably a bad hangover.*

But the next day, his pain was worse. Doctor Beth took him to the hospital, where they ran tests finding no cause, only symptoms. Soon he was doubled over. Heavy doses of drugs alleviated his suffering. But the glassy stare of his eyes, his rumpled hair, his silence, his weight loss, all helped me guess how much he'd taken on the chin, how much he hurt.

"And Brian isn't some pussy," Jesse said in the fo'c'sle as he threw some last items in his bag—another empty bunk.

"I know. Listen, Jesse, there's something I want you to have." I walked over to my bunk and reached behind my sea chest, pulling out a serving mallet, a tool for quickly wrapping wire rope in marline that I'd made out of apple wood in preparation for the voyage. A few fathoms of marline were wrapped loosely on its spool. I handed it to him, knowing his dedication to seamanship, knowing he was going to sign on another ship soon, knowing in my heart that I was not. I felt my eyes swell. A lump lodged in my throat.

"Thanks." He saw me struggling. "It's one of my favourite things now." Jesse clutched the handle close to his chest then plunged a hand into his duffle bag and pulled out half a bottle of amber rum. He spun off the cap and passed the bottle. I tipped it back. Hot liquor burned the lump from my throat. Then it soothed, warmed. I felt stronger passing the bottle back to Jesse. He took a drink. We said goodbye. He left the ship.

Over the next few days, the rest of the crew departed with all the ceremony of leaves falling from a tree. Don and Annie headed for Montreal in a rented car with a quick goodbye. I gave Crista a hug one morning before she got into a car bound for Massachusetts. Vicki sailed off on the HMS *Rose* and a couple of us watched her go. I heard that third mate Tom broke into tears as he left the ship. But most people drove off smiling, eyes firmly fixed on the future.

Brian had recovered some by the time I left. I felt his ribs through his sweatshirt as we hugged, and realized that he'd given everything he'd had to see that the ship made it all the way around.

I wrote a note for Captain Dan, thanking him for the voyage. Then I tore Maggie the Cat from the only world she ever knew, and left.

The new world took us both time to adjust to. Half my clothing had rotted in a bucket of sea water when I left my dirty laundry to soak in the Galapagos and then neglected it for days. I'd lost my glasses in Cape Town and accidentally burned my passport in Zanzibar. My wallet had been stolen in Bali and I'd lost my boots in Panama. My sandals gave up the ghost in Africa, and Tom had given me an extra pair of shoes that I'd cut the heels out of so they wouldn't give me blisters.

I felt out of place in my old home. In a grocery store that played hollow music from its warehouse ceiling, and aisles lined with sterile packaged goods, I was hit with deep melancholy. But that feeling didn't last.

I'd left the *Picton Castle* a journeyman sailor. In a matter of months I had my captain's ticket and was now unemployable as a tall ship deckhand. I became the relief captain of a cruise boat in Tampa, Florida, and then first mate of the barquentine *Gazela Primeiro* before taking the part-time sales job that helped allow me to write this book, a process every bit as rich and arduous as the experience I wrote about.

Brian and Beth live on Martha's Vineyard. Brian enjoys his exacting work as a high-end carpenter, and he likes that the work makes him part of a team. Beth is a full-time family doctor. She likes how the pace of her practice allows a deep commitment to her patients, and she likes to watch sailing ships in the harbour on her lunch break.

One of Kim's sons now works with him at the Dory Shop, while he and his wife, Jill, are the King and Queen of Big Duck Island, off Lunenburg. Soon after the voyage Kim bought the island from a woman who didn't even realize she owned it.

"You've got something I want: Big Duck Island," he announced.

"No I don't."

"Yes you do, and I'm gonna buy it."

Marcello's absconding with the ship's provision money attracted some press coverage in Canada, but no legal action. Now he's a stuntman, actor and photographer in Montreal and Rome. He's in love with a rising Italian actress, and has said he would like to play himself in the dramatization of this book.

Second mate Karen and bo'sun Josh live in Colorado. Karen is now a massage therapist, and Josh, who led the Seward, Alaska, high school wrestling team to win the state championship after the voyage, is working towards being a full-time wrestling coach.

Patricia continues to be one of the few women lobbyists on Beacon Hill, choosing her battles and throwing parties in between.

Third mate Tom is now captain of the *Harvey Gamage* out of Maine. Jesse is chief mate of the US Brig *Niagara*.

The year we returned, Captain Dan was named *Sail Trainer of the Year* by the American Sail Training Association. His successful refit and safe voyage won the admiration of his peers.

Since the end of the voyage, I have seen six of the Barque *Picton Castle*'s crew marry each other in three unforgettable ceremonies: Claire and Nobby; Rebecca and Bill; Karen and Josh. Though memories have faded, bonds remain strong.

Maggie and I have lived with Ariel in Savannah, Georgia, since 2001, and it has been everything that I'd hoped for on the voyage. On a nearby river we sometimes sail in the boat I built as a kid. When the tide gets low, we anchor off the mud flats, put on our boots and collect some of the best oysters in the world. They're sweet, and a little salty.

Over those last days in Lunenburg, someone had placed an easel on the dock next to the ship. It held a sign announcing the 2000 World Voyage of the *Picton Castle*.

Selfishly, I found it hard to believe the voyages would go on without us. They would. Dan Moreland and the ship would be the only constants. I felt humbled by the fact that he would do it again. And again.

Acknowledgments

THIS WORK SHOWS MANY PEOPLE COPING WITH THE rigours of life aboard ship on a long maiden voyage. I believe that every one of them was doing the best they could, and all shone brighter as a result. I'm deeply grateful to the captain and crew of the *Picton Castle* for sharing their lives with me and the readers of this book. I have changed some names and biographical information.

My deepest thanks to Michael Schellenberg for enthusiastically fostering this work. I can hardly imagine an editor more incisive, committed and inspiring. Also at Knopf Canada, for their professionalism and integrity, I thank Diane Martin, Louise Dennys, Jennifer Shepherd, Angelika Glover, Deirdre Molina, Scott Richardson, Julie Chivers, Ron Eckel, Cathy Paine, Janine Laporte and freelancers John Sweet and Liba Berry.

Many people have helped me improve my writing. I thank Dinty Moore and Martin Lammon of the Arts & Letters Writing Workshop, Alex Gunn; and for their conscientious critiques: Samson van Overwater, Professor Terry Craig, Jennifer Bowers, James L. Nelson, George Dawes Green, Steven Clark and Eric Curl.

For supplying me with books, archives and knowledge, I thank Arthur "Skipper" Kimberly, Jon Kalish, Robert Denham, Chris Miller, Anthony Pizzo of the Ships of the

Sea Museum in Savannah, Ralph Getson of the Lunenburg Fisheries Museum, and David Walker of the Maritime Museum of the Atlantic in Halifax.

For their love and support, I wish to thank Laurel and Drew, the Janzen Family: Richard, Donelda, Damian and Margaret, and good friends Opollo, Jimmy, Don, Michael, Tim, Matt and Darren.

For his encouragement, mentorship, and for reaching back to pull me up the ledge, I'm indebted to John Vaillant. For having the faith to give me a head start, I am deeply grateful to my grandmother, Margaret Crockett. For always believing in me and working to help me cross the finish line, I thank my parents, Bob and Sue Crockett. I'm especially grateful to Ariel Janzen for her unending support, and because, more than anyone, she has helped me learn to write.

For the chronology of events and a deeper understanding of sailing history, the tall ship movement, and the phenomenon of the *Picton Castle*, I gratefully acknowledge the following works: Villiers, Alan. *Men, Ships and the Sea*. Washington, DC: National Geographic Society, 1962; Villiers, Alan. *The Way of a Ship*. New York, NY: Charles Scribner's Sons; 1970; Jarrell, Todd S. *Slow Dance with the Planet*. Audiocassette. Minneapolis, MN: HighBridge Company, 2001; Moreland, Daniel D. "Captain's Logs." *Picton-Castle.com*. Online. 22 January 2001; Peers, Neil. "Emergency at Sea." *Picton-Castle.com*. Online. 22 January 2002; Ellison, Kristin. *Various Articles*. Soundings. March 1998, November 1998, and January 1999; Vaillant, John. "Five Hundred Days Before the Mast." National Geographic Adventure. Summer 1999; Kalish, Jon. "Sailing." Radio Documentary. NPR. 8 September 1998; Gilkerson, William. "Captain Daniel Moreland and the *Picton Castle*." Maritime Life and Traditions. Summer 2001; United States Coast Guard records relating to search efforts for the *Picton Castle*. 1998.

Permissions

Rigel Crockett was born in Lunenburg, Nova Scotia, and currently lives in Savannah, Georgia. A graduate of Mount Allison University, he also holds a 100-ton master's licence and a 1600-ton mate's license in sailing and motor-ships.